Bridging Decades, Embracing the Future
Lancaster Mennonite School celebrates 75 years

**Bridging Decades, Embracing the Future:
Lancaster Mennonite School celebrates 75 years**

Copyright © 2016 Lancaster Mennonite School

Published by
Lancaster Mennonite School
2176 Lincoln Highway East, Lancaster
Pennsylvania 17602

ISBN: 978-0-9895651-9-6

All Scripture quotations, unless otherwise indicated, are taken from the Holy Bible, New International Version®, NIV®. Copyright ©1973, 1978, 1984, 2011 by Biblica, Inc.™ Used by permission of Zondervan. All rights reserved worldwide. www.zondervan.com The "NIV" and "New International Version" are trademarks registered in the United States Patent and Trademark Office by Biblica, Inc.™

Writing, research and editing team: Jeff Hawkes, Eileen R. Kinch, Joanna Lynch, Andrea Peifer Martin, Beth Oberholtzer

Design and layout by Beth Oberholtzer

Photographs: From the archives of LMS (unless credited otherwise), including those by Jonathan Charles, Fern Clemmer, Gary Hiller, Paul Jacobs, Elton Moshier, Eli Passage, Stephanie Weaver; additional photographs by Keith Nisly (keithnisly.zenfolio.com), Donovan Roberts Witmer (www.donovanwitmer.com), Son Nguyen and Ben Wong.

*Printed in the United States of America by
DavCo Advertising, Inc., Kinzers, Pennsylvania*

Contents

Welcome: Legacy and promise at LMS	4
Partnering across cultures and traditions	7
Building bridges to the future	14
Unity in diversity	18

Centered in Christ — 20

Aaron Kauffman (1997): Remembering LMS	22
Sara Wenger Shenk (1971): Remembering LMS	27
Karen Weaver Sensenig (1972): Remembering LMS	28
Fikeveni Dlamini (2008): Remembering LMS	33
Steve Good (1987): Remembering LMS	36

Transforming Lives — 40

Gievanne Gonzalez Garcia (1999): Remembering LMS	48
Madeline Bender (1989): Remembering LMS	52
Liz Hess (1983): Remembering LMS	60
Anson Lam (2013): Remembering LMS	72
Hans Weaver (2009): Remembering LMS	76
Rod Lefever (1984): Remembering LMS	90
Anna Groff (2002): Remembering LMS	96
Karla Santiago (2006): Remembering LMS	102
Susan E. Weaver Godshall (1961): Remembering LMS	106
Fred Kniss (1974): Remembering LMS	108
Peter Dula (1988): Remembering LMS	110

Changing Our World — 118

John W. Eby (1958): Alumni of the Year 2000	120
Miriam Book (1966): Alumni of the Year 2000	121
Daniel S. Hess (1966): Alumni of the Year 2001	122
Evanna F. Hess (1966): Alumni of the Year 2001	123
Angie Miller Petersheim (1975): Remembering LMS	124
Allon Lefever (1964): Alumni of the Year 2002	125
Janet N. Gehman (1952): Alumni of the Year 2003	126
Sam Beiler (1983): Remembering LMS	127
John L. Ruth (1948): Alumni of the Year 2004	128
Donald B. Kraybill (1963): Alumni of the Year 2005	129
Phyllis Pellman Good (1966): Alumni of the Year 2006	130
David Shenk (1955): Alumni of the Year 2007	131
Lena Horning Brown (1952): Alumni of the Year 2008	132
Dan Charles (1978): Remembering LMS	133
Connie Heisey Stauffer (1955): Alumni of the Year 2009	134
J. Alex Hartzler (1986): Alumni of the Year 2010	135
Margaret L. Allen (1958): Alumni of the Year 2011	136
Joseph P. Leaman (1998): Alumni of the Year 2011	137
Edith Yoder (1983): Alumni of the Year 2012	138
Jessica King (1992): Alumni of the Year 2012	139

Looking to the Future — 140

Appendix — 143

LMS Board Members 1992–2016	144
LMS Administrators 1992–2016	146
Lancaster-Lebanon League Athletic Titles 1980–2016	148
LMS Graduates 1992–2016	150
Linford Fisher (1993): Alumni of the Year 2013	152
Tashya Leaman Dalen (1992): Alumni of the Year 2013	157
J. Nelson Kraybill (1972): Alumni of the Year 2013	160
Ty Bair (1995): Alumni of the Year 2014	165
J. Michael Eby (1990): Alumni of the Year 2014	168
Lynette J. Eby (1991): Alumni of the Year 2014	168
Rhoda Reinford Charles (1972): Alumni of the Year 2015	173
William K. Poole (1979): Alumni of the Year 2015	176

Bridge Builders for the Future — 179

"'Not by might nor by power, but by my Spirit,' says the LORD Almighty." –ZECHARIAH 4:6

Welcome
Legacy and promise at LMS

A school, by definition, is a hub of learning. The energy, enthusiasm and creativity I see every day at one or more of Lancaster Mennonite School's five campuses never fails to inspire and reinvigorate.

There are times, however, when it's instructive to pause from the busyness and to reflect on the big picture: the purpose of a school, its accomplishments, its vision for the future. A major anniversary offers just that opportunity for reflection, and that's the reason for this book. Lancaster Mennonite in 2017 is celebrating its 75th anniversary, and this book tells our story. You'll find compelling stories of LMS alumni recalling what their days at the school meant to them. You'll also find fun and poignant photographs of life at LMS over the years. For three-quarters of a century, Lancaster Mennonite has strived to prepare young people for life in an ever-changing world, encouraging in them a hunger for truth and knowledge and also a desire to be disciples of Christ, responding to humanity's brokenness with love, hope and compassion.

On a Monday morning in September 1942, a time when war cast an appalling shadow across much of the world, Lancaster Mennonite High School opened its doors for the first time. Was the new school an act of faith that God's love remained eternal and had the power to cut through the darkness? On that morning, 151 teenagers, all from peace-affirming Anabaptist backgrounds, headed into classes taught by six teachers. Among the 30 course offerings were German and Latin.

Lancaster Mennonite clearly met a need because parents continued to entrust their children to the school year after year. Freshmen arrived. Seniors graduated. The cycle repeated. And with each graduating class came renewed commitment by parents, alumni and the wider church community to help the school grow and extend its mission in new, life-giving ways.

The last 30 years alone have brought spectacular improvements to facilities at the Lancaster campus: the media center in 1985, the Calvin and Janet High Fine Arts Center in 1991, the Alumni Dining Hall in 1996, Gym B in 1999, the Park G. Book Building in 2004, the turf field and stadium in 2007, the Rutt Academic Center in 2008, and Millstream Hall in 2015.

But over the decades, Lancaster Mennonite became more than a high school. Other campuses joined the fold to extend the school's mission to pupils as young as 4 years old. Today, Lancaster Mennonite teaches 1,500 students on five campuses in two counties, including Locust Grove, New Danville, Kraybill and Hershey. Each of those campuses has its own personality. At Locust Grove, Spanish immersion instruction begins in kindergarten and extends to sixth-graders. New Danville is an extraordinarily diverse school where almost half the children have African, Latino or Asian ancestry, including the children of recently settled refugees from Burma. Kraybill has a strong middle school that puts on a play each year and has a long tradition of winning sports teams. And Hershey, the newest addition at LMS, has only 200 students, but in covering the spectrum from kindergarten to 12th grade, it creates an extraordinarily connected and supportive school family.

All told, LMS is 178 acres with buildings encompassing 560,000 square feet.

While change has been a constant at LMS, a core foundational value has never changed: to offer a strong academic program centered in Christ. Today, students can prepare for higher education by taking any of 12 advanced placement classes or participating in dual enrollment opportunities with HACC or Eastern Mennonite University, earning college credits. Partnering with Millersville University, instrumental students spend part of each day at the high school and part on the university campus. LMS also offers a diverse selection of agricultural courses, some of which—small engines, horticulture, fish and wildlife—prove valuable

On facing page. Top photo: LMS Superintendent's team in 2016, left to right—Heidi Stoltzfus, Director of Advancement; Miles Yoder, Assistant Superintendent; Marlin Groff, Chief Financial Officer; Richard Thomas, Superintendent; Joyce Thomas, Administrative Assistant, Superintendent's Office. Bottom left photo: Leadership team in about 1990, left to right: Miles Yoder, Richard Thomas, Marlin Groff. Bottom right photo, Superintendent Thomas reads The Little Engine That Could *to students on the first day of school.*

to those who aren't future farmers. Business classes, computer science, family and consumer science, four languages, drama and music round out the curriculum. Enhancing classroom learning are mini-course offerings that include travel overseas.

LMS also offers an abundance of extracurricular activities to enrich student life. Starting in the early 1970s, LMS began offering sports, and today it fields 16 athletic teams. The Lancaster campus' highly ranked boys' soccer program achieved a PIAA state championship in 2011. Another exciting area of student endeavor is drama, including the three theatrical performances the high school features each year at the Lancaster campus. And music thrives here, with band, orchestra and Campus Chorale only part of a rich tradition.

The past 75 years have seen tremendous changes, perhaps none greater than the influx of international students. Today, they number 130 and come from twenty countries. These courageous students, many of whom come from very different cultures and life experiences, complement the learning of our American students, helping to broaden their understanding of the world and furthering the school's global vision.

I've relied on numbers to try to give a sense of LMS's growth. But know that at its core LMS is really about something that can't be quantified. We believe LMS is most successful when it is touching hearts. If we can assure each student that he or she is loved and valued, just as God holds each one, then we are truly doing the Lord's work. We believe love begets love, and our hope is to launch graduates into the world who have learned how to love one another and how to bring light to the world.

Lancaster Mennonite is 75 years old, and it's not done yet. We have new generations to teach and new opportunities to explore. This year, as we look back on 75 years of growth and accomplishment, we are, indeed, excited about the work we've done, but even more excited about what we can achieve in the next 75 years.

—*J. Richard Thomas,*
LMS superintendent
July 2016

The LMS executive board in 2016 included, below, left to right: Diane Umble, Gerald Horst, Richard Thomas, Harold Mast, Cindy Mast, Anne Weaver, Andy Dula, and John Rutt. Chad Hurst is missing from the photo.

6 WELCOME

Partnering across cultures and traditions

"Grace, mercy and peace from God the Father and from Jesus Christ, the Father's Son, will be with us in truth and love." –2 JOHN 1:3

A look back at the history of Lancaster Mennonite must start long before the founding of any school. The real beginning occurred when some idealistic Anabaptists pulled up stakes in the Old World, crossed an ocean, and resettled in Penn's Woods, grateful to have the freedom to create their own Christ-centered community. On the former homelands of the Susquehannock and Conestoga natives, Swiss/German Mennonites, led by Hans Herr, established the first permanent European settlement in Lancaster County in 1710. The newcomers built a thriving farming community on lands that now include the Lancaster and New Danville campuses of Lancaster Mennonite School.

Over time, the Mennonite community's roots grew deep into the rich soil of its new homeland. Families lived and worked together to build a strong foundation that bridged old and new traditions. Scholar Donald Kraybill noted in *Passing on the Faith*, his 1992 book about Lancaster Mennonite School, that Mennonites established some of the first schools in Lancaster County, and "they operated these small village schools for youth from various religious backgrounds." This continued for many years until Pennsylvania adopted the Free Public School Act of

7

1834. At this time, Pennsylvania Mennonites relinquished their schools and buildings, and many became public schools.

By the 1930s, social pressures challenged Mennonites with questions of how best to pass on their faith and values to the rising generation. These discussions led in 1939 to the first twentieth-century Mennonite school in Pennsylvania, the current Locust Grove campus. One year later, the now New Danville campus opened as an independently run Mennonite school. The trend continued with the 1942 opening of Lancaster Mennonite School (LMS), followed by the 1949 opening of Kraybill Mennonite School. In *A School Grows in Donegal,* Elaine W. Good wrote that the LMS board bought additional land and paid for renovations of the Kraybill church building that was donated by Kraybill Mennonite Church for the purposes of starting a school. The Lancaster Mennonite School board was in charge of educating students in grades nine and ten at this Mount Joy campus while the Kraybill Mennonite School board operated the lower grades. In grade eleven, these students then transferred to the Lancaster Mennonite campus to complete their high school education.

This relationship continued until 1971, when the two school boards agreed that the Kraybill school board would operate the entire school at the Mount Joy campus, rather than just the elementary grades. In spite of a petition from parents, the Kraybill school board discontinued grade ten and added kindergarten, noting that improved roads made travel to the Lancaster Mennonite High School (renamed to make clear its high school focus) easier.

The creation of Lancaster Mennonite Middle School in 2000 created a climate for new considerations with Mennonite schools in the area. A committee on cooperation was established between Lancaster Mennonite School, now both a middle school and a high school, and nearby Locust Grove Mennonite School. Judi Mollenkof, the principal at New Danville Mennonite School, questioned why there were so many independent Mennonite schools and why the elementary schools were not connected to the high school. Mollenkof knew about the cooperation committee and asked if Lancaster Mennonite School and New Danville could explore a merger, a request that

LMS denied. Talks between Locust Grove and Lancaster Mennonite continued, leading to the belief that long-term cooperation was contingent on structural change, but neither school was ready to talk officially about merging.

In 2001, Mollenkof again asked for merger talks between New Danville and Lancaster Mennonite, and this time LMS said yes. These talks led to a recommendation to merge, which was approved by both Lancaster Mennonite and New Danville school boards, as well as the New Danville parents' association. A school press release in the Lancaster *New Era* on August 18, 2001, stated, "We believe the merger will address the educational changes and challenges of the twenty-first century more effectively and increase program efficiency as schools combine resources in curriculum, staffing, co-curricular activities and finances." At the point of merging, both schools had been in operation for about sixty years. The merger became official on July 1, 2002.

In a similar process, Lancaster Mennonite later merged with Locust Grove Mennonite School in 2003 and Kraybill Mennonite School in 2006. In some ways, the merger reflected the earlier involvement between

Sites in the Lancaster Mennonite School system in 2016, facing page from left: Lancaster campus, Locust Grove campus, New Danville campus; this page from left: Kraybill campus, Hershey campus.

PARTNERING 9

TRADITIONS & TRANSITIONS
Gathering in the classroom

Remember, not so long ago, when students sat at desks in neat rows and listened as the teacher lectured from the front of the classroom—and sometimes strolled down the aisles to make sure everyone was paying attention? "Hands-on" education meant holding a pencil and writing on paper, then collecting the papers and handing them in.

Today's classrooms still include pencil and paper, but also an array of technical tools, including electronic tablets, laptop computers, and Smart Boards. Projects might be team-based, collaborative, online or individual. Students may also collaborate to create digital stories, PowerPoint presentations, videos or podcasts instead of traditional projects. Research is often conducted on the Internet, and a "paper" may be an electronic document.

LMS administrative team in 2016, left to right: Eloy Rodriguez, New Danville principal; Judi Mollenkof, Kraybill and Locust Grove principal; Brenda Bare, Director of Curriculum and Instruction; Miles Yoder, Assistant Superintendent and principal at Hershey; Richard Thomas, Superintendant; Elizabeth Landis, Lancaster campus middle school principal; Elvin Kennel, Lancaster campus high school principal.

Kraybill and Lancaster Mennonite in establishing the Kraybill school in 1949. In each case, the elementary school merged into Lancaster Mennonite School, and together they will celebrate the 75th anniversary of the school in September 2017, recognizing that two of the campuses were established before this date. In 2013, Hershey Christian School approached Lancaster Mennonite School about becoming a part of LMS. The schools spent time discerning if there was compatibility. Eventually, they reached the conclusion that they could work together, and in February of 2015, Lancaster Mennonite acquired Hershey Christian School. Miles Yoder has been appointed principal of the Hershey campus and continues to serve as the LMS Assistant Superintendent.

Now LMS has become one school on five campuses, rather than five schools trying to operate as one.

Three Eras for Lancaster Mennonite School

Lancaster Mennonite School was founded in 1942 by Lancaster Conference of the Mennonite Church. The school and related congregations were closely connected, and for years changes in the churches were mirrored in the school. But as the school matured, it became more independent and also affiliated with Atlantic Coast Conference of Mennonite Church USA, reflecting changes in the church. Mennonite Church USA also asked its institutions to better represent the diversity in their communities and the world. Lancaster Mennonite changed to reflect the racial/ethnic diversity of the church and the broader community, and it began to welcome international students and students from a range of non-denominational and denominational congregations.

Nonconformity and Nonresistance: 1942–1970

During a time of nationalism and militarism in public schools, Mennonite schools understood their role to be havens of protection from the world's evils. Lancaster Mennonite was a place to preserve Mennonite values and to create a nonconforming and nonresistant Mennonite community.

PARTNERING 11

"I appreciated the opportunity to become friends with others who shared my values and to be taught by teachers who encouraged and cared for me as a person and helped nurture my spiritual development."
–Sam Thomas, alumnus and parent

Students who did not feel comfortable at public schools felt accepted and nurtured at Lancaster Mennonite.

The school emphasized unity through common practice. Most students were from Mennonite congregations, and they saw the school as an extension of congregational life. Students were expected to follow the church regulations on outward separation from the world through plain dress, which meant no ties for men and required head coverings for women. Separation from the world also meant no interscholastic sports, dances or plays. Students accepted this as part of their Christian commitment. Common farming backgrounds, worship practices (such as four-part harmony singing), and understandings about Christian life united students and teachers in a sense of community and discipleship. Chapel speakers, student-led chapels, and friendships encouraged mission work and challenged students to deepen their Christian walk.

Community and the Individual: 1970-2001

When the draft ended in the 1970s, Mennonites no longer needed to resist militarism in public schools. More exposure to non-Mennonite culture through radio and television also made public schools more attractive. A new generation of Mennonite students wanted training for more individual, professional futures. Lancaster Mennonite School then turned its attention to excellence in education with an emphasis on curriculum development. The school began offering Advanced Placement and other high-level courses, special education programs, agricultural education, and peacebuilding.

As LMS added drama, athletics, and dance to school life, the school focused less on unity through dress codes and more on unity through service in the kingdom of God. Mennonites were now interested in peacemaking, exploring the connection between peace and justice, and living a life of service. Living simply also became an important part of the peace witness. Students at Lancaster Mennonite did voluntary service after graduation through Eastern Mennonite Missions and other service agencies in other cultures and countries. The curriculum now required global studies courses, and some teachers led overseas field trips. Students outside the Anabaptist community started attending the school, as well as those from other countries.

Where Global and Local Meet: 2001-Present

For much of the school's history, students from Anabaptist backgrounds were in the majority. In 1973, ninety percent of Lancaster Mennonite School students were Mennonite. This percentage decreased to twenty-five percent by 2014, reflecting the growing diversity as more students of varied backgrounds began attending, including international students that comprised twenty percent of the high school student body.

Although the composition of the student body is different than it was in the 1940s, Anabaptist understanding still provides a framework for community and spiritual life at Lancaster Mennonite School. Anabaptists believe that Christian commitment should be at the center and then pervade all aspects of life. At LMS, a Christ-centered education means that students will be instructed by the power of the Spirit and enabled to grow more fully into the image of God. Education in character, academics, and interaction with each other flow from this understanding.

12 PARTNERING

As Lancaster Mennonite becomes more diverse, the school seeks to prepare students to be global citizens, to connect with churches around the world, and to learn from those churches what it means to be faithful disciples of Jesus Christ in today's world. The emphasis is not only going into the world to serve, but also on receiving gifts from the global community, allowing others to serve and teach them. LMS also invites students to model a warm ecumenical spirit as they explore the Anabaptist heritage, while also extending a hand to people of different faiths and Christian denominations.

Today, Lancaster Mennonite is a safe and nurturing place for students to explore difficult questions of Christ-centered discipleship as they relate to issues such as terrorism, the environment, and economics, as well as war and peace. As in its early days, LMS takes its commitment to peace seriously. Peace must begin inwardly with God before it can take outward shape in a life of reconciliation that, for many, includes saying no to military participation. The school also practices restorative discipline as a way to model the transforming power of the gospel. Peace means to care about environmental and economic justice—and to build a life-giving culture that works with the community and political structures to resist violence and to create a just peace.

Lancaster Mennonite is no longer a school for only Mennonites; it is now a missional school that serves the local community and the the entire world. The school values and finds wisdom in the Bible's vision of "persons from all tribes, languages, and peoples" as it tries to create a dynamic, diverse, Christ-centered community, informed by the best of the Anabaptist tradition that both gives and receives from other Christian traditions. LMS is a loving environment where spiritually transformed students can become world-changers, sharers of their faith, servants to their communities, peacemakers, justice-seekers, and ministers in a broken world.

PARTNERING 13

"There is a river whose streams make glad the city of God, the holy place where the Most High dwells." –PSALMS 46:4

Building bridges to the future

When Lancaster Mennonite School opened its doors, the school had a Christ-centered mission of encouraging loyalty to the Mennonite church, instilling knowledge of the Bible, and encouraging evangelism and service. LMS offered an alternative to public schools, which promoted militarism, taught evolution, and modeled less strict moral behavior.

Now, seventy-five years later, the interpretation of that Christ-centered mission has changed. Dances, drama, and interscholastic sports, once opposed by the founders of the school, are now part of a Lancaster Mennonite education. They are viewed as God-given venues outside the classroom that are important aspects of faith formation, leadership development, and community collaboration toward a common goal.

The most iconic symbol of the Lancaster campus is the 1890 bridge spanning Mill Creek, or as it is called on campus, Mill Stream. Prior to the bridge, traffic forded the creek about one hundred feet south of the current bridge. With the bridge's construction as a public thoroughfare, horses, wagons, and cars could cross even if the creek was high.

The bridge and Yeates Hall are the only surviving structures on the Lancaster campus that were present when the school opened. Both the New Danville and Locust Grove campuses moved from their initial locations, leaving behind no original buildings. The only other original building is the restored meetinghouse on the Kraybill campus, which was built as a Mennonite church in 1898. These three structures connect the school to its past, and each brings memories and meaning. The Kraybill meetinghouse is a symbol of the importance of the students' congregations and the role of the school in Christian formation. Yeates Hall, formerly called Gardiner Hall, is a reminder of Lancaster Mennonite School's commitment to educational excellence and a well-rounded education, which also reflects the vision of the former Yeates School, the previous owner of the property on which the Lancaster campus currently stands. The bridge is also a symbol of reconciliation, which is understood to be the central to the work of following Jesus.

For seventy-five years, Lancaster Mennonite schools have been in the business of building bridges. In the early years, bridges were built between education and the church. These years were also times of building bridges among other Mennonite communities. LMS was the first Mennonite high school in Pennsylvania. The residence hall became an important part of the educational program as Mennonite students from other parts of Pennsylvania, Delaware, Maryland, and New York came to attend.

The high school also built bridges to the larger Mennonite church. Connie Stauffer, class of 1955, said, "Our chapel speakers were like a list of who's who in the Mennonite church. It was like all the better-known leaders of the church at one time or

Yeates Hall, top, in the early days on the Lancaster campus and currently, above. Left, the restored Kraybill Mennonite meetinghouse on the Kraybill campus. Below, flood waters pour over the Mill Stream bridge.

BUILDING 15

another spoke in chapel, at commencement or at special programs." Another bridge between Lancaster Mennonite School and the broader church occurred when LMS dean Noah Good was elected secretary of the newly formed Mennonite Secondary Council in 1948 during a meeting in Kitchener, Ontario.

In the late 1960s, bridge-building began to include more students from other than Mennonite backgrounds. Some came from Lancaster Christian School, which had not yet developed a high school, while others were children of parents who were on staff at Lancaster Bible College. Still others came from evangelical congregations and had parents who were seeking a faith-based education that valued educational excellence, interscholastic athletics, music, drama, and other activities beyond the core curriculum.

Bridge-building took an international turn in the mid-1980s, when students, fleeing a Marxist government in Ethiopia, began enrolling at Lancaster Mennonite School. This global trend has continued, and in 2013 a staff member focused on international recruitment so that by 2015 over twenty percent of the high school population came from twenty countries. The school has now reached the point where being considered a "local" student means the student came from somewhere in the United States.

In an increasingly global society, Lancaster Mennonite equips students to interact positively with those of different backgrounds and cultures. The school also seeks to create and maintain an atmosphere that encourages Christian community and peacemaking. LMS is a place where students can feel supported and challenged to deepen their spiritual journeys. The fruit of the Spirit knows no cultural barriers, and this fruit is needed in a broken world that turns to violence and hatred to solve its problems. Love is the greatest bridge-builder.

Building on its heritage, Lancaster Mennonite School desires that its students grow academically and spiritually. Through local and global bridge-building in a Christ-centered community, students' lives will be transformed, and they will change the world around them. LMS prepares students to navigate life issues through the power of Christ-like love and service.

16 BUILDING

TRADITIONS & TRANSITIONS
Both an end and a beginning

Commencement is both the culmination of high school and the bridge to higher education, work and a life lived with meaning. For many years, students wore suits and dresses. Caps and gowns were introduced in 1984.

The evening before commencement is Class Dedication, a student-planned program featuring student speakers chosen by the graduating class and the faculty.

Commencement itself features an outside speaker chosen by the faculty. There are no cords of distinction at commencement. Everyone is treated equally, and each graduate is celebrated for having achieved this milestone.

Following commencement, graduates assemble on the front lawn for the long-standing tradition of the class circle. Graduates are surrounded by staff, parents and family, a gathering that symbolizes the community invested in the students as they are commissioned for life after high school. The class circle concludes with students tossing their caps into the air.

17

"There before me was a great multitude . . . from every nation, tribe, people and language, standing before the throne and in front of the Lamb." –REVELATION 7:9

Unity
in diversity

Lancaster Mennonite School operates with the understanding that its diversity is what gives the school its unique blend of past cultural and religious heritage combined with integration of various religious, ideological, and global perspectives. This more complex unity is based on the idea that differences enrich human interactions. The body of Christ, although one, has unique and varying gifts.

In the early years, teachers and guest speakers who had served as missionaries, teachers and aid workers overseas brought their knowledge to share with students. In the 1980s, Lancaster Mennonite began welcoming international students, many from Ethiopia. Students from Korea and other countries soon followed, enriching and diversifying the student body.

New contacts in 2010 brought a dramatic increase in the number of international

students, Chinese in particular. In 2016, students from China and Korea lead the numbers. Country flags exhibited at each of the schools represent students in the high school who hail from more than twenty countries.

Over the past years, Lancaster Mennonite administrators and staff have worked intentionally to become a school that welcomes people of all races, ethnicities and socioeconomic levels in alignment with the missional vision of embracing an increasingly global society. LMS values its heritage and equips students to walk in the way of the risen Christ, interacting with and connecting to people of all faiths and cultures.

The school currently reflects this growing diversity. A guiding principle of Lancaster Mennonite is that students learn how to relate to each other positively across racial, ethnic, socioeconomic and other human divides, while keeping Christ at the center of their interactions. Although not all students who attend LMS are Christian, particularly among international students, many become followers of Jesus by the time they graduate.

Unity in diversity bridges the ideological, religious and cultural divides that may exist among students and staff, forming a community called the Body of Christ, with the common goal of working together, unified by faith, for peace, prosperity and justice.

Donovan Roberts Witmer

UNITY 19

Lancaster Mennonite cherishes a diverse community. The students and staff come from many faith perspectives and cultures, and some, especially students from Asia, have never heard of the Bible.

But while we strive for diversity, we also value unity, and we try to do that by affirming a Christ-centered perspective. We try to view all that we do and stand for through the lens of how we believe Jesus would respond to the complex world we know today.

School leaders seek to instill in students a sense of discipleship and lives motivated by compassion and love. This is accomplished in numerous ways, including service projects that strive to meet the needs of people around the world, chapel speakers who promote discussion and prayer about crises around the world, and a focused curriculum that examines current events, history and literature from a broad cultural, social, and theological perspective.

The school's holistic approach strengthens faith and nourishes care for creation and love of neighbor, empowering students to seek justice and promote nonviolence as they try to model Jesus' life in these turbulent times.

CENTERED IN CHRIST   21

REMEMBERING LANCASTER MENNONITE

School trips to the third world called him to service and faithfulness

"That day of service drove home the importance of just being a presence in the lives of the poor."

AARON KAUFFMAN

During a high school trip to Guatemala, Aaron Kauffman was moved by an unexpected scene: children in worn T-shirts combing through a city dump. The heart-wrenching sight "caught me off guard," recalled Kauffman, who watched as the children scavenged for items that might bring them a few coins.

The teen was staying with a host family to learn about Latin American culture and to improve his Spanish, but the visit to the dump became more than just a lesson about the third world's grinding poverty or a reminder that he should be grateful for the relative affluence of his life in the United States. "I remember thinking it isn't right what these children have to live through," he said, "and I need to do something about it."

Earlier that year, Kauffman had arrived at a crossroads in his faith journey. It happened as he turned to an assignment for Bible class. He was supposed to reflect on belief in God, and as he considered what to write, he came up blank. He mentioned his struggle to his father, who in a non-challenging way asked him, "Well, do you believe in God?"

Kauffman wasn't sure, but as he thought about the people in his life he admired because they exemplified lives of service, compassion and faithfulness, he realized God, indeed, must be working in their lives. He had his answer, and from then on belief, compassion and faithfulness would become hallmarks of the life he chose.

Another school trip, this time to Kenya and South Africa with the choir, helped to reinforce Kauffman's thinking. One day as he looked out of the bus window and his eyes gazed upon row after row of tin-roofed shacks, he felt a surge of compassion. "I remember praying a simple and naïve prayer, 'Lord, please somehow show them your love,'" he said. And at that moment Kauffman felt he experienced a response: "You show them my love."

His senior year Kauffman went overseas one more time. It was a 19-day trip to India for Mennonite World Conference. The trip with four other students included a visit to Mother Teresa's Missions of Charity, where they volunteered for a day. Kauffman's duties included helping to bathe and shave destitute men, some of whom had disabilities. It was service at such an intimate level that it deepened Kauffman's call to be a vessel of God's love.

"One can get exercised about issues of injustice," Kauffman said, "but that day of service drove home the importance of just being a presence in the lives of the poor."

"I was probably the one changed," he said.

Kauffman is president of Virginia Mennonite Missions.

Aaron Kauffman | Harrisonburg, Virginia | Class of 1997

Teach me thy way

"Teach me thy way, O Lord" is the LMS motto, and it never grows old. A youngster encounters the motto on the first day of elementary school. And it's displayed on banners in the high school fine arts center. At LMS, education is more than classes and homework. It's about encouraging students to always turn to God for guidance.

"I never want my students to feel like they are forced to participate in something that they don't want. There's a balance . . . I want to open the door, but I think we have to trust God that He's helping us with that. I really try to open myself up to the Holy Spirit's guiding."
—Alejandro Ulloa, high school world history teacher

CENTERED IN CHRIST 23

Chapel services connect

What happens at high school chapel is rarely predictable, but one thing never changes at the school-wide assemblies: the opportunity for the entire school community to come together for illumination and inspiration.

Variety is the spice of chapel with student council one day putting on a skit about the upcoming talent show, a church leader the next day sharing stories, and a student band the next day performing a rousing rendition of "Amazing Grace."

Opportunities for building community happen in other divisions as well. Middle school students gather weekly, and elementary students participate in classroom devotions. The gatherings help answer this question, "How do we walk in this life together?"

"Chapel isn't just about the religious experience. It's about coming together and experiencing both the joys and sorrows we face together, and the things that matter. We have learned that when we have chapel, we stop our world for a little while." –Devon, high school student

Faith and worship

Worship is more than chapel gatherings. Worship is a way of relating to God in a meaningful and ongoing way. LMS's long history of teaching and demonstrating Anabaptist ways of thinking and living helps students build a strong foundation upon which to grow their faith.

There are many ways to live a Christ-centered life and many ways to demonstrate discipleship. Meeting others—teachers, mentors, family, alumni—who demonstrate how they live faithfully is critical in passing on faith. Young people navigate a complicated world. Building a habit of worship helps young people remain committed to God's values, from peacebuilding to caring for a broken world.

"The rootedness that has been developed for many years is alive and well in the school, in different ways than it was 75 years ago, but still there foundationally. It's a lens you can look at the world through. That's powerful for me. I've had those experiences, so I want them for my kids, too." –Andy Dula, alumnus and parent

CENTERED IN CHRIST 25

A clear commitment to peace

Peacemaking has long been a central tenet of LMS. The understanding of shalom, or peace, integrates internal affirmations of peace with self and God, and the external affirmations of peace with others and nature.

Little ones learn about how to be peacemakers in their own worlds by sharing, helping others and being kind. "May Peace Prevail On Earth," inscribed in different languages on the four sides of peace poles at the Kraybill, Lancaster and New Danville campuses, serves as a reminder that everyone is part of a broader peace community.

Large gatherings marking International Peace Day serve as both celebrations and witness to neighbors, while small groups participate in the day-to-day work of mediation to resolve differences. Restorative justice sessions seek to bring healing when harm is done.

Older students, further exposed to the model of Jesus as a peacemaker, may study peacebuilding in more depth. Some pursue it as a vocation, others as an avocation.

"The regenerated do not go to war, nor engage in strife. They are the children of peace who have beaten their swords into plowshares and their spears into pruninghooks, and know of no war.... Since we are to be conformed to the image of Christ, how can we then fight our enemies with the sword?... Spears and swords of iron we leave to those who, alas, consider human blood and swine's blood of well-nigh equal value."
—Menno Simons (1496-1561)

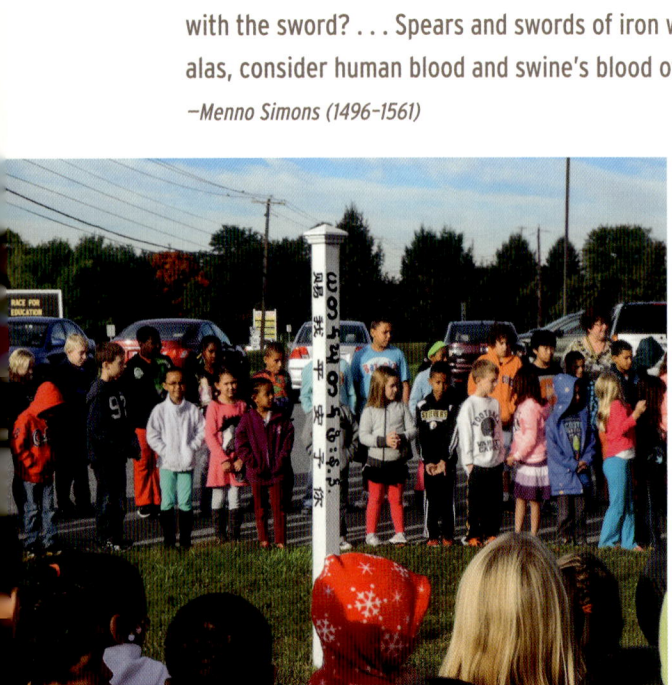

26 CENTERED IN CHRIST

REMEMBERING LANCASTER MENNONITE

SARA WENGER SHENK

Special teachers and beautiful experiences broke through the routine

"I experienced a sense of excitement sitting in his class and realizing this is who we are."

The daughter of Mennonite missionaries, Sara Wenger Shenk spent most of her childhood in Ethiopia amid a lively, multi-cultural milieu. Little wonder she felt newly constrained as a freshman at Lancaster Mennonite High School in 1967 by the conservative culture, particularly the closely enforced dress code governing hairstyle and the length of dresses.

But at times the rules and routine faded into insignificance as Wenger Shenk found herself caught up, even transported, by inspired teaching and uplifting school experiences.

One such occasion happened when literature teacher Janet Gehman turned the classroom into a mini-production of Shakespeare's *Macbeth*. Students read aloud and acted out scenes. Suddenly, mere words on a page—the chanting of the witches around the cauldron, or Macbeth's lament that life is "but a walking shadow"—came alive in the way the playwright meant the story to be experienced. "It quickened something in my imagination," Wenger Shenk said, "opening it to the mystical, to the lyrical dimensions of the universe."

Similarly, Wenger Shenk said, history teacher Myron Dietz saw nothing humdrum about the story of the first Anabaptists, but lifted up their radical, countercultural understanding of the gospel as prophetically relevant to these times. With his big beard, his River Brethren garb, his gift of laughter and sparkling eyes, Dietz easily engaged at a surface level with students. But Wenger Shenk appreciated how intent Dietz was also trying to connect with their minds. He saw the ideals of nonviolence, simple living, community and reconciliation that animated the lives of the first Anabaptists as being powerfully relevant to a twentieth century defined by racial strife, militarism and ruthless capitalism.

"He communicated the potential for social transformation," Wenger Shenk said. "He made those connections in ways that came alive for us. I experienced a sense of excitement sitting in his class and realizing this is who we are."

And then there was the moment her senior year when every singer from every choral group on campus filled the stage to perform Haydn's magnificent piece, "The Heavens are Telling." It was a complicated, challenging work, even for talented amateurs, and Wenger Shenk knew from rehearsals that pulling it off was not a sure thing.

"Would the soloists soar? Would the tenors remember to come in on time? Would it have that transporting, rapturous outcome, or would we have to stop and start again because the tenors missed a beat?"

Her worries proved to be unfounded. The students sang, the beauty of their voices became all that mattered, and Wenger Shenk thrilled to being a part of it through to the last note. And it was magnificent.

Shenk is president of Anabaptist Mennonite Biblical Seminary in Elkhart, Indiana.

Sara Wenger Shenk | Goshen, Indiana | Class of 1971

CENTERED IN CHRIST

REMEMBERING LANCASTER MENNONITE

KAREN WEAVER SENSENIG

Always the "new girl" at school, she found a home at LMH

"People drew me out and helped me see myself as a person of value."

Shy and quiet, Karen Weaver Sensenig, a freshman at Lancaster Mennonite, was content to be a spectator at chapel. Most mornings, other students went to the microphone in front of the student body and talked about how God was working in their lives. Not Sensenig.

For as long as she could remember, teachers were telling her to speak up. But it just wasn't her nature. The lack of confidence came in part because she was frequently the new girl in school. Family moves to Ethiopia, Virginia, Maine and Pennsylvania meant Sensenig attended five schools by the time she entered Lancaster Mennonite in 1968.

Only at LMH, though, did she begin to feel she had found a home. Teachers there, she said, took the time to get to know her, to draw her out and to make her feel valued. Her peers, too, welcomed her, and she began to feel like she belonged.

Later in her freshman year, Sensenig ran for class office. "People drew me out and helped me see myself as a person of value," she said. "That surprised me."

Sensenig finished as a runner-up. It was hardly a defeat for someone who had never imagined she had leadership potential.

Sensenig's parents returned to Maine after two years in Lancaster, but she stayed at Lancaster Mennonite and lived in the dorm. Her junior and senior years offered opportunities to become close to a roommate and others living on campus. She joined friends each morning for devotions.

Those mornings offered lessons in the value of vulnerability. Among friends she trusted, Sensenig started to share about her personal doubts and struggles. It was risky to confess weakness. "At that age, you really care about what people think about you," she said. But she took the risk to share from the heart, and she found that being authentic strengthened the relationships that were most meaningful to her. Taking that risk remains a life lesson.

One day at chapel, Sensenig felt a call to share. Her heart pounded as she considered what she felt she had to do. She had to stand, walk down the aisle, wait her turn and then look out upon the students and faculty and speak. She didn't want to get up.

She got up.

Drawing from 1 Peter, Sensenig spoke to her peers about life's trials testing faith and thereby strengthening it. When she finished and returned to her seat, she felt triumphant. She had overcome fear and obeyed the call. "I was finding my voice," Sensenig said.

Today, Sensenig, a former teacher, is a pastor and spiritual leader. The seeds were planted at Lancaster Mennonite.

Sensenig is pastor at Habecker Mennonite Church in Lancaster County, Pennsylvania.

Karen Weaver Sensenig | Ephrata, Pennsylvania | Class of 1972

28 CENTERED IN CHRIST

Lift your glad voices

"I love the energy that music brings to people, and I love helping children discover more of who God made them to be." —*Darlene Hein, elementary music teacher*

From pre-kindergarten students who love the simplest melodies to teens who belt out songs with enthusiasm, it is clear that the musical tradition is strong at LMS.

Fall festival hymn sings are filled with alumni voices blending, just like in the old days. Voices soar when the occasional community-wide call brings hundreds together to sing Handel's "Messiah."

"LMS influenced me in music through friendships with other musical people—in Campus Chorale and musical theater. With those connections, I discovered a way to express myself and my faith through music. I remember being inspired by other students or visiting musicians who performed in chapel." —*Mindy Nolt, alumna*

CENTERED IN CHRIST

Music binds all together

"There's something about music that brings friends, schools and people from around the world together . . . I learned so much about people, hospitality, racism and faith."
–Renae Gochnauer, alumna

There's nothing like music to bring people together and touch hearts. Young students at LMS learn about others through music. Guests or classmates may share songs or put on concerts to share their musical heritage. Maybe an unfamiliar instrument is featured. Where on the map does that instrument come from? What does that tune from across the seas have in common with your community?

In the upper grades, international students may share or music groups present global music on campus and in the wider community. Sometimes travel abroad is a part of the equation.

"I was impressed with the power of singing and the joy and strength it brought to the people. In South African culture, chorale music is a reflection of a cherished way of life, a way that we know is modeled through Christ."
–Marcella Hostetler, middle school and high school music teacher, Campus Chorale director, parent

Donovan Roberts Witmer

30   CENTERED IN CHRIST

TRADITIONS & TRANSITIONS
Campus Chorale directors

LMS's select choir, Campus Chorale, has been the school's ambassador for 57 years, performing for tens of thousands at churches and many other venues. Gifted directors have helped the Chorale establish a tradition of excellence.

Arnold Moshier was the first director, and from 1959 to 1982 his singers set the tone. Moshier was tireless in the pursuit of perfection, inspiring the singers to work hard to meet his high expectations. Moshier returned after retirement to lead an alumni choir during the high school's fall festivals. He continued to lead with gusto, inspiring the adult singers to sing with the same verve that they had as students.

Clyde Hollinger also put his mark on the Chorale. Hollinger, who directed from 1983 to 1992, is remembered as a warm and patient leader with a jolly laugh who delighted in sharing his great love of music that included classical music as well as traditional Mennonite hymns.

John Miller, director from 1992 to 2008, insisted on discipline and quality, but he also displayed a deep and genuine enthusiasm. An accomplished singer and professional actor, Miller helped broaden the school's music and drama programs. He also expanded the singers' horizons by taking his choirs on tours of Africa and Eastern Europe.

Marcella Hostetler, who became director in 2008, brought both a wealth of experience and a new perspective. Under her direction, Campus Chorale broadened its repertoire of Western classics to include music from around the world. Whether she was engaging with students during rehearsals or taking them overseas, Hostetler encouraged students to grow musically and personally.

Faith celebrations

At Lancaster Mennonite, faith-centered holidays are much more than days off. The school celebrates Christ's birth with beautiful music and awe-inspiring programs, worships the risen Lord at Easter and is mindful of the spirit of Thanksgiving year round.

"It is satisfying to have a program that is both educational and community-building. We share the good news, *Si Cristo Me ama* (Jesus Loves Me), no matter where we live or what language we speak." –*Jan Stauffer, elementary music teacher, parent*

32   CENTERED IN CHRIST

REMEMBERING LANCASTER MENNONITE

Examples of faithfulness reopened his heart to God

"There's beauty in waking up each morning and asking, 'How am I going to serve today?'"

FIKEVENI DLAMINI

Humbled that classmates chose him for commencement speaker, Fikeveni Dlamini, a native of Swaziland who entered Lancaster Mennonite High School as a sophomore knowing no one, rose and faced the audience. His topic: being centered in Christ.

Dlamini could speak about Jesus as the foundation of a purposeful life because teachers had modeled it. They had inspired him by the passion they brought to the classroom and by the genuineness of their service-filled lives.

"They were so different from each other," Dlamini said, "but the one thing they had in common was dedication to their job, and not just to teaching but to the calling God had on their lives through teaching."

But the young man who could recognize the power of Jesus-directed lives and expound upon it in a graduation address was, in fact, not sure he believed any of it.

Dlamini returned to southern Africa with more questions than answers. In part, it was his nature. His creative, curious mind impelled him to arrive at his own conclusions.

Another factor was confusion over what to do with his life. Dlamini had long felt pressure to conform to what others wanted for him. But was he just currying favor and mimicking the behaviors of a good Christian, one who had during his student years performed as part a musical trio at churches and Christian camps as far away as Arkansas?

Not comfortable with feeling like a fraud, Dlamini went through a phase of mild rebellion for several years after he left LMH. He smoke and drank, for instance, behaviors that were in conflict with his heart. He also began to identify as an atheist.

"I was reading and asking questions that I had never asked," he said. "It was very invigorating, but it was very dangerous at the same time. I lost my gentle spirit. I think I developed a divisive nature. I became a prideful person. By trying to find my identity, I lost it."

Was it open-mindedness that led Dlamini back to God? What he can say is he continued to ask questions and to reflect on what is a life well lived. His heart remained open, and he arrived a place where he saw himself as a child of God, one imbued with a faith in the transformative power of striving to be Christ-like.

"One of the challenges that Africans have is they associate success with money and status," Dlamini said. "I always knew that can't govern what you do. It has to be more than that. It's about doing what you love. It's about following God's calling. At Lancaster Mennonite, I got that."

He knows that a follower of Jesus will continue to have struggles. "But there's beauty," Dlamini said, "in waking up each morning and asking, 'How am I going to serve today?'"

Dlamini is chief sound engineer at Challenge Ministries Swaziland and Potter's Wheel Church. He hosts "Gospel Impact" on Swaziland Televison.

Fikeveni Dlamini | Mbabane, Swaziland | Class of 2008

CENTERED IN CHRIST 33

TRADITIONS & TRANSITIONS
Singing a capella

Is there a sound simpler, purer and sweeter than unaccompanied voices rising in song?

Years of singing in church as youngsters prepared many students for the celebration of singing in the early days of LMS. Opportunities to sing abounded. There were vocal groups for all willing participants, from duos and trios, to single-sex and mixed-sex quartets, to quintets, on up to school-wide choruses. Most social events included group singing and often, special vocal music.

Today, the music program at LMS continues to resound from that strong tradition of four-part singing favored by many Mennonite churches. Elementary and middle school students sing in class, school choruses and in special programs, while the upper grades enjoy a wide variety of singing opportunities from small groups to school musicals to choral competitions.

Campus Chorale, LMS's select vocal choir, was formed in 1960 and is still going strong. While today's Chorale sometimes adds instrumentation, the focus remains on the beauty of vocal harmony.

Keith Nisly

34   CENTERED IN CHRIST

The power of prayer

"Prayer is a part of their life here; it's a touchstone while they are in school. Every day somewhere in the day, prayer touches their lives, and I think that is a blessing."
–Carol Wanner, parent

Teachers lead elementary students in prayer at devotions and often conclude the school day with a prayer. Another way schools promote prayer is through "prayer walks" during which small groups of children walk throughout the school to pray for their school, families and the wider community.

Prayer time is woven throughout the older students' days. It takes place during chapel and devotions, and is welcome in times of stress and thanksgiving. Public prayer at sporting events brings the team together and serves as a witness to others.

Prayer can also be a stillness, an openness to God's voice that can take place any time.

"Prayer walks have been very meaningful for our students and teachers. It's a wonderful way to come together as followers of Jesus."
–Judi Mullenkof, Locust Grove and Kraybill campuses elementary principal, parent

CENTERED IN CHRIST **35**

REMEMBERING LANCASTER MENNONITE

Farmer's son got a kick out of soccer, and a life lesson

"Being a Christian is not only something we teach. It's something we live."

Steve Good was a member of an impressive soccer team during his senior year at Lancaster Mennonite High School. The team finished with a 22-3 record, won the district championship and headed into the state playoffs with a chance to go all the way to the top.

Playing soccer was a new passion for Good, a dairy farmer's son who wasn't able to play a sport until his junior year because he had to be home after school to milk and feed cows. Good's father relented after the coach wrote a letter encouraging him to allow his son to experience the joy and life lessons of playing a sport. The coach allowed Good to leave practice early to get home in time to still attend to the livestock.

Good loved finally being able to play a sport. "We had a lot of fun together," Good, who played center midfielder, said of his teammates. "It was the team aspect that I really enjoyed. Each person felt they were there because they were needed on that team, whether you were a starter or coming off the bench. And each player had a responsibility within the team. You were accountable to each other, on and off the field."

For Good, the excitement of getting ready for the state playoffs was diminished when he learned that several teammates had made a poor choice that had consequences for the entire team. The school, following its policy on sportsmanship, informed the players who had gotten into trouble that they would sit out a portion of the game. The team played hard without them, but in the end it went down to defeat in the first round, and hopes for a state championship were over.

The episode offered an unexpected life lesson from playing soccer. Good saw clearly how actions have consequences. Student athletes knew what could happen if they fell short of the school's high expectations, and the school didn't hesitate to assess a penalty. It held firm to its requirement that student athletes strive for excellence and be good examples. It didn't compromise on its principles at a time when abiding by them was inconvenient. It's something that stuck with Good.

Throughout his years at LMH, Good likewise appreciated how Bible teachers reinforced both his family's and the school's Christian values. Teacher John Landis, for example, stressed that being a follower of Jesus means that Christian life is lived out every day. It was a classroom lesson learned on the soccer field.

"Being a Christian is not only something we teach," Good said. "It's something we live."

Good is the co-operator of Lime Valley Farms. He also co-owns a car wash, laundromat and mulch business.

Steve Good | Strasburg, Pennsylvania | Class of 1987

CENTERED IN CHRIST

The nature of God's gifts

Spending time in nature can be a powerful way of connecting with God. Enjoying the natural world while walking across the campus—or simply looking out the window—and seeing the marvels of God's creation enriches the soul.

Each fall, amidst the sports practices and other activities, students may pause to appreciate the sight of yellow leaves glowing in the golden light. As the days shorten, geese fly overhead and honk plaintively.

After the sleep of winter, the green bursts forth. Add water and light and a tiny seed grows into a hearty plant. A newly emerged butterfly stretches its delicate wings before flying off. At each turn of the season, there is a farewell and a greeting. And thoughts turn toward the Creator.

"The beauty of each LMS campus creates an atmosphere of peace and a deeper appreciation for the Lord and all God has entrusted to us." –Miles Yoder, assistant superintendent, Hershey campus principal, parent

Portrayals of faith

In the early years at LMS, "plays" were classroom demonstrations, or skits that told Bible stories. Over time, the interest and involvement in drama and public performances grew. Stories of Jesus and religious-themed plays, such as *Godspell, The Robe, Joseph and the Amazing Technicolor Dreamcoat,* and *Fiddler on the Roof,* are still an important part of the mix.

"I feel so privileged that I can help students realize that the gifts they are given are from God and that they can use them to bless many people in both the sacred and secular realms without compromising their own beliefs and values. The arts are created by God and we can use them to honor Him, wherever we choose to exercise our gifts." –Dean Sauder, *high school Bible teacher, parent*

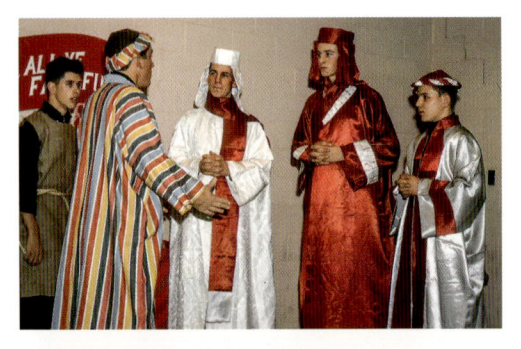

CENTERED IN CHRIST

Faith is both the roots and wings of the LMS experience. It is integral to every aspect of school life, both inside and outside of the classroom.

LMS Faith Practice Statements

1. In this school, students know they are loved and valued by God which enables them to value and love each other.

2. Peacebuilding, including the use of restorative discipline, is regularly modeled and practiced as a lifestyle of nonviolence, seeking justice and being part of a reconciling faith community.

3. Our school values and is responsive to cultural, racial and socio-economic diversity.

4. Our school provides a welcoming community where it is emotionally safe to raise questions, to value and learn from differences, and to care for each other.

5. The school enables students to practice global awareness, cultural sensitivity, anti-racism, and compassionate living.

6. Students grow in their understanding of stewardship of all God has entrusted to them, including the natural environment.

7. Staff members in our school are committed to modeling the life of Jesus Christ.

8. Students grow in understanding the process of biblical discernment by asking questions, practicing spiritual disciplines, and engaging with other Christians.

9. Students are encouraged to grow in relationship with Jesus and to follow Jesus daily in life through attitudes and practice.

10. Our school does everything it can to eliminate the obstacles that exclude or hinder the ability of students to receive a faith-infused education of excellence.

11. Stories and symbols of faith and reconciliation are regularly shared in our school community.

12. Our school invites parents to become partners in the faith formation of their child.

13. Our school is a community that lives the gospel message through praying, serving others, and enabling students to grow in understanding that they can make a positive difference in the world globally and locally.

14. Our school builds a strong faith and learning community in which students and staff support each other.

15. Our school enables students to live a life of curiosity, wonder and mystery as they join with God to bring the reign of God on earth as it is in heaven.

CENTERED IN CHRIST

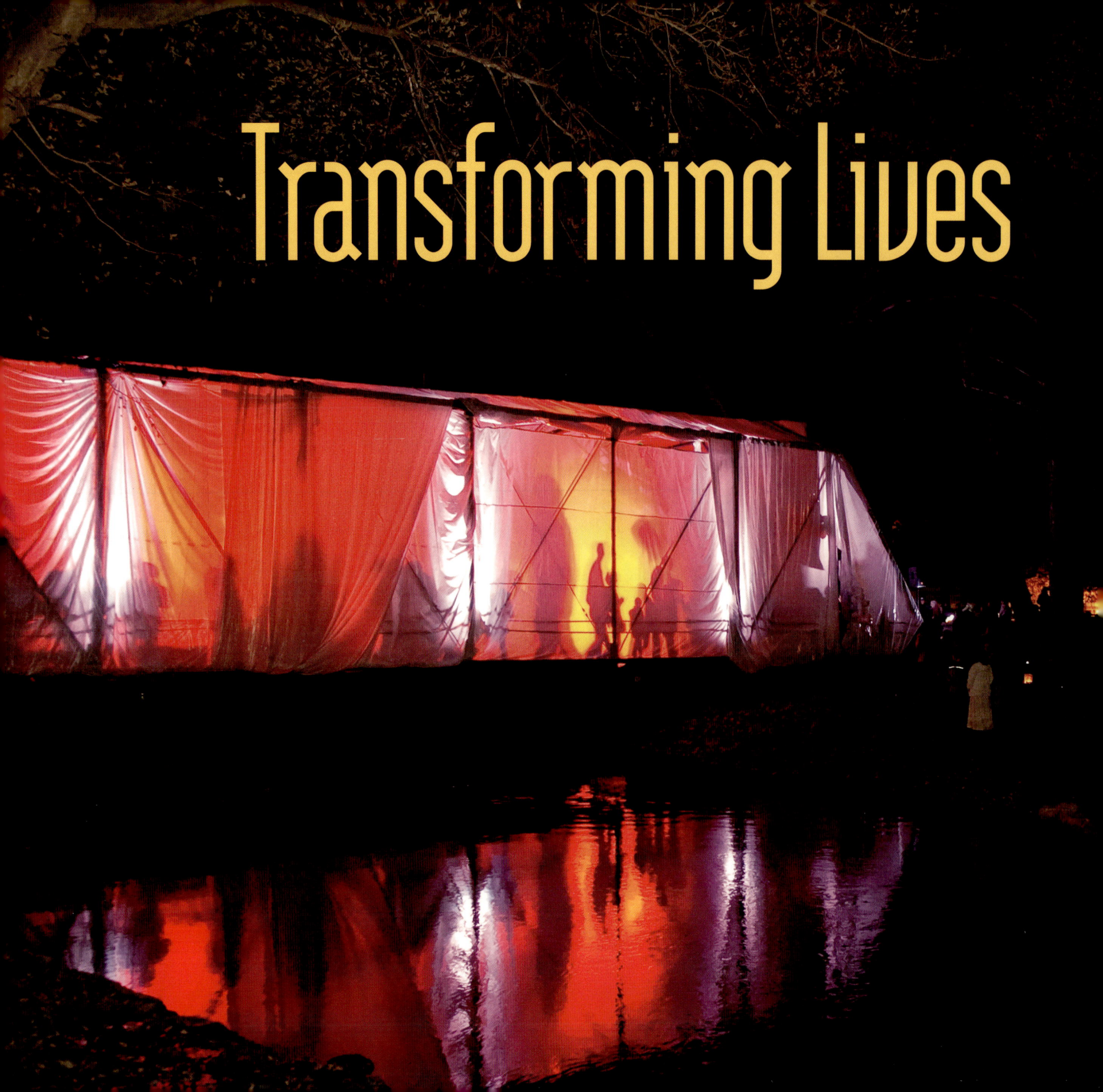

Transforming Lives

Everything that happens at Lancaster Mennonite School is aimed at transforming lives—from spiritual growth through worship and leading Christ-centered lives, to thought-provoking academic experiences in the classroom. LMS provides the context through which true faith can be nurtured and acted upon. Holistic transformation cannot separate the spiritual from academics in the classroom because the two are intertwined.

The intent is to teach students the skills necessary for success in life, career, and in relationships. Transformation means so many things—to grow spiritually, to learn skills, to grow in empathy, to grow in emotional intelligence—and all of these are skills people need for success in life.

Transformation occurs through academic discussions to understand the human side of history, and through social and service opportunities where students come together to work for justice, share experiences to build up each other's faith, and to model for others what it means to be a Christian in today's world.

At all levels, Bible classes, devotions and chapel provide students with the opportunity to think, examine, and express how faith impacts their lives. This leads to spiritual transformations that transcend the typical academic experience and teaches students how to meet life's daily challenges.

TRANSFORMING LIVES   41

"Blessed are the peacemakers: for they shall be called the children of God." —MATTHEW 5:9

Camaraderie on campus

Strolling across campus between classes offers a refreshing breath of fresh air and a nice stretch of the legs. And experiencing the weather between classes, whether it's summer's last gasp or a wintry gust, is something students of varying ages and interests can always chat about.

Breaks are built into each day in a variety of ways: standing up to stretch, changing classes and heading to lunch. Young students enjoy dashing outside for recess; that break is echoed when older students enjoy a semi-monthly break for community-building.

"Our world stops together; students can have conversations, or throw a Frisbee. We recognize the importance of socialization to emotional wellbeing. We work hard, but we stop and play. . . . it enhances our community."
–Elvin Kennel, Lancaster campus high school principal, alumnus, parent

42   TRANSFORMING LIVES

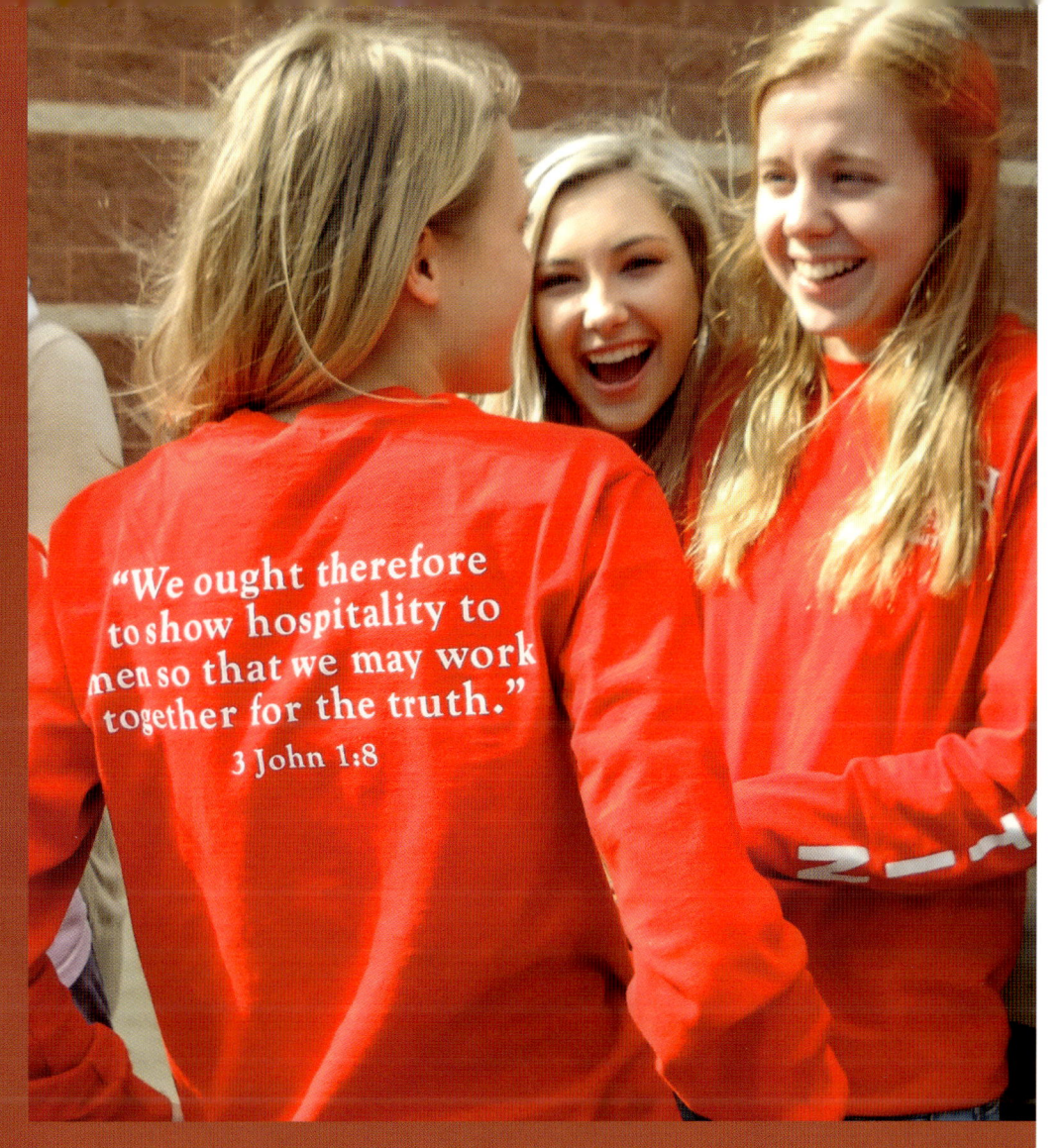

Friendships that build community

In the mid-1960s, it was games on the lawn. At a later time it was a reason to wear red T-shirts. Whatever the occasion, friends have a way of pulling each other into a variety of activities. Belonging to a campus club or organization provides a way for students to get to know others who share their interests. Even with diverse backgrounds, friendships are built through spending time together and working toward a common goal.

Check with alumni and current students and you'll find stories of bonds strengthened through participation in student government, yearbook, newspaper, sports, choir, orchestra and FFA Organization.

"Everybody is so friendly on campus. In some schools there are lots of individuals in one spot and you kind of feel alone, but at LMS it's more of a community, and I feel like I know everybody I see." —*high school student*

TRANSFORMING LIVES

Lasting bonds

Maybe you've shared secrets since your elementary school days. Or maybe you met because of assigned seating at chapel or in homeroom. Or maybe it was the challenge of competition that forged your relationship.

Your friends may be people who are similar to you or who draw you into unfamiliar social circles. Friendship is about meeting and learning about other people, valuing your commonalities and differences, but most important of all, caring about each other.

At the end of the year it's hard to say goodbye, but you know you'll keep in touch.

"LMH is my home. I've met wonderful people who have been best friends, family, and mentors. I've learned a lot through the different cultures represented and have grown spiritually." –*Darshika Kirubaaharan, high school student*

44 TRANSFORMING LIVES

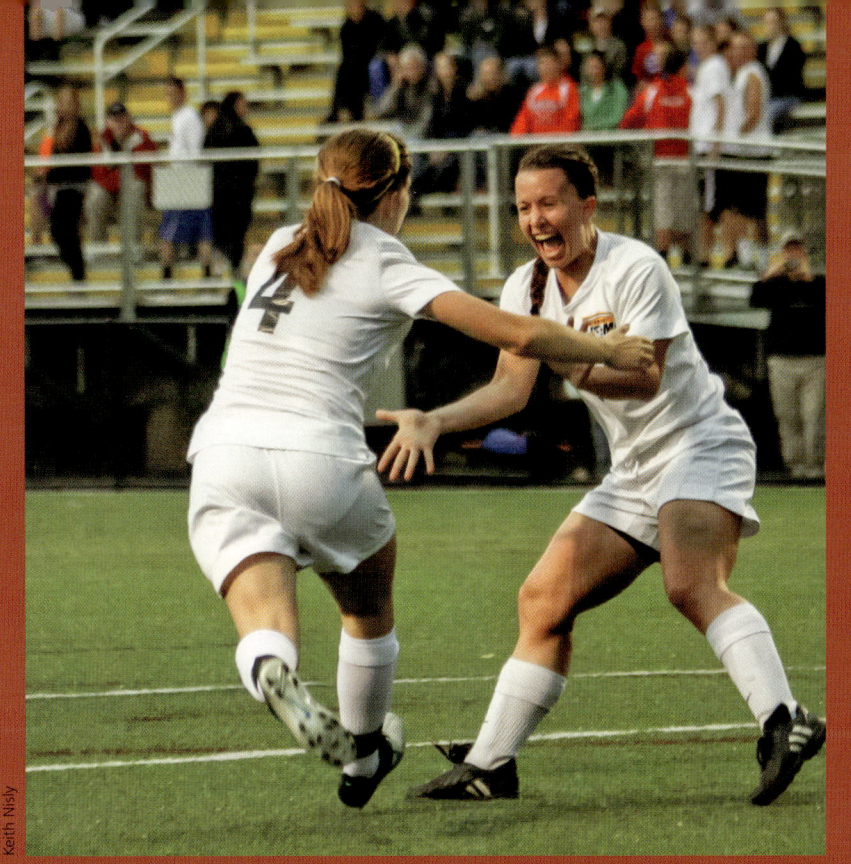

"As a parent of three LMS students, I see the school as a place where life-long friendships can be fostered. I have a group of close friends from my time at LMS and we are still important parts of each other's lives 30 years later. I hope my children have this same experience; from what I have witnessed of their friendships, I believe this tradition will continue for them." —*alumna and parent*

TRANSFORMING LIVES   45

A sense of belonging

Your teacher's face lights up when she sees you. Your friends shout your name and punch you on the arm. Another friend goes with you to class. Walking onto campus after summer break feels like coming home. You belong here.

Teachers foster the sense of belonging by mentoring their pupils. Classmates build community through deepening friendships. Feelings of safety and a freedom to trust come through knowing that others share the same values. Financial aid to attend the school can provide a welcome like no other.

"LMS has been like an additional parent for my two children. My son had a lot of anger and I worried he would be asked to leave, even though he wanted to stay. I appreciated the gentle and respectful guidance related to his behavior. Then my son turned it around completely! Now, I refer other families here."
—Bernadette, middle school parent

46 TRANSFORMING LIVES

TRADITIONS & TRANSITIONS
A place to call home

Students have been living on campus from the beginning, when 60 of the first 151 students called LMS home. Initially housing students in Eshelman's Mill, Gardiner Hall, the farmer's cottage, and faculty homes, the school built Graybill Hall in 1949. A typical student in the early days through the 1980s lived in the residence hall during the week and went home on weekends.

Over the years, LMS began attracting international students. Because going home to South Korea or Ethiopia for the weekend was not an option, they lived in Graybill Hall during the week and stayed with host families on weekends

Built in 2015, Millstream Hall houses students during the week and on weekends, plus many holidays. Conversations in Chinese, Swahili and Korean can be heard throughout the facility.

Residence hall students may come from around the world, but at LMS they form close bonds as they study and have fun together. Dorm life is a community within a community.

47

REMEMBERING LANCASTER MENNONITE

GIEVANNE GONZALEZ GARCIA

LMS opened her eyes to the beauty of diversity

"I saw God's love, mercy and grace through many other people and cultures."

The only thing Gievanne Gonzalez Garcia wanted to do was go home. A native of Puerto Rico who had spent her childhood in Chicago and Queens, New York, she felt completely lost as a freshman newly moved into the dorms at Lancaster Mennonite High School.

"I cried for two weeks almost every day," Garcia recalled. "I missed New York, my friends, my family."

Garcia remembers vividly her rocky start at LMH because it stands in sharp contrast to the rest of her four years there. As she gradually got over her homesickness and culture shock, Garcia started to warm to the others in the dorm and to the welcoming and supportive adults.

Jim Yoder, the dorm director, became like a big brother, and English teacher Janet Banks was like a second mother. "She was the one I could talk to about anything, including boys," Garcia said. "She took me under her wing, guiding me on a personal and spiritual level." Even during semesters when Garcia didn't have Banks for class, she felt comfortable stopping by her classroom after school to chat.

Garcia began to appreciate that the world was wider than her Latino and Disciples of Christ background in New York City. She came to love the diversity of her new friends in the dorm, girls from places like Ethiopia, Ghana and South Korea. "We became a big family," she said.

Garcia loved, too, getting to know faculty members who opened her eyes to new ways of thinking about how to follow Jesus. Bible teacher Myron Dietz, in particular, struck her as so unusual with his full beard and conservative attire: black pants, solid shirt, black suspenders. He was loud, funny and wise. "I could cut any other class," Garcia recalled, "but I never wanted to miss Bible with Mr. Dietz."

One day when she was down, Dietz took the time to listen, and then he asked to pray for her. "It truly touched me," Garcia said. "I didn't have that positive, male role model in my life. I had love for him like a grandfather."

LMH changed Garcia in profound ways. When she heard about two girls at school getting ready to fight, she instinctively took on the role of peacemaker. She stepped in and urged them to resolve their differences by talking it over. It worked, and Garcia felt proud when assistant principal Miles Yoder thanked her.

Garcia entered Eastern Mennonite University eager to learn more about other cultures and Anabaptist heritage. "LMH was the beginning of who I am now," Garcia said. "I saw God's love, mercy and grace through many other people and cultures. It opened the world to everything I've done so far."

Garcia is an elementary instructional specialist at Faith Family Academy in Dallas, Texas.

Gievanne Gonzalez Garcia | Grand Prairie, Texas | Class of 1999

TRANSFORMING LIVES

Finding your place

Students have many places to pursue their gifts and find a place to shine. Some may enjoy a moment in the spotlight while others prefer to work behind the scenes in a supporting role. Many students blossom after their teachers and friends recognize their gifts and encourage them to get involved.

"I think some of the best things about LMS are still what I experienced as a student. Many students find a place for themselves and can be successful here in a way that they weren't wherever they came from. I've had students who came from negative experiences, but had a chance to really bloom here." –*Jane Moyer, high school English teacher, alumna, parent*

TRANSFORMING LIVES **49**

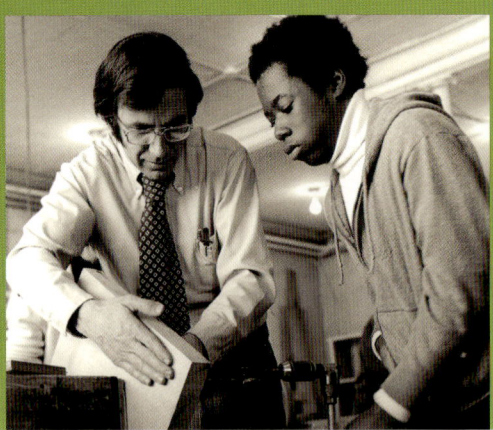

Connections with caring adults

When LMS graduates are asked about their school experiences, they most often tell about the encouragement and direction they've gotten from teachers. They value the adults who mentored and served as role models, who saw something special in them. Sometimes teachers stay in touch with their students for years.

"Teachers are really excited about their subjects, which helps tremendously. And they are not only willing for us to ask questions; they say, 'please ask us questions, please visit us, we are here to help you.'" —Maya Dula, high school student

50   TRANSFORMING LIVES

A genuine interest

"It is a blessing to have a school where teachers take a genuine interest in kids beyond the classroom. Our children have had the privilege to have mentors that we as parents respect and trust. It broadens the community of influence beyond family and church." –*parent of middle school student*

Positive interactions take place in and outside of the classroom. From a clear demonstration in technology education class, to a kindly worded correction at a music lesson, to casual conversation in the dining room, adult respect for each student is evident. The model of Christ-like love helps build a strong base of support from which each young person can grow.

"Teaching gives me the opportunity to challenge students to take risks, see things in a new way, and strive for excellence. It also allows me the chance to share my love and enthusiasm for the arts. It's a blessing to see the student's joy and sense of accomplishment."
—*Kathy Ciaccia, high school art teacher, parent*

TRANSFORMING LIVES 51

REMEMBERING LANCASTER MENNONITE

MADELINE BENDER

Their enthusiasm cultivated a life-long love of learning

"When you think about it, loving your subject is what you need in any field."

Soprano Madeline Bender poured her heart into developing her God-given voice and pursuing a career as a world-class opera singer. But her biggest role models weren't singers or musicians. They were high school teachers who taught art and science, subjects far removed from musical productions. The lessons that had the greatest impact weren't ones the teachers emphasized at the lectern. What made the greatest impression was how they taught.

Biology class with Charles Longenecker, for example, was like a magical tour of ecosystems and the amazing living things within them. Mr. Longenecker came into class, Bender recalled, so filled with excitement and wonder about the day's topic that she couldn't get enough. She got caught up in his enthusiasm and appreciated how he stimulated her intellectual curiosity.

One day Mr. Longenecker announced they were going into the woods where they would collect samples, make measurements and get their hands dirty. Bender's reaction? "Hurray!" she said. She couldn't wait to put down the text and do real science. On another occasion, Longenecker took them for an overnight trip to the beach, where students traipsed across dunes and pine barrens to study the sturdy organisms that thrived in the salty, punishing environment.

"That was the kind of teacher Charlie Longenecker was," Bender said. "Even if you hated biology, nobody would doubt that man was completely committed."

Similarly, Bender found art teacher Mary Lou Houser a compelling instructor whose passion for the visual arts and, more importantly, for the creative process helped the teen see herself as one who creates. "She wanted us to explore our own ideas so that we would teach ourselves," said Bender, who took every class Mrs. Houser taught. "That's the sign of a true teacher. They teach you to learn."

Bender employed that lesson her senior year when her English teacher, Janet Gehman, allowed her to pursue an independent study project to fulfill a course requirement instead of having to drop a course she preferred. Thankful that Mrs. Gehman relaxed the rules, Bender threw herself into the assignment, giving her topic far more effort than if she had been stuck taking a class.

Those experiences at Lancaster Mennonite High School, and many others that developed Bender's sense of self worth and cultivated a love of learning, would in years to come influence her own creative and entrepreneurial journey.

"When you think about it, loving your subject is what you need in any field," Bender said. "Those teachers inspired me to reach my full potential. They shared what they loved, and I wanted to be like that."

Bender, an international opera singer, is the founder and operating director of Musical Theater Builders. She also is founder and operating director of nonprofit Voices of Hope.

Madeline Bender | New York City | Class of 1989

TRANSFORMING LIVES

Commitment and care

There is a sense of teamwork and a circle of caring that students often feel and parents appreciate. Not only do teachers support students, but families help uplift and support faculty.

"The LMS teachers are committed to and care for the students. When I expressed concern, one faculty member told me, "You know what? Some of the students get it while they're here, and some of them get it later. It's just our job to love them while they're here." –*parent of high school student*

TRANSFORMING LIVES **53**

Generations of support

LMS is one big, multi-generational family. Elders share their wisdom, and the youth inject new life. Younger students invite older friends and relatives to participate in Grandparents' Day. Families come together for all kinds of activities, whether it's to read to one another, cheer at sporting events or celebrate graduations. From the nuclear family to the extended family to the school family, everyone feels at home.

"At LMS there is a consistency that weaves together education, church, faith and career. There's also a sense of legacy. I felt nostalgic when walking these halls and thinking of my parents and grandmother doing the same thing." –Daryl Eshleman, alumnus and parent

54 TRANSFORMING LIVES

"I was eager to go to LMS because I had family and lots of friends there. While a student, I felt like I got a good education and that the teachers really cared about us. And I met my husband at school—we started dating in the final weeks of our senior year." –*Ann Wenger Miller, alumna and parent*

TRANSFORMING LIVES 55

Coming home each year

The annual Fall Festival and Homecoming at the Lancaster campus is more than an opportunity to enjoy a tasty meal, run a 5K race, or bid on a work of art. It is a chance to reconnect with old friends and the school community.

Growing from simply an auction in the early days, the current two-day celebration offers a full farm breakfast, basketball tournaments, children's activities, concerts and a barbecue dinner. Yum! The 5K Iron Bridge Run, originally a fundraiser for the new track, now attracts hundreds of runners and walkers each year. They cross the iron bridge and traverse the cross country course through the woods and over rolling fields. Meanwhile, the auction has grown to include much more than quilts. The proceeds from the spirited bidding benefits the community.

"I am grateful for all of the experiences LMS has given me over the years. We make it a priority to contribute financially and enjoy attending plays and concerts. I graduated in 1953 and have kept in contact with six other women from my graduating class. I was pleased to see three of our children and two grandchildren graduate from LMS. I pray God's continued blessing on the school." –Loretta Lapp, alumna and parent

56   TRANSFORMING LIVES

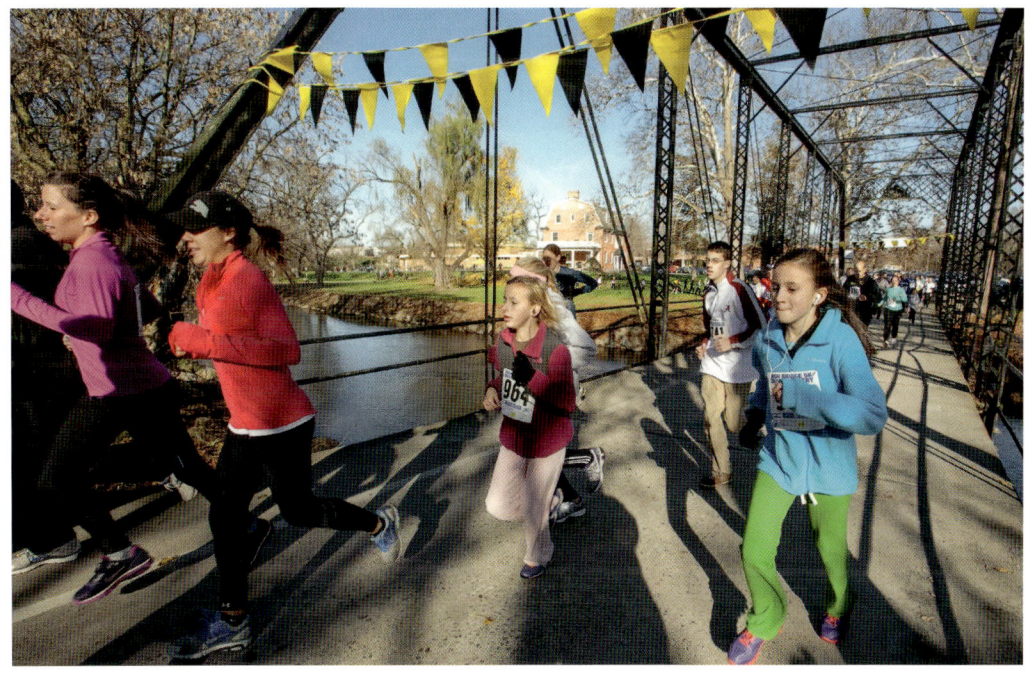

"At LMS I experienced affirmation, validation and a sense of connectedness. It prepared me for a life of commitment to the church and to the broader community. Our commitment to God and church and community remains strong."
—David A. Wenger, alumnus

TRANSFORMING LIVES

Learning to see

Over the decades Lancaster Mennonite High School has expanded its art education program. In 1977 the school hired its first certified art instructor, increasing students' opportunities for creative expression and career exploration that hadn't been fully available in earlier years. Photography joined class offerings in the 1980s, and in 1991 the Fine Arts Center opened.

Students look forward to entering work in the Scholastic Art and Writing Awards program, and some captured national honors. Meanwhile, on every LMS campus, art teachers expose younger students to the concepts and techniques of artistic expression. Students learn that art is about imagining, experimenting and taking risks. At the same time they develop critical thinking skills useful in all endeavors.

"It was an honor to explore the connections between aesthetics and creativity in a spiritual context." –Mary Lou Weaver Houser, former high school art teacher, parent

58 TRANSFORMING LIVES

"Art expands the mind. It teaches us to appreciate beauty, the visual culture we live in and understand that images have meaning. We create because our creator God creates. What a joy!" —Wendy Weinstein, elementary school art teacher

TRANSFORMING LIVES

REMEMBERING LANCASTER MENNONITE

LIZ HESS

She experienced a wake-up call, in art and faith

"At LMH I was standing on solid rock."

Art came easily to Liz Hess. Maybe too easily. Beginning in kindergarten and continuing through junior high, she was known for her artistic abilities, collecting awards along the way. But coming to Lancaster Mennonite High School in 1979, Hess discovered that she had a lot to learn and could no longer coast on talent.

Art teacher Mary Lou Houser recognized Hess was far ahead of her classmates, but that only meant she held her gifted student to a higher standard. "She was encouraging, but she was not easy," Hess said. "This wasn't the typical 'craft times' of art classes past." Hess thrived in her classes.

Calligraphy was a case in point. Hess had taught herself the fancy script, or so she thought. Her calligraphy, indeed, was ahead of most of the other students'. But Houser recognized Hess didn't understand proper technique. She required her to go back to square one, for which Hess would become thankful.

Likewise, Houser challenged Hess to aim high in other artistic processes, and her critiques were more demanding than what she expected from other students. "I needed that challenge," Hess said.

A wake up call came in art history class. Hess hated it. She wanted to create art, not study artists from past eras. Once when Hess told Houser how dreadful she found the class, the teacher was blunt. "Then don't plan on going to art school," she told her, "because you will be expected to study art history far more in depth than what you are getting here in high school." Hess took the advice to heart. "It challenged me to try harder," she said.

Although Hess lived for art class, her experience at LMH wasn't single-focused. Hess surprised herself when she warmed to algebra, for example. Math had always been her weakest subject, and one in which she always received the lowest marks. But teacher Stanley Kreider helped Hess make sense of algebraic formulas by explaining concepts in ways she could grasp.

It didn't hurt that Kreider's quirky sense of humor kept students engaged. Hess said he was known for his dramatic reactions to student mistakes, such as by feigning a liver attack, pulling out a medicine bottle, breathing deeply from the empty container, and pretending to experience sudden relief after nearly dying from the student's incorrect answer. Hess also appreciated Kreider's insistence that students apply math to their lives, such as by having them open checking accounts. While Hess had always been on the verge of failing math before coming to LMH, she became a 'C' student in Kreider's class.

One other faculty member left an impact on the high school student. Hess appreciated the sincerity of Glen Sell's role as campus spiritual director.

"You could see he had an earnest desire for students to become excited about a personal God," Hess said. "For four years we had this wonderful spiritual adviser, but the sad thing is I wasn't that interested."

During Hess' high school years, she had little desire to pursue God any further than what was required to fit into her Christian community. It was several months after graduating that Hess had a spiritual turning point that altered her life and put her on a completely different course than what she had been pursuing.

"I shudder to think how I would have turned out if I had not been given the opportunity to learn under such influential Godly role models during my impressionable school years," Hess said. "At LMH I was standing on solid rock."

Hess is an artist and owner of Liz Hess Gallery in Lancaster, Pennsylvania.

Liz Hess | Lancaster, Pennsylvania | Class of 1983

TRANSFORMING LIVES

Observing anew

Student photographers have lots of reasons to shoot photos. Their images end up in the yearbook, the campus newspaper and on the web. They take photos for class and their own projects. They learn through the selection of a subject and its position in the viewfinder. They focus on the singular or the mass, on a still life or a moving target, on a landscape or up close and personal. The result speaks volumes without a word.

"My LMH classes in film and digital photography and work as a yearbook photographer paved the way for me to pursue a degree in photography at EMU. I gained the confidence I needed to see my own identity as an artist and photographer." –Molly Kraybill, alumna

61

A new way of interacting

It's too bad no one thought to take note of when the first selfie was taken at LMS. In any case, selfies have become quite the phenomenon on campus. And why not! Who wouldn't want to document the first day of classes—or the last day, for that matter!—and every occasion big, small or in-between? Say it with a selfie!

Of course, at a community-minded school like LMS, selfies often aren't a solo activity. Everybody gets involved for group selfies! And then everyone gets involved in looking at their selfies, texting their selfies, and posting their selfies. How did people get by before cell phones? Say "cheese!"

"Taking photos of students taking group selfies has been fun because it shows personality and groups of friends interacting with each other." —Keith Nisly, photographer for school events, parent

62 TRANSFORMING LIVES

It was such fun!

The movement of dancers can seem effortless, but behind their fluidity is dedication and hard work. The reward for this pair was a flawless performance as the orchestra played and the audience watched in awe.

Who said school is no fun?

During a particularly cold winter in the mid-1960s, Mill Stream froze solid, and delighted students knew just what to do. Many laced up their skates and streamed onto the ice, including these two girls who glided gracefully together.

Sometimes hanging upside down with friends is just what's needed to refresh oneself between classes. Here, three friends did just that, gaining a new perspective.

"We had a blast in high school! Even though we worked hard, my friends and I took time to have fun and laugh, too." –*Kristina Roth Martin, alumna and parent*

TRANSFORMING LIVES 63

Instruments of self-expression

LMS is a place where instrumental music comes to life. Students of any age may learn an instrument and join a band or orchestra. Performance opportunities include concerts, the pit orchestra, chapel, talent shows and special programs. Acoustic or electric, solo or in a group, soulful or pounding, instrumental music makes the spirit soar.

"I'm a musician, and it's just phenomenal. Everyone in the music department is great. I feel like I have a connection with all of the teachers. Our orchestra conductor is also a mentor. It wasn't just about teaching music, but also about how I can grow as a person through music."
—Adam Harnish, alumnus

"Peacebuilding and social justice work influence what I do musically. I am no longer interested in using music for entertainment only. I am interested in the deep layers of transformation that can take place when engaging with the creative arts and in opening up the space for positive change through music."
—Frances Miller, alumna

TRADITIONS & TRANSITIONS
Music classes

When some schools are cutting back on music, LMS continues to hold up music as a mainstay of the curriculum. Students are not dragged into participation; they're drawn in by the beauty, energy and fun.

The days of sitting sedately at one's desk, book propped open, are gone. Students are on their feet, standing tall and breathing deeply. The teachers' enthusiasm is contagious. All are encouraged: "Everyone together now!"

Maybe a new tune is introduced on the piano; maybe the beat of a djembe drum sets the rhythm. Along the way a new vocabulary of pitch, melody and dynamics is absorbed.

Students both find their voices and learn to listen to others as they join together in song. Lone voices become a strong community voice. The appreciation for music they gain lasts a lifetime.

Discerning and determining

Discernment is about studying and comparing varied elements to gain insight and make good decisions. Agriculture students use it when judging fowl, preschoolers use it when recognizing letters, scientists use it when identifying specimens.

Analyzing all the facts allows one to come to an informed conclusion. A student group in the 1960s discussed the wisdom of preserving the family farm. Students in 2015 were called upon to look at issues in the news and analyize them through a historical context.

"It was powerful to listen to the students process how they experienced the play, *To Kill a Mockingbird*, especially their reactions to characters who were racist. The kids expressed ideas about how to end the racism that persists in our culture. Art can have an important role in highlighting injustice."
—Beth Weaver Kreider, high school English teacher, alumna

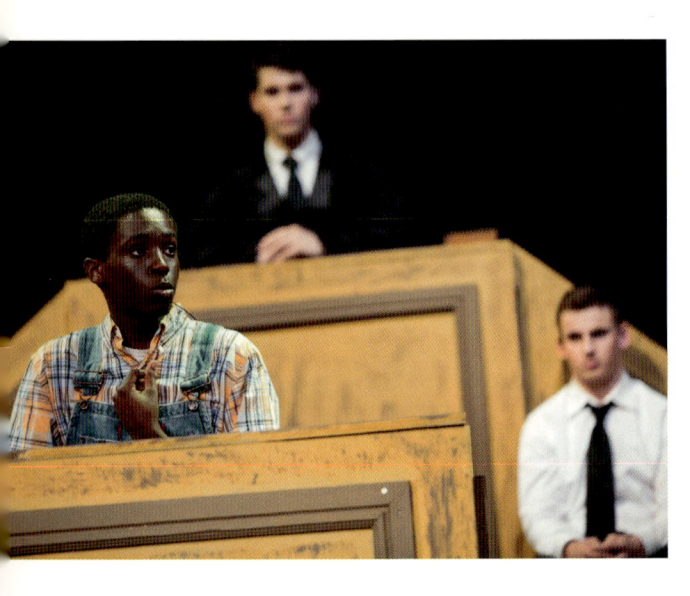

66 TRANSFORMING LIVES

"The goal was not to come away scared of [different world religions], but to focus on the ways we're the same. That's the kind of message I think my kids need to hear. We spend plenty of time focusing on how we're different. I like to focus on how we are alike." —*Andy Dula, alumnus and parent*

TRANSFORMING LIVES **67**

Campus family fellowship

Auctions and festivals bring families together. Kids are thrilled when items they made leads to a bidding frenzy. The money raised benefits their school.

Each campus' auction has its own flavor, offering special items such as artwork, quilts, themed baskets and crafts. There are wagon rides and dunk tanks, farm displays and bull riding, bouncy castles and face painting, games and demonstrations. And, of course, there's food. Lots of yummy food!

"I remember women from the church community coming to New Danville and setting up quilt racks in the front lobby and quilting right here during school hours in preparation for the auction. It certainly added to the feeling of family and connectedness to the school."
—Edie Hess, administrative assistant, parent

TRANSFORMING LIVES

TRADITIONS & TRANSITIONS
Quilts at auction

Piecing together fabrics and sewing decorative patterns is an art form many cultures share. Pattern choices, color selection and the style of stitching often give clues to the people who create.

Creating quilts has not just been an art form, but also a source of entertainment and community building for Mennonites across the United States. Quilters give free rein to imagination as they experiment with a riot of colors and admire the subtlety of a fine stitch.

LMS naturally drew upon the quilting tradition for fundraising auctions. Early supporters of the school sewed quilts individually, in families and at church sewing circles. The most beautiful quilts could set off fierce bidding.

The tradition of quilts at auction continues today. Maybe the design is a contemporary abstract; maybe it's a more traditional tumbling block. But bidders know that each quilt was worked with love, and they come eager to raise their hands in support of the community.

69

Students + running = school support

"The Race for Education not only helps to raise money for LMS, but it's a wonderful family event. Many of the parents come out and run with their children. It helps to foster a love for running, but also a love for each other and our school community as students, teachers, parents, and grandparents all cheer each other on to keep on running!"
–Eloy Rodriguez, New Danville campus principal, parent

"I thought it was a marvelous opportunity to be physically active and raise money for the school." –Soleil Yoder Salim, elementary student

Engaged and involved

What happens when students feel valued? For one, they don't hesitate to raise their hands when they have a question or an answer. They speak up, demonstrate what they know and are quick to volunteer.

"Knowledge is only one part of being a successful student. Students also need to be able to give to the world. If we can create an environment where students feel support, they will be able to be life-givers." –Elvin Kennel, Lancaster campus high school principal, alumnus, parent

71

REMEMBERING LANCASTER MENNONITE

ANSON LAM

Seven thousand miles from everything he knew, he learned independence

"I'm very glad my parents sent me. I learned a lot."

Anson Lam was only 16 when he said goodbye to his parents, left Hong Kong and flew for his first time to the United States. He was heading to a school he had never seen and knew little about. Moving into a dormitory with other international students, Lam knew he had to try his best. He was ready to throw himself into his studies.

Why did Lam's parents in January 2011 send their son to Lancaster Mennonite High School in the middle of his sophomore year? It was a Christian school where they hoped an Asian student would be safe, welcomed and prepared well for the future. It also was affordable.

Their decision paid off. LMS turned out to be exactly what Lam needed. Living so far from his parents and everything that was familiar forced him to become independent and to make good choices. The classes also stretched him academically.

Lam appreciated the rigor of Matthew Weaver's accounting class, and he enjoyed getting to know Mr. Weaver on a personal level, a friendship that extended to the teacher visiting him in Hong Kong during summer break.

Lam also appreciated teacher Dean Brubaker's passion for statistics and the clarity of his instruction. Lam had entered the Advanced Placement class with trepidation, but soon that gave way to fascination. "He made us not afraid of numbers," Lam said.

As Lam contemplated college and a field of study, Brubaker encouraged him to consider actuarial science. "I'm thankful for his advice," said Lam, who went to Penn State University and majored in risk management with a focus on actuarial science.

But life at LMS wasn't all about schoolwork. Lam joined the bowling team even though he had never bowled. As his average climbed above 180, he developed friendships with teammates and loved the competition and camaraderie. "I still keep in touch with them," he said.

"I'm very glad my parents sent me to LMS," Lam said. "I learned a lot," not the least of which was how to handle freedom, stand on his own feet, tackle life's issues and make good decisions.

"After you graduate from college, you need to face challenges, either in your life or at your workplace," Lam said. "I started earlier than some people."

Life at LMS taught him independence and gave him the courage to venture beyond the familiar.

"It's hard in a new culture and environment, but the first thing is you need to try," he said.

Lam is a student at Pennsylvania State University's Smeal College of Business.

Anson Lam | State College, Pennsylvania, and Hong Kong, China | Class of 2013

TRANSFORMING LIVES

Here, let me help

We start to learn the importance of taking turns and helping one another in preschool. The lessons continue through our school years and last a lifetime. Students who are paired to tackle an assignment learn to lead and follow. All of us need practice in knowing when to respectfully offer help and when to gracefully accept help.

73

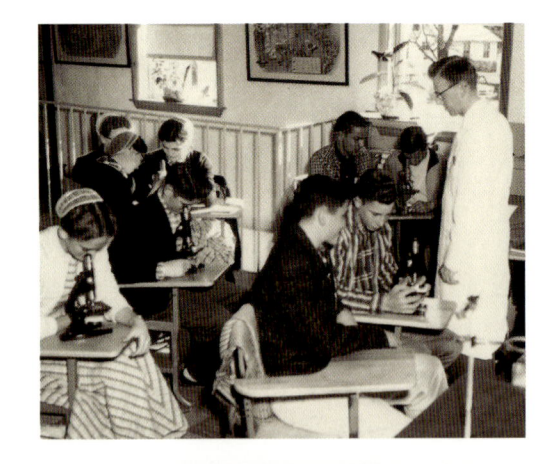

Academic excellence

Founded in the days when only the privileged few went to college, LMS today enjoys a reputation of academic challenge that gets students ready for post-high school learning. Students may take Advanced Placement courses and earn college credits through dual enrollment with HACC or Eastern Mennonite University. Participation on the award-winning quiz team challenges young minds to stay sharp.

"LMS was central in my development as a Mennonite and lifelong learner. I specifically remember a conversation John Weber had with me and several other students, impressing upon us the importance of higher education, specifically Mennonite higher education. I've spent the rest of my life doing things I first learned well at LMH." —Fred Kniss, alumnus, Provost at EMU

"I felt great pride with this quiz bowl team that could name the song and then sing the verses, name the play and then quote the lines or identify the country and then describe the economy because they had been there." –*Galen Sauder, middle school teacher, quiz bowl coach, parent*

75

REMEMBERING LANCASTER MENNONITE

HANS WEAVER

He started a coffee fundraiser, became an entrepreneur

"I actually enjoyed waking up and being part of the café every morning. I knew business was something I needed to explore as a career."

Hans Weaver was a sponge at Lancaster Mennonite High School, soaking up knowledge from a variety of experiences. But one unexpected lesson was how to make strong coffee.

If the coffee he served to his customers every morning at the Cup of Job Café in the school's old gym was too weak, Weaver heard about it.

There's more to say about Weaver and coffee. But Weaver, a bright, curious, personable student, turned his attention to other interests as well.

He learned, for instance, the joy of choral singing. Choir director Marcy Hostetter taught her students to experience music as meditation, as prayer and as a way to build community. Weaver ever since has explored hymns and other music for their hidden depths.

Weaver also learned that the world is a big, fascinating place, filled with rich cultures so different from his own in Lancaster County, Pennsylvania. His eyes were particularly opened on a student trip to Argentina led by Brent Hartzler. Weaver joined about 20 other students for the three-week trip. Knowing only a little Spanish, he found himself stretched as he lived with a Spanish-speaking host family in rural Patagonia. And yet he thrived.

"I fell in love with the culture and the people," Weaver said. The trip "caused me to become more curious and hungry to know different cultures." He continues to travel to Latin America, helping farmers import coffee to the United States.

Yes, coffee.

Strong coffee.

It was meeting consumer demand for coffee at LMH that awakened Weaver's entrepreneurial spirit. He got permission to start the Cup of Job Café as a way to raise funds for the student council. He hoped to attract students and faculty who stopped at convenience stores before school. He figured if he offered quality coffee and doughnuts at a cheaper price, he could beat the competition.

It worked. The café regularly served 60 to 70 customers a morning. For every dollar customers spent, the student council reaped 70 cents.

"I actually enjoyed waking up and being part of the café every morning," he said. "I knew business was something I needed to explore as a career."

Weaver sensed how different LMH was the first day he visited while an eighth-grader at Garden Spot Middle School. Weaver loved how the students chatted outside while changing classes, and he loved how teachers were passionate about their lessons and encouraged students to speak up and debate.

"It felt more like a college," he said, and he decided that day LMH was the place for him.

Its impact continues to reverberate.

Hans Weaver is co-CEO of Menno Tea.

Hans Weaver | Lancaster, Pennsylvania | Class of 2009

TRANSFORMING LIVES

Across cultures and borders

Speed of communication and ease of travel have made the broader world more accessible. Students learn about and experience other cultures more readily than ever, bridging cultures and building relationships through international trips. China, Argentina, South Africa, Brazil . . . new foods, new music, new sights and new understanding beckon.

"LMS global trips are often unique because they connect with places in other countries where LMS staff members have either lived, or are with schools where we have had connections for a long period of time." –Brent Hartzler, high school Spanish teacher, parent

"The trip to Argentina changed my life through experiencing a new culture, becoming more proficient in a second language, but most importantly, creating lifelong friendships." –Abby Beiler, high school student

TRANSFORMING LIVES 77

"I love the outdoors and to have an opportunity to take students to a place where they are unplugged. There are no cell phones, no technology. Reminds me of when Jesus went into the wilderness." —Lee Thurber, middle and high school health and physical education teacher

78 TRANSFORMING LIVES

Learning through experience

LMS began offering minicourses in the mid-1970s and they've become a valued part of school life. Minicourses, such as the Stratford Shakespeare Festival or a Grand Canyon hike, are offered every two years. Juniors and seniors choose among options that afford a chance to learn beyond the classroom. "Grade experiences" are offered to freshmen and sophomores and outdoor and cross-cultural events are planned for middle-schoolers.

Field trips are another school highlight, creating some of the most memorable moments of a student's experience.

"The students didn't know each other very well when we left, but everyone came back feeling like a family. Something magical happens when you create the right social context for sharing. I see students open up to others in a way that happens most naturally in the midst of shared experiences." —*Michael Charles, high school history and global studies teacher, alumnus*

TRANSFORMING LIVES   **79**

Broadening horizons

The high school media center has seen big changes over the last 25 years. More contemporary fiction and books for young adults have joined classics on the book shelves. The number of desktop computers increased from one in 1993 to 35 in 2016. And teachers now sign out carts loaded with laptops and iPads. The media center staff helps students with research, teaching them to discern what is relevant and credible and to acquire critical thinking skills.

"I enjoyed getting to know my students in order to help them find a topic they were interested in, guiding the research and recommending good books." –Carl Laws Landis, former high school media center director, parent

80 TRANSFORMING LIVES

TRADITIONS & TRANSITIONS
Broadening the reach

Wasn't cooking and sewing a girl thing in the 1960s? Not for these intrepid young men who didn't let traditional gender roles stop them from joining the cooking club.

These days, the family and consumer science department offers a broad menu of classes. Fashion and design teachers instruct students in the creative, hands-on aspects of making clothes as well as the related disciplines of merchandising and consumer science.

Food and nutrition classes—including Chinese culinary arts—are also student favorites. Maybe it's the camaraderie. Maybe it's the teacher's enthusiam. OK, we know. It's really the giant cookies. Yum.

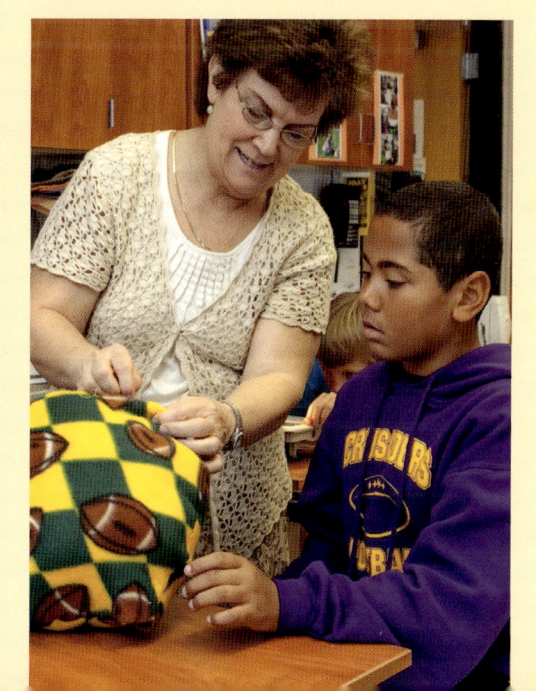

81

"LMH has a great cafeteria! The food is a lot better than at my last school. I always like the chicken croquettes." —*Josh, high school student*

82 TRANSFORMING LIVES

Gathering around the table

Mealtime is about enjoying tasty and healthful food and spending time with friends. Caring food service workers make sure each day offers an array of appetizing and wholesome options.

The Lancaster campus not only feeds lunch to hundreds on weekdays, it is open six days a week to provide three daily meals to more than 50 residence hall students.

Longtime favorites include chickenetti and the famed LMS Cookie, a tasty combo of chocolate cookie with peanut butter or chocolate chips.

"I am grateful for the dining hall staff. They work hard and help each other. There is a strong sense of camaraderie in the kitchen. During staff appreciation week, students write notes of thanks to the cooks. It really means a lot." —Dottie Weber, director of food services, middle and high school family and consumer sciences teacher, parent

TRANSFORMING LIVES **83**

Learning by doing

Reading and listening are time-honored ways to learn. Add the hands-on component and information retention shoots up. Preschoolers match and trace shapes, elementary students spell words with craft sticks and tend plants, middle schoolers shape models and build shelters, and high schoolers study chemistry and aerodynamics. Connections fostered through touch light up the brain.

"A project-based system engages students in deeper learning while helping them practice vital, lifelong skills, such as problem-solving, critical thinking, creativity, inquiry, communication, flexibility, collaboration and adaptability." —Elizabeth Landis, Lancaster campus middle school principal, alumna, parent

"My daughter comes home from school excited to share with us what she is learning and researching. I see her becoming more confident in her ability to express herself."

—Dennette Alwine, parent of middle school student

TRANSFORMING LIVES   85

All seventh- and eighth-grade students at the Kraybill campus take classes that teach practical living skills. Students are given hands-on experience with simple house wiring, plumbing, carpentry and painting. They also learn about automobile maintenance, fire safety and budgeting. These hands-on experiences are vital to a well-rounded education. *—Jim Baer, Kraybill campus middle school home technology teacher, alumnus, parent*

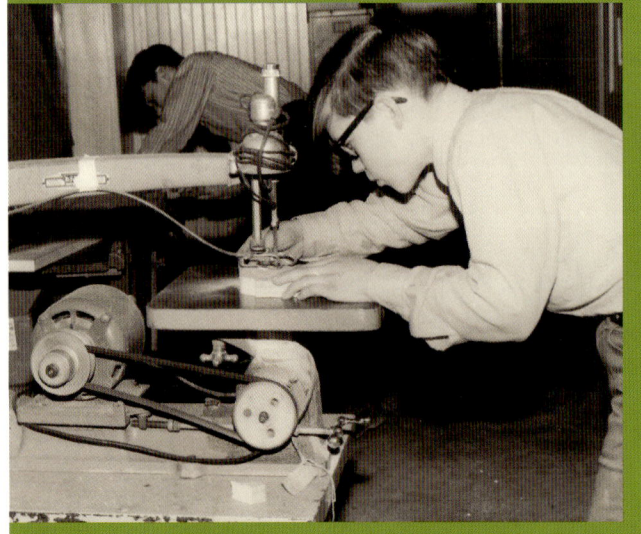

86 TRANSFORMING LIVES

The satisfaction of a job well done

Once considered for boys only, "shop" classes at LMS have evolved into "technology education" for boys and girls.

Students in middle school participate in small group problem-solving and model-building, then test and analyze the results. Each year eighth-graders at the Kraybill campus team up to build a garden shed or some such item to sell at the spring auction.

Meanwhile, those who take woodworking or metalworking in high school may be introduced to a career or a lifelong hobby.

Doing work with your own hands, whether it's a simple home repair or the meticulous crafting of a chair or table, offers a sense of satisfaction you rarely experience staring at a computer screen.

"I enjoy seeing students' sense of pride and accomplishment when they finish a semester-long project, and it is always fascinating to see what projects interest them." –Aden Stolzfus, *high school advanced manufacturing technology teacher, alumnus, parent*

TRANSFORMING LIVES **87**

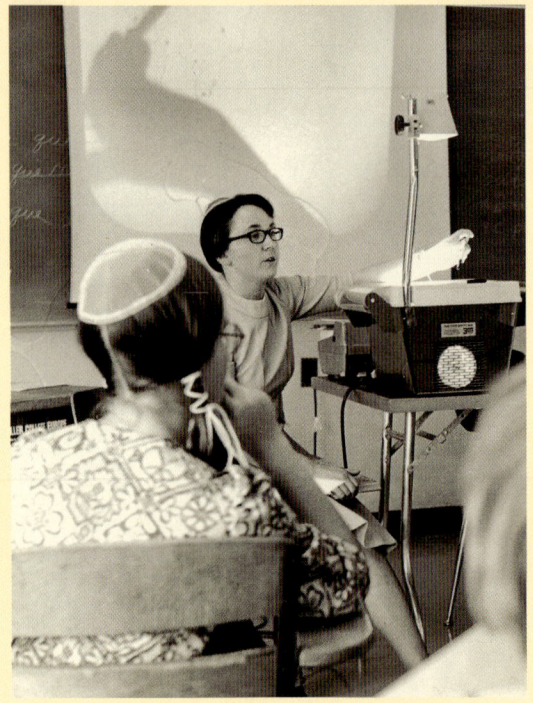

TRADITIONS & TRANSITIONS

From manual to electronic

Written communication has changed dramatically over the years, and LMS has kept pace. Though the QWERTY keyboard stayed with us, fingers moved from manual to electric typewriters—used primarily in business courses—to early word processors, then personal computers, which all students use to learn keyboarding and gain computer competency.

Digital video players replaced reel-to-reel film projectors while Smart Boards and PowerPoint presentations took the place of the overhead projector and slides.

In 2016, when everyone can carry a computer in his or her pocket, portable devices such as laptop and tablet computers enhance many classroom experiences. Preschoolers play matching games, elementary students practice newly acquired math skills, middle-schoolers plan projects, and high school scholars research everything from the life span of a mayfly to literary allusions.

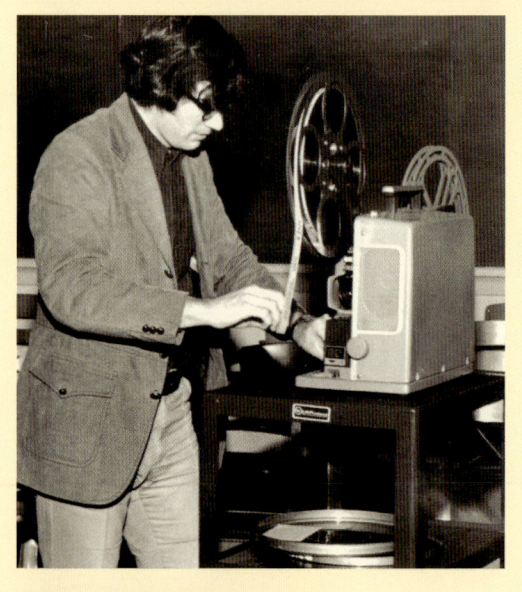

88 TRANSFORMING LIVES

"I value the ways in which my own kids are being challenged to live lives aligned with Jesus' message of peace, love, inclusion, justice and service." —*Janelle Thomas, middle school teacher, alumna, parent*

TRANSFORMING LIVES   **89**

REMEMBERING LANCASTER MENNONITE

Teachers saw his potential and made him feel he mattered

"You're learning team dynamics and how to organize the work of a group of people."

ROD LEFEVER

For a math whiz like Rod Lefever, the new opportunity at Lancaster Mennonite to study computer programming could not have come at a better time.

He was a junior who had gotten by his first two years of high school without putting forth a lot of effort. What mattered more than school was his close-knit group of fun-loving friends and his part-time job at a busy restaurant.

But heading into his junior year, Lefever realized he needed to get serious about school if he wanted to go to college and have a more significant career than restaurant work. It was at the same time he started hitting the books harder that he also found school work that excited him: the rapidly evolving field of computer science. "Although I had access to a computer at home, that programming class was formative," he said.

As a senior, he got to dive even deeper because LMH offered Computer Programming II for the first time. In that class Lefever rose to the challenge of working as part of a team to create applications. "It's a very different environment needing to work with several people putting something together versus doing it yourself," he said. "You're learning team dynamics and how to organize the work of a group of people." A major achievement was writing the program for tracking school attendance and grades, a system that worked so well, he said, the school started using it.

Lefever thinks the lesson that teamwork matters was part of a wider dynamic at LMH that made students feel that they mattered as people and that nurtured growth in every aspect of a student's life, not just the academic. LMH graduates, he believes, often develop a strong sense of emotional intelligence that serves them well in the workplace and in society in general.

Even during his first two years at LMH when he wasn't giving his best effort, Lefever said he felt teachers valued him and worked at pulling him out of his shell.

"They cared very much, and they recognized the potential even when the effort may not have initially been there," he said. "Those high school years are so formative. Having a supportive environment in terms of the friendships you develop and the teachers who are guiding you probably kept me from straying in ways that I might have been inclined. A lot of things at LMH set me on the course for the rest of my life."

Lefever is a partner/business manager at Hoober Inc. of Intercourse, a farm equipment dealership.

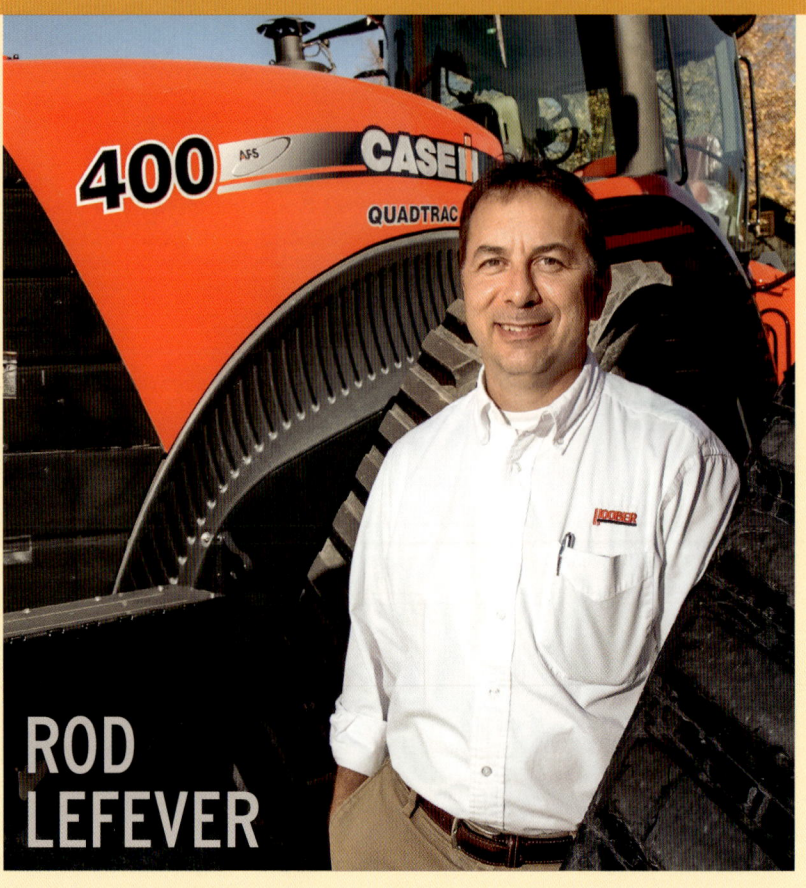

Rod Lefever | Neffsville, Pennsylvania | Class of 1984

TRANSFORMING LIVES

"The FFA realizes that whatever career a student may pursue, whether agriculturally related or not, he or she needs to obtain leadership qualities, such as team building and communication, in order to be successful." —Jasmine VanSant, alumna

The FFA team

LMS students have long participated in agriculture clubs, which led in 1993 to the school becoming the first private institution in the country to receive an FFA Organization charter.

FFA members compete as livestock judges and agriculture mechanics, give speeches, participate in community service and develop leadership skills. About much more than agriculture, FFA is a vehicle for students to explore a wide range of career paths. Graduates have gone into business, banking and teaching. They've taken to heart the FFA motto, "Living to serve," and have put their experiences to work in the community in myriad ways.

"Since I grew up on a family farm, the agriculture department and FFA was an immediate niche for me at LMS. Agriculture is a part of everyone's life, whether the setting is rural, urban, or international. It is vital in education and I am thankful that it was a part of mine."
—Katie Andrews, alumna

The outdoors as a classroom

For generations of LMS students, putting on waders or rolling up pant legs and stepping into the Mill Stream for a lesson has been a rite of passage. Peering into the net brings excitement and a bit of trepidation. There's a world of difference between looking at a photograph in a textbook and holding a dripping wet crayfish.

Quickly wielded binoculars helped students to identify the different species of birds that made their homes in the woods in the 1960s. More recent outdoor forays have students planting and tending gardens and discussing interrelated ecosystems. One middle school developed a pollinator garden after learning how colony collapse disorder threatens honey bee populations.

Learning scientific facts is empowering. More powerful is being able to bridge with integrity the worlds of science and faith, respecting both.

"The earth is the Lord's, and everything in it, the world, and all who live in it . . ."
–Psalm 24:1

92   TRANSFORMING LIVES

"We are so blessed to have a wetland, stream and woodland. These natural settings give kids the types of learning experiences they remember long after the classroom lectures are forgotten." —*Wayne Lehman, former middle school science teacher, parent*

TRANSFORMING LIVES 93

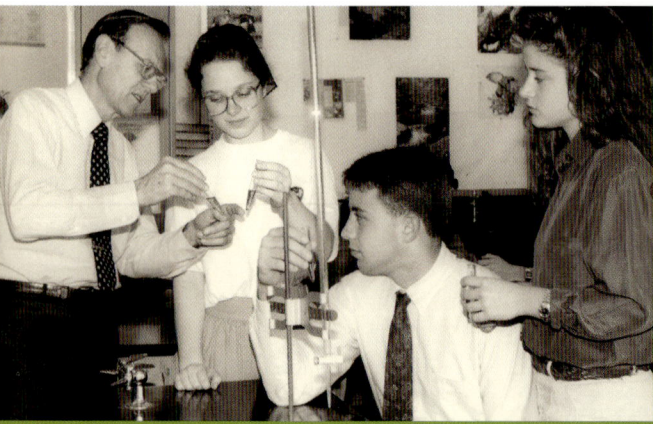

"From the beginning we wanted to combine high academic standards with a definite church relatedness. We wanted our students to have science courses as good or better than they would receive in public school." —*Noah Good, founding dean of LMS, in* Passing on the Faith

94   TRANSFORMING LIVES

Scientific collaboration

The advancement of science today takes collaboration and cooperation. LMS understands that students need to learn how to work with others who will test their ideas and build upon them. And even students who don't see science as part of their future get caught up in the thrill of discovery when they collaborate with classmates. Students develop critical-thinking and problem-solving skills that will help them be successful in all kinds of endeavors.

"We need to continue to develop students who can think outside the box, since the problems they will encounter and need to solve have not yet even been discovered." –*Duane Evans, high school science teacher, parent*

REMEMBERING LANCASTER MENNONITE

Wanting to run races and be in the play, she got the green light

"I learned the importance of teamwork, and at the same time I experienced the weight of responsibility."

ANNA GROFF

Anna Groff was in a quandary the fall semester of her sophomore year at Lancaster Mennonite. She went out for cross country because she had enjoyed the sport as a freshman and because teammates had become good friends. But Groff also decided to try out for the fall play.

When she got a role in Shakespeare's *Much Ado About Nothing*, Groff didn't want to quit cross country. But she also didn't want to pass on the opportunity to try her hand at acting.

Groff decided she would try to persuade the cross country coach and the play director to let her do both. She explained to them that she could leave cross country practice a little early and sprint over to the Fine Arts Center, where she would be a little late for play practice, but not that late.

Groff couldn't have been happier when the coach and the director agreed to accommodate her request.

Looking back, Groff appreciates the way the school understood that a student could be excited about participating in conflicting activities and yet be motivated to make both work.

"They let me try different things and didn't expect me to be amazing at any of them," said Groff, who sees herself as a generalist with a range of interests. "It was a busy time (that fall), but I got to do two things I really wanted to do."

Groff as a senior plunged into another passion: journalism. She became editor of the *Millstream*, and under the guidance of advisor Dan Deitzel, she honed her writing and editing skills. Groff also got her first taste of managing people, encouraging them to write pieces and to meet deadlines. She developed leadership skills that proved useful in college and in professional work. "I learned the importance of teamwork, and at the same time I experienced the weight of responsibility," she said.

Throughout her time at Lancaster Mennonite, Groff always felt support and affirmation from faculty. In the wider Mennonite community, congregations were wrestling with the question of female leadership, and Groff found the discord unsettling. But at school she never doubted that she was as free as any male student to pursue any opportunity that interested her. "I felt that whatever I wanted to do, the sky was the limit," Groff said. "I remember teachers saying, 'I'll be curious to see where you go from here.'"

Groff said Lancaster Mennonite's high standards, particularly in writing and critical thinking, prepared her for adult challenges. But at the same time that she felt academically challenged, she also saw the school as family.

"I still feel that people there care about me," she said.

Groff is executive director of Dove's Nest and the former executive director of The Mennonite.

Anna Groff | Tucson, Arizona | Class of 2002

TRANSFORMING LIVES

TRADITIONS & TRANSITIONS
Good sports

In the early days, LMS didn't have sports teams in uniform, but students always enjoyed competition and working up a sweat. Class socials featured games between mixed volleyball teams. On field day students assembled for races and other events. Pick-up basketball games offered workouts before anyone heard of cardio.

Over the years, LMS started fielding teams to compete with other schools. LMS built a soccer field surrounded by a track. Volleyball moved into the gym, and basketball required time-keepers and coordinated cheering.

Athletes today now tread on the shiny wooden floor in Gym B, where bleachers rise to the ceiling and courts are marked for basketball and volleyball. Outside, a rubber composite track surrounds a multipurpose field. Near the baseball fields and tennis courts is the artificial turf field with towering light standards for field hockey, lacrosse, and soccer. Cheering throngs fill the stadium for big games.

What hasn't changed over the years is the fun competitors have as they try their best.

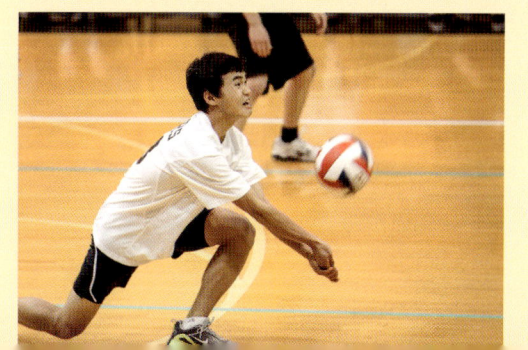

Working together for success

Playing sports at LMS is about building self-confidence, making friends and having fun. But just as important is the life lesson of teamwork, individuals sharing a goal and working hard to try to achieve it.

In team sports, seasoned players assume leadership roles, helping new teammates fit in and start building for success in coming seasons. It is important to learn to win with humility and to lose without a loss of self-esteem. A sure sign of a cohesive team is when players on the sidelines are engaged and rooting for their teammates in the game.

At LMS, coaches try to instill in their athletes the idea that Christian values should guide them and that they are, as the saying goes, "playing for a greater purpose."

"Do you know why LMS is winning? It's because they are a selfless team—you can't even pick out their stars because they do so well at teamwork." – *opposing coach, overheard at a soccer game*

"The combination of strong academics and the lessons learned on the soccer field and the basketball court gave me what I needed to be successful in business—leadership skills, teamwork, discipline, and a strong work ethic. I don't think people understand how much athletics can make persons great employees."
—Jerry Hostetter, alumnus and parent

TRANSFORMING LIVES

Essential community support

Parents haul their chairs and their enthusiasm from game to game. They carry in fruit snacks for the little ones and conjure up spaghetti dinners on game night for the older players. They shout unabashedly for their kids and their teams.

LMS Blazer support may take the form of dramatic black and gold paint on a few of the faces among the hundreds filling the stands or simply a collection of teammates and a few friends beside the track, but community support is vital on and off the field.

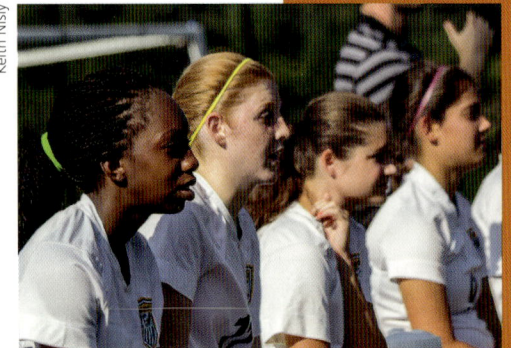

"My friends and family have provided me with relentless support at my cross country races and tennis matches throughout my four years at LMHS. Tennis and cross country are very psychological sports and having my friends and family backing me up along the course or beside the tennis court was an immense help to me when coping with the pressures of competing." —Seth Weaver, high school student

100 TRANSFORMING LIVES

"It has honestly meant so much to me when friends and family came to watch me play. Their support gave me added motivation to play better. It's almost like I would try even harder just to put on a good game for them." –*Maia Garber, high school student*

101

REMEMBERING LANCASTER MENNONITE

KARLA SANTIAGO

A great teacher helped her find her voice and set her course

"Now that I'm a teacher and putting together musicals for my own students, I think back about how my teachers conducted rehearsals."

Karla Santiago entered Lancaster Mennonite High School her junior year with a vague idea of wanting to become a teacher. She pictured herself teaching English or kindergarten. Those ideas vanished, however, when she fell under the spell of an inspiring music teacher: John Miller. His example made Santiago want to be a music teacher, and his memory continues to inspire.

A great teacher gets to know his or her students, their strengths and potential, and then finds ways to challenge them to try new things and grow. So it was that Miller zeroed in on Santiago's perception of herself as an alto. Miller thought her voice had sufficient range to also sing soprano parts, and he wouldn't take no for an answer. "I fought it really hard. I didn't want to be a soprano," Santiago said. But Miller was sure he was right. He insisted she sing the soprano parts, and he encouraged her efforts. In time Santiago realized Miller was right. "I found my voice!" she said, and later in college she performed as a solo soprano.

Her senior year Santiago was thrilled to be cast as the character Cat in the Hat in *Seussical*. It's a fun, audience-pleasing role. But Miller, who was directing the show, saw the role as an opportunity to push Santiago out of her comfort zone and grow as a performer. Miller did that by giving Santiago the assignment of improvising her own movements to the short but snappy song, "How Lucky You Are."

"That scared me a lot," Santiago said. "I like being told exactly what to do, where to stand, etc. It was hard for me to figure out what to do with the song without feeling completely forced and awkward."

Miller had some ideas for how Santiago could approach the task. He suggested she sing the song to herself as if she were trying to talk herself out of being glum by reminding herself of the good things in her life. She said Miller asked her, "How would I convey the emotion of the song if I had to tell myself, 'How lucky you are!'"

Santiago did as Miller had suggested and found herself connecting with the song in a way she hadn't before. She figured out how to move and gesture while she sang the song. She gained confidence as a performer. More importantly, she learned something about teaching. She recognized that great teachers step back from telling students what they need to know so that they have space to figure out things on their own.

"Now that I'm a teacher and putting together musicals for my own students, I think back about how my teachers conducted rehearsals," Santiago said. "I want my students to feel confident about the roles they are playing. I want to be the kind of teacher that encourages them, but also pushes."

Santiago is a music teacher for elementary students at the Santa Cruz Christian Learning Center, a private, international school in Bolivia. She directs the Christmas program and choir.

Karla Santiago | Santa Cruz, Bolivia | Class of 2006

TRANSFORMING LIVES

In the spotlight

Being a performer takes courage. It takes self-confidence to stand before an audience and put all of your diligent preparation on the line. Whether you are standing alone in the spotlight or are part of an ensemble, the moment of truth comes when the curtain rises.

"The arts taught me the value of teamwork. No choir, cast or band can operate as a group of individuals. The arts bring out the best in everyone and allow them to act as a part of a greater whole. That communal experience has been invaluable to me going on to college."
—Logan Ressler, alumnus

103

Backstage performance

The tech crew engages in performance of a different sort. Ten students run sound and lighting for each daily chapel service at the Lancaster campus. The crew for a play or musical, often 20 or 30 students, stage-manages, builds the set, paints, collects props and coordinates a series of microphones, lighting affects and video using state-of-the-art systems. Students on the tech crew practice leadership and teamwork. They show respect and service to others, along with the necessary technical skills, while making an important contribution to a larger whole. And they have fun along the way!

"I really enjoyed building the set for the musical and made a lot of good friends. Tech crew taught me valuable skills, like how to mix with professional equipment and to produce video." —*Ethan Beiler, high school student*

"Many students graduate from LMS and continue in the theater and entertainment industry. It is a good to know that working with the tech crew and on stage productions has a positive impact on students' lives and future careers." —*Ryan Rohrer, technical director*

104 TRANSFORMING LIVES

"I enjoy the interaction with students, helping them develop their God-given talents and giving them opportunities to perform in a variety of settings." –*Jim Fairman, middle school music teacher*

Working in harmony

A score is the carefully conceived documentation of a composer's vision, but not until the conductor raises the baton and watchful musicians start to play or sing does a piece of music come to life.

A well-rehearsed musical group is a wonder to experience as individual voices and instruments blend and rise, creating something truly greater than the sum of its parts. Such harmony stirs an audience's soul.

"LMH was a positive place of growth for me. I had a lot of fun performing in the pit orchestras for the musicals. John Miller and Marcy Hostetler both provided influence and support, and encouraged me to believe in myself. They truly changed my life and helped set me up for success." –*Eric Umble, alumnus*

TRANSFORMING LIVES 105

REMEMBERING LANCASTER MENNONITE

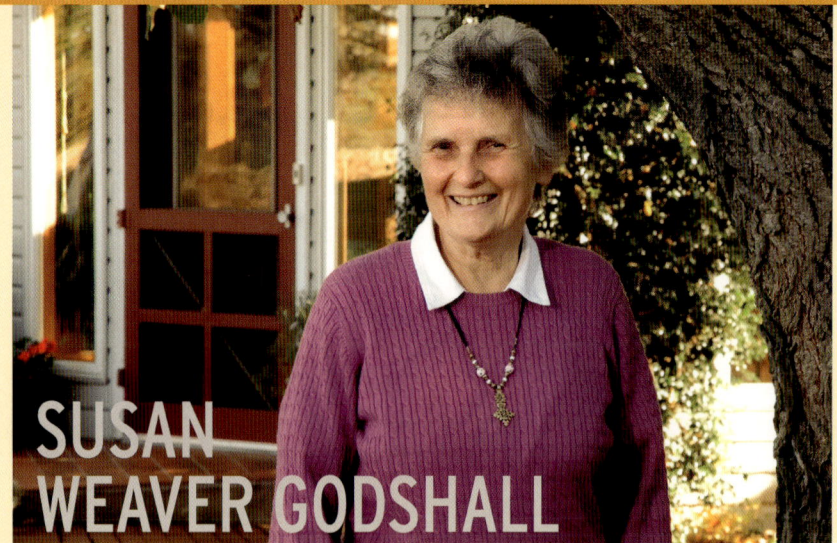

SUSAN WEAVER GODSHALL

More than school, it was a journey of surprises

"When faith is dim or troubled, there is something about the wonders of creation that pull me back to the Creator."

Students and faculty, 400 voices strong, began to sing. It happened every morning at Lancaster Mennonite High School. Chapel and hymn-singing were synonymous. But for Susan Weaver Godshall, on her first day as a freshman in 1957, the moment was novel and thrilling.

She was a farmer's daughter from East Earl who had attended a one-room school through the eighth grade. Suddenly, she was part of something bigger. She joined her soprano voice to the soaring, four-part harmony and felt swept up. That's what Lancaster Mennonite was: a journey of surprises, opening her world to the unexpected.

Godshall joined the choir and was introduced to Handel's "Hallelujah Chorus" and other inspiring classics. Later, she toured with the elite singers of the Choraleers, organized outside of the school by Arnold and Maietta Moshier. The young people gave concerts as far away as Canada. "I found out there were more kinds of music than we sang at my church," she said. "Music came to inspire me and to enrich my worship experience."

Godshall's four years at Lancaster Mennonite expanded her world in other ways as well. Her country school had not prepared her for algebra. She felt embarrassed by the 'D' she received on her first test. But the teacher, Luke Shank, continued to patiently explain concepts and to encourage her. She passed the next test with a 'B.' "I got a sense that I can learn things that I think are beyond my grasp," Godshall recalled. "If Mr. Shank had belittled and not cared, I might have failed. But he was there to help us learn."

While math remained a challenge, Godshall took Latin I, a required course for those preparing for college, and she discovered she had a knack for languages. She later majored in Spanish at Eastern Mennonite University.

Likewise, the hands-on lessons in a 10th-grade biology class taught by Charles Longenecker widened Godshall's appreciation of nature. "I came to realize the natural world has so much intricacy and grandeur," she said. "When faith is dim or troubled, there is something about the wonders of creation that pull me back to the Creator."

As she soaked in the lessons on writing and literature taught by sisters Edna and Grace Wenger, Godshall had another epiphany. Here were two Mennonite women, yet they were educated and flourished in a professional setting. "That was a very new idea for me," said Godshall, recalling how she felt her own horizons started to expand.

Godshall's years at Lancaster Mennonite broadened her outlook and gave her freedom to explore in a way that respected cherished relationships. She continued to honor the faith traditions of her upbringing, but she also accepted a call to stretch herself and prepare for the world beyond East Earl. She learned she could bridge two worlds.

Godshall is Chaplain Associate at Philhaven, Mount Gretna, Pennsylvania. She was formerly Representative to Africa for Eastern Mennonite Missions.

Susan E. Weaver Godshall | Mount Joy, Pennsylvania | Class of 1961

A yearly record

A yearbook is more than a publication. It's a trove of memories to be savored for years to come. It takes a dedicated team of students working throughout the school year to create each edition of *Laurel Wreath*. The photographers compose compelling shots. Writers convey the stories. Page designers create reader-friendly layouts. And the sales and production staff makes sure the work gets done on time and within budget. The students' hard work has been affirmed over the years by many scholatistic press association awards.

While their work is less comprehensive, students staffing the middle school yearbook teams are just as enthusiastic.

Working on a yearbook is a real-world experience that teaches lifelong skills, not the least of which is teamwork. Many students go on to careers making use of things they learned producing the yearbook. And all members of the staff help create something they can page through and treasure, remembering all the fun they had.

"Putting together the yearbook was a really fun time! I collaborated and worked with my friends to create a book that I know will be enjoyed for many years to come." —*Sophia Martin, high school student*

TRANSFORMING LIVES 107

REMEMBERING LANCASTER MENNONITE

FRED KNISS

A collaborative activity called learning

"That connection between book learning and real human problems captured my imagination."

Fred Kniss was a fresh face on campus in 1972, a pastor's son who had grown up attending public schools 600 miles away in Florida. Only two years from graduation, Kniss chose to leave home and try a new school knowing it might be difficult to fit in. He convinced his parents it was what he wanted.

Kniss looks back on his decision to attend Lancaster Mennonite High School as one of the best he ever made. Two extracurricular activities stand out.

Kniss worked on the *Millstream*, an experience that improved his writing and leadership skills. It also gave him a chance to test boundaries. The newspaper staff surveyed students on drug use and found a small number, less than 10 percent, admitting to experimentation. Kniss thought it was newsworthy. The principal, however, wasn't sure it should be printed.

Merle Good, a faculty member who advised *Millstream* staff, backed the students, and the principal relented. The story went to press. "It was probably the best-read issue of that year," he said.

Kniss found himself once more testing boundaries. This time it was putting on a play. Some believed theater conflicted with Mennonite values, but the school knew others saw it differently and agreed to a single-day performance of *The Miracle Worker,* which tells the story of Helen Keller. The actors agreed to abide by the dress code and other school rules.

Students got out of class to see the performance, and more than a dozen Mennonite bishops occupied a row of seats. Kniss, who played Helen's father, thought the performance went well. His grandfather, one of the bishops, had one complaint. He pointed out that Kniss had picked up the girl playing Helen and carried her down a ladder. Kniss' grandfather saw it as a violation of a rule against physical contact between male and female students. But the play proved successful, and dramas became highlights of the school year.

Student activities helped shape the adult Kniss became. And so did a sociology course taught by Myron Dietz. Kniss thought he would follow his father in becoming a pastor, but the sociology class and a research project opened his eyes to other possibilities. Kniss examined marketing's impact on consumer behavior, interviewed staff at advertising agencies and analyzed their work. "That connection between book learning and real human problems captured my imagination," Kniss said.

Kniss said one big thing stood out about Lancaster Mennonite: how the faculty cared about each student. "It's something I tried to model in my career in education," Kniss said. "I want students to get the sense that they are valued and that they and I are engaged in a collaborative activity called learning."

Kniss is provost at Eastern Mennonite University in Harrisonburg, Virginia, and was a professor of sociology at Loyola University in Chicago.

Fred Kniss | Harrisonburg, Virginia | Class of 1974

"Working on the *Millstream* has made me passionate about writing. It has made me realize that what I write has an impact on others, not just myself."
—Abby King, high school student

Campus communications

Since the beginning, the *Millstream,* the student newspaper for Lancaster Mennonite High School, has covered events, people and issues—whether they are campus concerns or related to the wider world. The student journalists practice the concepts of accuracy, fairness and accountability, and learn that free speech is no excuse for irresponsible speech. Administrators have allowed writers to tackle controversies, including those related to faith, such as patriotism and women in church leadership. Each issue engages the *Millstream* staff in lively conversation. The influx of international students has enriched the experience.

Another vital publication is *Silhouette,* the literary and arts magazine publishing poetry, short stories, essays and visual arts for over 35 years. Students handle every aspect of the magazine: editing, production and sales.

For over nine years, until 2015, LMS students ran the school website as part of a class. The experience students gained in designing and maintaining the website proved valuable in their careers.

"I was looking into web development as a career, so to get hands-on experience through the web team and to work with students with similar interests was amazing."
—Nick Walter, high school student

TRANSFORMING LIVES **109**

REMEMBERING LANCASTER MENNONITE

As LMH student and teacher, he benefited from both

"I was always an obsessive reader, but maybe I became an adult reader in that class."

PETER DULA

The 36-line, 17th-century love poem, dense with obscure language, took more than one reading to grasp. Peter Dula discovered the payoff was worth the effort. He was a student in Janet Banks' English class, and his first reading of John Donne's "A Valediction: Forbidding Mourning" could easily have been his last. But Mrs. Banks patiently opened his eyes to the power and beauty of metaphor in expressing the ethereal. "I was always an obsessive reader, and still am," Dula said, "but maybe I became an adult reader in that class. Mrs. Banks taught me the pleasures of poetry and the possibilities of language."

Reading and writing were reinforcing passions of the academically inclined Dula at Lancaster Mennonite. He wrote for the *Millstream* and appreciated the guidance and affirmation of adviser Dan Dietzel. "It gave me space to feel I had a gift that was worth sticking with," Dula said. Principal Dick Thomas was also an encouraging presence, telling Dula that his opinion pieces in the *Millstream* were better than the papers he wrote for the Bible class Thomas taught.

Dula graduated from LMH never suspecting he would return as a teacher. But in 1996 he came back from missions work in Burundi with plans to attend graduate school. When he missed the application deadline, he needed something to do and was grateful for the opportunity to return to LMH to teach social studies and Bible. "I loved it," Dula said. "Those were two of the best working years of my life."

Dula was surprised by how often students—he remembers them "bright-eyed and ready to go"—beat him to the classroom in the morning as he scrambled to get ready for the day. "We did a lot of discussion" in class, he said. "I was impressed with how engaged the students were and how willing they were to speak up and toss around issues."

Dula said he came to realize that teens wanted to be listened to and to be taken seriously. "They are often getting preached at," he said. "If Bible class was a place where they could talk and not get preached at, I think that was a real relief for them."

"That's what I've tried to keep doing," he said.

Dula's fondest memory teaching at LMH was taking students to a Trappist monastery in Massachusetts and exposing them to Catholicism and monastic traditions. The spiritual beauty of a vespers service, in particular, seemed to impress some of the students more than any class could have, Dula said. Dula overheard two students walking into the sunset afterward and talking about what they had just experienced. "They felt like they had entered a completely different world of spirituality," he said.

Dula is chair of the Bible and Religion Department at Eastern Mennonite University in Harrisonburg, Virginia.

Peter Dula | Harrisonburg, Virginia | Class of 1988

TRANSFORMING LIVES

TRADITIONS & TRANSITIONS
Reading for life

Young students progress through elementary school, moving from "learning to read" to "reading to learn."

Studies have found that becoming a lifelong reader has many benefits. Reading, of course, helps one master a subject. But lovers of reading also become stronger writers and deeper thinkers.

At LMS kids have many opportunities to read. Individualized reading programs seek to motivate students to become stronger readers. One important strategy is encouraging students to read what attracts them. When young students delve into books that interest them, they not only become more fluent readers and learn new things, they also start to develop a habit of reading that will enrich their lives.

TRANSFORMING LIVES 111

Building a strong base

The very nature of building invites cooperation. One may steady the base while another adds on, or one maneuvers materials while another directs. As each does his or her part, the structure all comes together.

Constructing walkways, stage sets and buildings in which to learn, worship and fellowship is a physical act. And then there is also the nurturing aspects of building community.

From little ones collaborating at playtime to a leadership that seeks to use resources wisely and to create an atmosphere of learning, LMS builds for the future.

"The diversity of the student body, the sense of community, and the moral basis of the education at New Danville are preparing our children to be caring, conscientious contributors to their world. This is the educational experience we want for them." –*Melissa Mattilio, parent*

112   TRANSFORMING LIVES

LMS construction projects, 1985–2016

1985 Offices and Media Center, Lancaster Campus
1991 Calvin and Janet High Fine Arts Center, Lancaster Campus
1996 Alumni Dining Hall, Lancaster Campus
1999 Gym B, Lancaster Campus
2004 G. Parke Book Building, Lancaster Campus
2006 Entrance and Offices, New Danville Campus
2007 Turf Field and Stadium, Lancaster Campus
2008 Fieldhouse, Lancaster Campus
2008 Rutt Academic Center, Lancaster Campus
2009 Palazzo Gallery, Kraybill Campus
2010 Track, Lancaster Campus
2012 Entrance and Offices, Kraybill Campus
2015 Millstream Hall, Lancaster Campus
2016 Dining Hall, Hershey Campus

113

TRADITIONS & TRANSITIONS
Spring banquet

Who are you going with? How did he ask you? What are you wearing?

The venue and activities have changed, but the enthusiasm remains. Preparations for the Junior-Senior Banquet are always electric.

In the early years, the banquets were sedate affairs with dinner in the dining hall, entertainment by vocal groups, and inspirational speeches.

More recently, students have enjoyed formal dinners at a variety of venues, followed by forays onto the dance floor. Later in the evening come the post-banquet festivities. Shine and sparkle is always in style. Parents and teachers get misty-eyed. Who are these groomed, mature young people, and how did they get past awkward adolescence?

Joyful celebrations

Celebration can be raising a state trophy high in the air or tossing one's mortarboard skyward. It can be gesturing exuberantly in song or tapping that final brick into the path representing a met fundraising goal. But always it's better with friends and family by your side or in the audience, sharing in the joy of accomplishment. They knew you could do it.

"I'll never forget the joy of pursuing a state title with my teammates and brothers. Going out on top was truly special, but it's the experiences that I shared with my friends that I will always remember." —Benji Kennel, alumnus

TRANSFORMING LIVES 115

Graduate Profile

Lancaster Mennonite School is a comprehensive PreK-12 school that prepares graduates for lifelong learning. The Christ-centered educational process develops the gifts of each student to live as a global citizen. It is expected that a graduate of LMS is a person who:

Academic

- Infuses a Christ-centered faith into learning and understanding

- Has a love for learning and has developed skills that enable him/her to be a lifelong learner with the ability to solve problems, think critically, and to work collaboratively with others

- Exhibits competency in basic subject matter, possesses knowledge in the academic disciplines, the arts and workforce skills

- Communicates effectively through speaking, writing and listening

- Incorporates technology appropriately and has the skills to analyze and manage information

- Has the knowledge and skills for success in his/her personal life, management of money, relationships, and self-understanding

- Has a love for God's creation and its diversity in the natural environment and peoples

Spiritual

- Is growing in relationship to Jesus Christ and a faith community
- Has a faith centered in Jesus Christ as the final revelation of God
- Is biblically literate, values and accepts the authority of Scripture, knows the history of the universal Christian church and the Anabaptist heritage and is able to bring these into discernment of faith questions
- Lives a life of discernment, spiritual growth and the discovery and development of gifts, by asking questions and seeking answers, through the practice of spiritual disciplines, the counsel of other Christians and the church
- Knows he/she is loved by God and shares this love with others by word and deed
- Cultivates a worldview informed by Christian Anabaptist teaching

Lifestyle

- Practices global awareness, cultural sensitivity and humility, respect, an anti-racist lifestyle and compassionate living
- Practices stewardship of all God has entrusted to him/her, including the natural environment and is generous in giving of time and money to bless and serve others
- Shows commitment to forgiveness, understanding, reconciliation and non-violent resolution of conflict, and respects all human life
- Participates and is accountable in the life of a church community
- Maintains healthy relationships with others in family, church, workplace and community
- Practices wellness of body, mind and spirit
- Practices a balanced ethic of work, service and leisure
- Lives with a sense of curiosity, wonder and mystery

The graduate profile is developed within the framework of *Confession of Faith in a Mennonite Perspective* that gives definition to the theological phrases in this profile.

"The greatest gift LMS can give to students is to let them know that there's a God of love who loves them more than they can ever love themselves. We envision shalom as being four things—peace with God, peace with yourself, peace with others, and peace with creation."
–J. Richard Thomas, LMS superintendent, parent

Changing Our World

Lancaster Mennonite School is five campuses and the people who populate it. But the school's impact is greater than the sum of its parts.

LMS is an engine of change making our world a better place.

We want students to see themselves as global citizens who ask what is best for the world and seek peaceable solutions. We prepare students for successful lives in which meaning is found, not in the pursuit of wealth and material things, but in building a more just and peaceful world. Our counter-cultural outlook encourages students to identify with the values of the Sermon on the Mount and to advance the Kingdom of God.

We encourage involvement that promotes social change. Often, chapel features speakers from around the world who call on the LMS community to pray for and act upon global needs. The LMS community responds in many ways, from going on mission trips to supporting refugee resettlement.

The impact of the LMS experience is reflected in the ways graduates go on to heal a hurting world. They are teachers who choose to accept some of the most challenging assignments in inner-city schools and poor countries. They are health care professionals, attorneys and counselors whose doors swing open to the indigent. They are entrepreneurs and managers who pay workers fairly, adhere to rigorous codes of ethics, and practice sustainability in their use of the world's resources. And they are spiritual leaders who comfort the aggrieved and inspire all to lead Christ-centered lives.

What is the legacy of Lancaster Mennonite's first 75 years? It's the lived witness of its alumni.

Alumni of the Year 2000

"LMH supported and reinforced values and commitments which had already been encouraged by my parents."

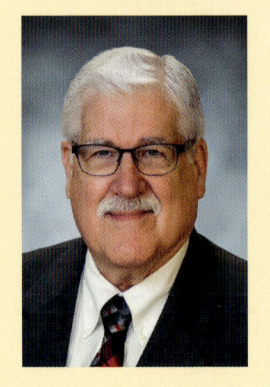

John W. Eby

Lititz, Pennsylvania
Class of 1958

Eby, a retired educator, was a professor of sociology at Messiah College and director of the college's Service Learning Program. Earlier, he taught sociology and business at Eastern Mennonite University.

Highlights: While at Messiah, Eby started an annual conference for service learning programs in faith-based colleges and became a spokesperson for these programs through writing and participation in conferences and consultations.

While he was a sophomore at Eastern Mennonite College, Eby was ordained by lot to serve the Blainsport congregation, a role that led to opportunities to serve as VS and 1-W director for Eastern Mennonite Missions, Mennonite Board of Missions and to chair the Mennonite Board of Missions.

In retirement, Eby chairs Landis Communities and is a board member for Welsh Mountain Homes and Camp Hebron.

Education: Eastern Mennonite University, bachelor's degree in chemistry; Cornell University, master's degree in development sociology; Cornell University, doctorate in development sociology
Spouse: the late Joyce Rutt, LMS Class of 1959
Family: two children, four grandchildren

Activities at LMS: Sports, chorus and yearbook
Church affiliation: Slate Hill Mennonite Church, Camp Hill, Pennsylvania

CHANGING OUR WORLD

From learning a new language to a deeper cultural immersion

While early class offerings may have stressed language as the entrée into a culture, more recent LMS programs include music, arts, politics and food as ways to understand other peoples. The elementary students enrolled in Spanish Immersion learn music and history as well as the language. The growing enrollment of students at LMS from other countries enriches the entire community with the diverse voices and experiences they bring.

Returning missionaries and teachers who had served in other countries gave early students glimpses of the world beyond. Reading maps, even as political lines changed over the years, has helped students understand their place in the world and to dream of travel. Young people grow to realize that God's love is not defined by borders and oceans. A broad perspective encourages global thinking.

Understanding the world and finding our place in it

Alumni of the Year 2000

"LMH impacted my journey in fantastic ways, calling me to a life of ministry, deepening my love for God and the church, giving me passion for cultivating an inner life."

Miriam Book

Harleysville, Pennsylvania
Class of 1966

Book is Interim Lead Pastor of Zion Mennonite Church, Souderton, PA and was Associate General Secretary for the Mennonite Church General Board in Elkhart, Indiana.

Highlights: LMH impacted my journey in fantastic ways, calling me to a life of ministry, deepening my love for God and the church, giving me passion for cultivating an inner life. I see followers of Jesus Christ creating communities of grace, joy and peace, so hope and healing can flow through us to the world. Christians should tend to their own souls before tending the mass of souls to whom we give leadership or are called to walk among. Leadership flows outward from within. Cultivating a deep relationship with God is of utmost importance in today's fast-paced living.

Education: Eastern College, bachelor's degree;
    London Bible College, diploma in pastoral studies
Spouse: James M. Lapp
Family: three children, seven grandchildren

Activities at LMS: Choraleers
Church affiliation: Zion Mennonite Church,
    Souderton, Pennsylvania

CHANGING OUR WORLD   121

Alumni of the Year 2001

"For me LMS was a doorway from the farm to the world—a challenging one, but manageable and safe. It allowed for exploration of identity, relationships and values, and the experience has enriched the journey ever since."

Daniel S. Hess

Lancaster, Pennsylvania
Class of 1966

Hess is a management consultant.

Highlight: In 1997, Evanna and I accepted a three-year assignment with Mennonite Central Committee, serving in Russia, Serbia and Albania. After we completed our term I returned to my psychotherapy and consultation practice but continued to take advantage of opportunities for international work and travel. Since 2008 I have been working with The KonTerra Group, a consulting firm that focuses on international humanitarian and development organizations, and my consulting assignments have taken me to five continents.

Education: Millersville University, bachelor's degree in psychology; University of Pennsylvania, master of social work
Spouse: Evanna Umble Hess, Class of 1966
Family: two children, four grandchildren

Activities at LMS: *Laurel Wreath* editor, student council, sophomore class president, junior class vice president
Church affiliation: Forest Hills Mennonite Church, Leola, Pennsylvania

Visiting and hosting internationally

LMS has long respected the insights of those who have had overseas experiences. Students today continue to learn about others by receiving cross-cultural visitors and traveling themselves. International visitors volunteer in LMS schools and speak at chapel while LMS partners with schools abroad.

When students travel abroad, they're not just tourists. Often they compete or perform music with their hosts. Travel opens the door to future service and career opportunities, and it builds global citizens.

122   CHANGING OUR WORLD

"I am always excited to host international students at our house. It's cool to learn more about another culture firsthand instead of just reading about it in textbooks or online."
—Ian Martin, high school student

"In the classroom we talk about who our neighbors are to build empathy for the whole world. I am grateful for a school that emphasizes becoming models of God's love." —Jenn Esbenshade, elementary teacher, parent

Alumni of the Year 2001

"LMS markedly expanded my worldview during an era when political and social upheaval shook our country. LMS nurtured my conviction that all people deserve justice and lives free of violence."

Evanna F. Hess

Lancaster, Pennsylvania
Class of 1966

Hess, a retired registered nurse, serves on her church council, is a member of the church's Syrian refugee support team and volunteers at Ten Thousand Villages.

Highlights: My nursing career in geriatrics included serving as the founding director of the Landis Homes Adult Day Services Program. My husband and I spent three years with Mennonite Central Committee in Russia, Serbia and Albania in a peacebuilding assignment and supporting organizations that worked with refugees. After returning, I was manager of MCC's Material Resources Center in Ephrata, Pennsylvania. In 2015, I served as Assembly Scattered Coordinator for the Mennonite World Conference Assembly Gathering in Harrisburg, Pennsylvania.

Education: Lancaster General Hospital School of Nursing, registered nurse diploma; Eastern Mennonite University, bachelor's degree in management and organizational development
Spouse: Daniel S. Hess, Class of 1966
Family: two children, four grandchildren

Activities at LMS: freshman class secretary, senior class treasurer, student forum member, officer of the Socratarian Society
Church affiliation: Forest Hills Mennonite Church, Leola, Pennsylvania

CHANGING OUR WORLD   123

REMEMBERING LANCASTER MENNONITE

Dorm experiences offered unexpected, lifelong lessons

"She led very gently, but she still was a decisive leader."

ANGIE MILLER PETERSHEIM

Conflict resolution was an early and unexpected lesson for Angie Petersheim after she moved into the dorm at Lancaster Mennonite High School her junior year.

The first in her immediate family to attend LMH, Petersheim, who grew up in Williamsport, Maryland, and had always gone to public schools, was excited about being away from home and experiencing a new school.

Petersheim's newfound independence brought opportunities for growth, including the challenge of learning how to stay on good terms with others in the dorm, some of whom pushed the rules or in other ways were different than her own low-key, easy-going family.

One girl in particular, to Petersheim's consternation, found a reason to be angry with her. Petersheim realized no one else was going to fix the problem, and it wasn't going to resolve itself. "I didn't think she had the right to be angry with me," Petersheim recalled, but for whatever reason, the girl was angry, and Petersheim had to deal with it. Fortunately, Petersheim said, the issue wasn't that big a deal, and she worked through it and reestablished harmony. The episode became a lesson for Petersheim about how to deal with a difficult person and later, when she was an adult and an educator, about how to help girls navigate their own rocky peer interactions.

Another benefit of dorm life for Petersheim was getting to know Charlotte Holsopple Glick, the dorm advisor, and to appreciate seeing a woman in leadership. "She led very gently, but she still was a decisive leader," Petersheim recalled. Glick's example helped to plant the idea that women can lead and can lead well, and that she, too, might have leadership qualities. And over the years as an educator and leader, Petersheim found Glick's leadership style influencing her.

Being at LMH, and away from her conservative home church, caused Petersheim to reflect on faithfulness and what it meant to be a Christian. Interacting with a variety of Mennonite women, Petersheim realized one did not have to wear a covering to love God. One could still follow Jesus and see a movie. "Here were adults I respected and appreciated, and they had different perspectives," Petersheim said. "Some of it may have been maturing, but I know LMH broadened my horizons."

Petersheim remained a member of her home church, but she appreciated returning home with different understandings and new ways of looking at what being a Mennonite means.

Petersheim is the administrator of Shalom Christian Academy, a private school in Chambersburg, Pennsylvania, serving 550 students.

Angie Miller Petersheim | Chambersburg, Pennsylvania | Class of 1975

124 CHANGING OUR WORLD

Mediation and conflict resolution

Talking about disagreements or conflict isn't always easy, but it is often effective. When someone wrongs you, it's natural to take offense. Peer mediation and conflict resolution allow students to work things out by meeting face-to-face. Listening to others, then explaining your point of view, is a valuable way to learn from a difficult situation. All work together to craft a solution.

Alumni of the Year 2002

"LMS shaped my values and ethics and assisted me in integrating my faith into my career, giving me the courage to represent the teachings of Jesus in many settings I would have never anticipated."

Allon Lefever

Lancaster, Pennsylvania
Class of 1964

Lefever is President of Lefever Associates and owns several small businesses. He formerly served as the Director of the Family Business Program at Goshen College, and as Director of the MBA Program at Eastern Mennonite University. Earlier, Lefever was vice president of Earthlink, Inc.; president of OneMain.com, Inc.; senior vice president of Afflilated Companies for High Industries, and group vice president of operations at Victor F. Weaver Inc.

Highlight: We took our Internet company public on NASDAQ in 1999. My senior executive positions at Weaver, Inc., High Industries and Earthlink, Inc. were wonderful experiences, most of all the opportunity to serve on fifty-nine boards of directors, twenty-nine nonprofit boards and two foundation boards.

Education: Millersville University, bachelor's degree in comprehensive social studies; Pennsylvania State University, master's degree in economics
Spouse: Doris Elaine Blank Lefever, Class of 1964
Family: three children, ten grandchildren

Church affiliation: Forest Hills Mennonite Church, Leola, Pennsylvania

CHANGING OUR WORLD

Alumni of the Year 2003

"I began to think more globally and also to think about how I fit into God's plan for the world and the church."

Janet N. Gehman

Strasburg, Pennsylvania
Class of 1952

Gehman, a retired English teacher, taught at Lancaster Mennonite School from 1965 to 1995.

Highlight: I spent a sabbatical year teaching in Tanzania and also accepted a two-year assignment with China Educational Exchange from 1986 to 1988.
   After I retired, I served for seven years as editor of Lancaster Mennonite Conference's newsletter, and also on the board of the Lancaster Mennonite Historical Society.

Education: Eastern Mennonite University, bachelor's degree; Millersville University, master's degree in education

Church affiliation: Hershey Mennonite Church, Kinzers, Pennsylvania

126   CHANGING OUR WORLD

Ties in the community

LMS reaches beyond the school campuses to the local community. Blazer values are on full display when runners team up in the Lancaster YWCA's Race Against Racism. Young agriculturalists share enthusiasm and knowledge with children as they show and discuss livestock. Prayer before a game and a salute to the opposing team's supporters at the close of a game represent beliefs far better than simply talking about them.

"I've run in the Race Against Racism since I was six years old. It's great to see so many people come to Lancaster city to support the YWCA program. Residents are sitting outside cheering, which makes it a fun run to be involved in." —Rein Wenger, high school student

REMEMBERING LANCASTER MENNONITE

Relationships matter in school and in business

"My time at Lancaster Mennonite strengthened me as a person, prepared me to deal with adversity . . . and set a standard for how to show caring for other people."

SAM BEILER

It happened every couple of months. Lancaster Mennonite High School principal Dick Thomas spotted shaggy-haired Sam Beiler, wrapped an arm around the student's shoulder and, with a chuckle, said, "About time for a haircut, isn't it, Beiler?" It was a friendly suggestion. Not a dictate. But it worked. Beiler made sure he got himself to the barbershop. The principal successfully enforced the dress code.

At the time, Beiler didn't give much thought to how school administrators and teachers guided student conduct. But later in life, particularly as his own children attended LMS, Beiler came to appreciate how faculty successfully motivated students to behave and to do good work by first developing caring relationships. When students made mistakes or misbehaved, Beiler said, they generally were more open to correction because they felt teachers and administrators knew them as individuals and were genuinely concerned about their wellbeing.

Beiler said as a high school student he was more interested in his social life than in excelling in his studies. He credits two teachers in particular, Mrs. Banks and Mr. Dietzel, for taking the time to get to know him and to challenge him to do better. Beiler said he didn't view their comments as negative or belittling, but as supportive and motivating. "What I felt was acceptance and encouragement," Beiler said. "I came to my own recognition that I could have done more." He said their manner made him want to improve. "I believe that my time at Lancaster Mennonite strengthened me as a person, prepared me to deal with adversity, which is a normal part of life, and I believe it set a standard for how to show caring for other people," Beiler said.

What Beiler learned about the primacy of relationships has influenced his management style as a business owner. He said he tries to accept employees as valued individuals, compliment their strengths and earn their respect. "I believe it motivates people when you are a positive force in their life," he said. And on those occasions when he has to address mistakes or failings, he said, "the employees are accepting and, perhaps, even welcoming of that."

At LMH, Beiler learned strong relationships make effective leadership possible.

Beiler is founder and chief executive officer of Spooky Nook Sports. He is the former president and owner of Auntie Anne's.

Sam Beiler | Lancaster, Pennsylvania | Class of 1983

CHANGING OUR WORLD

Alumni of the Year 2004

"LMS provides an excellent education in a nurturing environment that prepares students for lifelong learning and invites them to personal faith, Christlike mission, peacemaking and service in a global society."

John L. Ruth

Harleysville, Pennsylvania
Class of 1948

Ruth, now retired, was an English professor at Eastern University and the University of Hamburg, Germany. He is an author and was a Franconia Conference minister, ordained in 1950. From 1972 to 1993 he was associate pastor at Salford Mennonite Church.

Highlight: I taught English at Eastern University for a decade with a sabbatical in 1968-69 teaching at the University of Hamburg in West Germany. After that I made films and wrote books on Mennonite history, including *Conrad Grebel, Son of Zurich; The Earth is the Lord's: A Narrative History of the Lancaster Mennonite Conference;* and *Branch: A Memoir with Pictures*. I also served as a minister from 1950 to 1957 and from 1971 to 1993. I led European Anabaptist history tours for TourMagination from 1973 to 2015.

Education: Eastern University, undergraduate degree; Harvard University, master's degree and doctorate
Spouse: Roma Jacobs
Family: three children, nine grandchildren

Activities at LMS: chorus, editor of *Laurel Wreath*
Church affiliation: Salford Mennonite Church, Harleysville, Pennsylvania

"Spending time observing plants and learning how the laws of physics and chemistry have been created by God to keep our Earth in balance helps students understand what a gift our planet is and what our role is in protecting it." —Barbara Josephian, *middle school teacher, parent*

128 CHANGING OUR WORLD

Our relationship with the living world

Learning about the earth and its inhabitants, animal and plant, is key to being a good citizen of the community and the wider world.

When students have a direct connection as they research and learn—hands right in the soil or in the water—the knowledge gained remains a part of their experience. The realization that what each does has a clear impact on others, near and far, informs future decisions.

Students at LMS are encouraged to think beyond the local. Some accept the challenge to make a difference with broad gestures and brave voices. Others set forth in a quieter way, but still make strong and steady contributions. Each is committed to honoring God's earth by caring for the environment.

Alumni of the Year 2005

"Although I attended LMS only my senior year, it had a profound impact. It reversed my vocational direction, enriched my spiritual life, encouraged me as a fledgling writer, and gave me lifelong friends."

Donald B. Kraybill

Elizabethtown, Pennsylvania
Class of 1963

Kraybill is retired from Elizabethtown College, where he was distinguished professor and senior fellow at the Young Center for Anabaptist and Pietist Studies. He is the author of *The Upside Down Kingdom* and many other books. Kraybill was provost of Messiah College from 1996 to 2002.

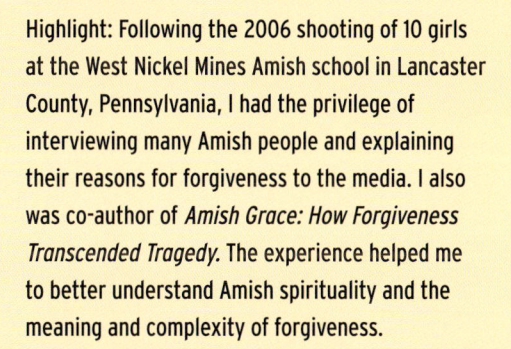

Highlight: Following the 2006 shooting of 10 girls at the West Nickel Mines Amish school in Lancaster County, Pennsylvania, I had the privilege of interviewing many Amish people and explaining their reasons for forgiveness to the media. I also was co-author of *Amish Grace: How Forgiveness Transcended Tragedy*. The experience helped me to better understand Amish spirituality and the meaning and complexity of forgiveness.

Education: Eastern Mennonite University, bachelor's degree in Bible and sociology; Temple University, master's degree and doctorate in sociology
Spouse: Frances Mellinger
Family: two children, two grandchildren

Activities at LMS: student council
Church affiliation: Elizabethtown Church of the Brethren, Elizabethtown, Pennsylvania

CHANGING OUR WORLD

Alumni of the Year 2006

"God bless you, LMS, for being a steady presence, for doing the long, slow work of shaping lives, ever so gently but persistently. For me. For our two daughters."

Phyllis Pellman Good

Lancaster, Pennsylvania | Class of 1966

Pellman Good is a book editor and an author on the New York Times bestselling list for the *Fix-It and Forget-It Cookbook* and *Fix-It and Forget-It Lightly*. She was the prior owner of Good Books, the Good Cooking Store and the Old Country Store. She was editor of *Festival Quarterly* magazine for 22 years.

Highlight: Having two books on the New York Times bestseller list. Other important experiences were serving on the executive committee of Mennonite World Conference, as editor of MWC's publication, *Courier*, and as a communication consultant and writer for MWC for more than 20 years.

Education: New York University, bachelor's and master's degrees in English
Spouse: Merle Good, Class of 1964
Family: two daughters and two grandchildren

LMS activities: literary editor of *Laurel Wreath*, choir
Church affiliation: East Chestnut Street Mennonite Church, Lancaster, Pennsylvania

130 CHANGING OUR WORLD

"Mill Stream is a perfect hands-on classroom. Students learn that what happens upstream affects what happens downstream. Streams affect the health of other waterways, so stream study is a good place to begin when learning about the role of water on this planet. We're talking about basic human need here— clean drinking water." –*Wayne Lehman, former middle school science teacher, parent*

Reviving the Mill Stream

In September 2013, 200 students on the Lancaster campus made a difference. They helped to plant 250 native trees and shrubs along the restored banks of Mill Stream. The added trees offer several benefits. Their shade keeps the waters cool, which aquatic life prefers. The roots stabilize the banks, reducing erosion. And the trees soak in heat-trapping carbon dioxide.

LMS saw the Mill Stream restoration project, coordinated by the Lancaster County Conservation District, as a way to care for God's earth. Students had a direct hand in practicing good stewardship by caring for the natural environment. Completion of the project is a step toward the goal of increasing the fish habitat, supporting the overall health of the ecosystem and restoring the Chesapeake Bay.

"It was fun to be outdoors and get dirty!"
– a tree-planting student

Alumni of the Year 2007

"I have a special interest in encouraging faithful Christian peacemaking, presence, and witness among Muslims."

David Shenk

Mountville, Pennsylvania
Class of 1955

Shenk is a global mission consultant with Eastern Mennonite Missions, focusing on ministry and witness among Muslims. He and his wife, Grace, served with Eastern Mennonite Missions in Somalia for ten years. Following that assignment, he taught for six years in the religious studies department of the Kenyatta University in Nairobi, Kenya. He is the author of over fifteen books and articles related to missions and the relationship of the gospel to other religions.

Highlight: From 1961 to 1963, I taught Bible and history at Lancaster Mennonite High School. "I loved teaching so much, that Friday evenings I wished it was Monday morning!"

Education: Eastern Mennonite University, bachelor's degree in social studies and theology; New York University, master's degree in social studies education and doctorate in religious studies education and anthropology
Spouse: K. Grace Shenk
Family: four children, seven grandchildren

Church affiliation: Mountville Mennonite Church, Mountville, Pennsylvania

CHANGING OUR WORLD

Alumni of the Year 2008

"Lancaster Mennonite helped to reaffirm my commitment to Christ and the church, and it gave me the foundation I needed to pursue my dreamed-of teaching career."

Lena Horning Brown

Denver, Pennsylvania
Class of 1952

Brown was an elementary teacher for 15 years at Weavertown Mennonite School, Gehman Mennonite School and with Eastern Mennonite Missions in Jamana, Somalia, and at Rosslyn Academy in Nairobi, Kenya. She also was deaconess and later associate pastor at Slate Hill Mennonite Church, where she was active in the resettlement of refugees from Vietnam and Laos. She was a board member at Eastern Mennonite Missions from 1985 to 1997.

Highlights: Teaching is a high calling. I count it a privilege to have been able to teach in Pennsylvania and with Eastern Mennonite Missions in Somalia and Kenya. It was also a privilege and honor to serve as a deaconess and a pastor.

Education: Eastern Mennonite University, bachelor's degree in elementary education; Millersville State College, master's degree in education
Spouse: Michael R. Brown
Family: two children, one grandchild

Activities at LMS: junior chorus
Church affiliation: Gehman Mennonite Church, Adamstown, Pennsylvania

Honoring the planet

LMS believes God calls on us to be wise stewards of the earth's resources. At the Kraybill campus, solar panels create electricity and reduce dependence on polluting power plants.

To reduce storm water polluting the Mill Stream, LMS created a rain garden of thirsty native plants around the Rutt Building. The facility also has a geo-thermal heating system and lots of windows to allow for natural lighting. Part of the roof has succulent plants to soak up rainwater.

Another Chesapeake Bay-friendly feature is the permeable patio outside Millstream Hall. Rainwater passes through the surface to recharge the water table.

All buildings have extra insulation. And the school composts food waste, a practice that enriches soil while reducing material trucked to the county incinerator.

132 CHANGING OUR WORLD

REMEMBERING LANCASTER MENNONITE

By way of LMH, a farm boy transitions to NPR journalist

"I got a little bit of a taste that there are big problems and big conflicts and inequities in the world."

DAN CHARLES

It wasn't Dan Charles' first trip to a big city. He had, as a youngster, visited Washington, D.C. and gone on a school trip to the Franklin Institute, a science museum in Philadelphia. But it was a trip to New York City in 1978, his senior year at Lancaster Mennonite High School, that gave Charles an understanding of just how big and different the world was from what he experienced growing up on a dairy farm in Lancaster County.

Charles remembers how he craned his neck at the skyscrapers and how he watched, fascinated, as pizza makers tossed and spun their dough. Just spending several days walking through the teeming metropolis and staying in a small room at a YMCA were experiences in their own right.

But the LMH teachers wanted their students to see more than the sites tourists visit. So they met with the daughter of Mennonite mission workers who as a college student had experienced kidnapping and torture during the repression of 1970s-era Argentina. And the students also found themselves touring the South Bronx and seeing how block after block had burned or been abandoned because of plight, poverty and government mismanagement.

"I was entranced," said Charles, recalling how the entire experience opened his eyes and remained a powerful memory. "I got a little bit of a taste that there are big problems and big conflicts and inequities in the world. But what do you do with that at that age, I didn't have any idea."

Charles struggled with social insecurity in high school. Feeling like a bit of an outsider, he found friends among students who had grown up in Africa and Asia as the children of missionaries. "Part of what made them enjoyable to me is they had seen more of the world than Lancaster and they had this different sense about them," he said. Charles also found success playing chess.

Charles would go on to become a journalist and author with opportunities to report on substantive issues. When he graduated from LMH, his career path wasn't set. In college he majored in economics and international affairs, fields he considered practical.

But looking back, Charles sees that the opportunity in high school to write for and edit the *Millstream*, the school newspaper, were formative experiences. "I felt like this was fun," Charles said of writing a mildly provocative piece and having it circulate on campus. "I'm not super proud of everything we did, but it was a really good experience to have a chance to take responsibility for something and work with other people and try to turn ambitions into reality."

Charles is the food and agriculture correspondent for National Public Radio. He has authored two books, including Lords of the Harvest: Biotech, Big Money, and the Future of Food.

Dan Charles | Washington, D.C. | Class of 1978

CHANGING OUR WORLD

Alumni of the Year 2009

"The benefit of investing in Mennonite education is clearly evident. Parents, church leaders and educators have a 'holy calling' to train, nurture, guide and instruct our children in the ways of God."

Connie Heisey Stauffer

Lititz, Pennsylvania
Class of 1955

Stauffer, a retired teacher, taught for thirty years in the Pequea Valley School District. She was a fourth-grade teacher, reading specialist and instructional support team teacher and leader. She also taught for two years at Eastern Mennonite University's Lancaster campus as an adjunct professor. Stauffer served 23 years on the LMS Board and was the first woman chair.

Highlight: From 1961 to 1965, Harold and I served in Somalia, where I taught English in the adult evening school. It was an enriching experience for us.

Education: Millersville University, bachelor's degree in elementary education and master's degree in education with a reading specialist certification; Pennsylvania State University, elementary principal certification
Spouse: the late Harold S. Stauffer, Class of 1955
Family: one daughter, two grandchildren

Activities at LMS: choir
Church affiliation: East Chestnut Street Mennonite Church, Lancaster, Pennsylvania

"True evangelical faith . . .

. . . cannot lie dormant. It clothes the naked, it feeds the hungry, it comforts the sorrowful, it shelters the destitute, it serves those that harm it, it binds up that which is wounded; it has become all things to all people." —Menno Simons (1496-1561)

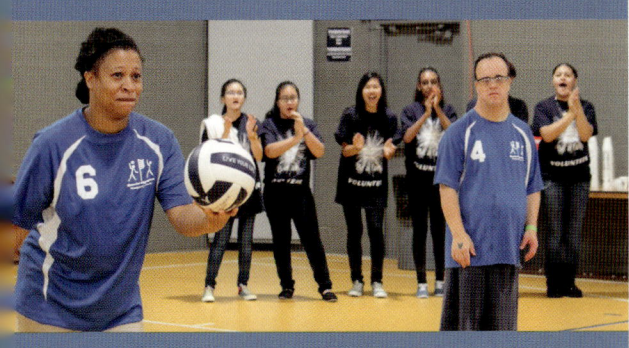

Relationships through service

Service is not a faceless, nameless exercise. It is an activity that connects people in a meaningful way. A high school student may give back to elementary students by telling them stories, and they respond by greeting her with enthusiasm and listening closely as she reads.

Making a greeting card isn't just an art project. It is a middle schooler thinking about what that elderly nursing home resident might like and piecing together cheerful decorations with a carefully chosen sentiment.

Organizing and supporting a Special Olympics volleyball team pulls people together. Members of the International Students Association become a part of the team as they encourage and cheer.

And helping someone select a coat at a charity shop is not just presenting an item. It is first understanding what the person needs, then working toward a solution.

Alumni of the Year 2010

"As millions of people seize on the opportunity to improve their lives through application of business principals and capital infusion, they are driving tremendous positive change throughout emerging markets around the world."

J. Alex Hartzler

Harrisburg, Pennsylvania
Class of 1986

Hartzler is the managing partner of WCI Partners, LP, a real estate development company.

Highlights: I served with Mennonite Central Committee in Santa Cruz, Bolivia. I was executive vice president and co-owner of Webclients.net which was sold to ValueClick in 2005. I formerly served as board chair for Ten Thousand Villages and on the board of Mennonite Economic Development Associates and currently chair Sarona Asset Management. I am also the publisher of *TheBurg*, a community newspaper in Harrisburg, Pennsylvania.

Education: Penn State University, degree in economics, and George Washington University School of Law. I was a Fulbright Scholar at the University of Cologne, Germany.
Spouse: Kristine Werley
Family: One son

LMS activities: Basketball and editorial page editor of the *Millstream*

CHANGING OUR WORLD 135

Alumni of the Year 2011

"I feel it was what the Lord was preparing me for. My passion is children. It was always my desire to be in service for the Lord, and every step of the way he has led me to care for children."

Margaret L. Allen

Philadelphia, Pennsylvania
Class of 1958

A retired child care director, Allen developed Bethany Child Care Center, serving as director from 1972 to 2013. Under her leadership, enrollment grew from 35 to 78 children. Earlier, she worked at New York City Head Start. She provided many years of board service to Eastern Mennonite Missions, Diamond Street Mennonite Church in Philadelphia and Diamond Street Community Center.

Highlights: Attending Ontario Mennonite Bible Insitute and visiting churches in Europe and Africa. I also enjoyed serving on many church boards.

Education: Ontario Mennonite Bible Institute, Hesston College, New York University, City College of New York, Community College of Philadelphia and Temple University
Family: one child

Activities at LMS: ice skating
Church affiliation: Deliverance Evangelistic Church, Philadelphia, Pennsylvania

Service in repair and maintenance

Clearing up debris, fixing a roof and painting a railing are practical ways to show Christ's love. Mennonites have a long tradition of service, and LMS embodies that spirit. Sometimes all it takes is a bit of time and willing hands.

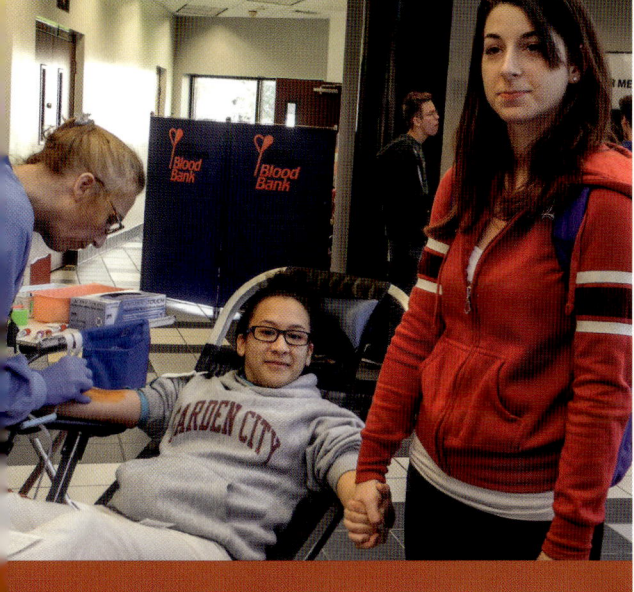

Giving of our riches

Giving to relieve suffering is as much a tradition as giving of time and talents. Food drives at LMS have spanned the years and the grades. Even the youngest students can understand how important it is for everyone to be warm and to have enough to eat, and maybe to also have a few toys.

Older students have responded to needs that they've heard about from their congregations, through appeals at chapel and their own burgeoning awareness. One recent winter, coats were collected for people suffering in war-torn Syria.

And what could be a more literal giving of oneself than donating blood at the annual blood drive at the Lancaster campus?

"We're grateful when students understand the importance of addressing world poverty. When they turn that into action they are living out the school mission to transform lives and change our world." –Judi Mollenkof, Locust Grove and Kraybill campuses elementary principal, parent

---

Alumni of the Year 2011

"Teachers and staff genuinely cared for students. I believe this care was the result of their personal relationships with Jesus Christ. Being surrounded by brothers and sisters in Christ had an impact which, even today, I probably do not fully appreciate."

Joseph P. Leaman

Lancaster, Pennsylvania
Class of 1998

A commercial insurance agent, Leaman works at the BCF Group. He is worship leader at Stumptown Mennonite Church and a member of the Partnership for a Missional Church steering team.

Highlight: Being married to Melissa and having our son Judah have been by far been my most significant life experiences. I learned very quickly that God uses a spouse and children to further sanctify me to Him on a daily basis.

Education: Millersville University, bachelor's degree in business administration
Spouse: Melissa
Family: one child

Activities at LMS: soccer and basketball
Church affiliation: Stumptown Mennonite Church, Bird-in-Hand, Pennsylvania

CHANGING OUR WORLD 137

Alumni of the Year 2012

"The church today can be polarized along many different lines, but I am energized by seeing local churches practice unity in Christ when it comes to befriending homeless single mothers and their children."

Edith Yoder

Philadelphia, Pennsylvania
Class of 1983

Yoder is executive director of Bridge of Hope National. She was executive director of Bridge of Hope, Lancaster and Chester counties, for 14 years. She was after-school director at Glad Tidings Community Center in Bronx, New York. She was co-editor of *Journeys of Hope* and *Amazing Hope: A Ministry of Friendship of Homeless Families.*

Highlight: Serving and leading at Bridge of Hope, first as a local ministry and then helping launch this work with homeless single mothers and children in thirteen states and Canada. All of it has been an incredible opportunity to see God at work on behalf of the poor and homeless.

Education: Eastern Mennonite University, bachelor's degree in accounting with a minor in religion; Temple University, master of education in adult and organizational development
Spouse: Garth Scott
Family: three stepchildren and three grandchildren, one of whom we are raising

Activities: field hockey, student council
Church affiliation: Frazer Mennonite Church, Frazer, Pennsylvania

Connecting with nonprofits

Partnering with nonprofits exposes students to the many ways they can make a difference. Young people pack cans of meat that Mennonite Central Committee sends overseas, stack cords of wood at the historic Hans Herr House, sort clothes for a thrift store, and much more.

Some LMS graduates go on to work in the nonprofit sector. Others make volunteering a way of life.

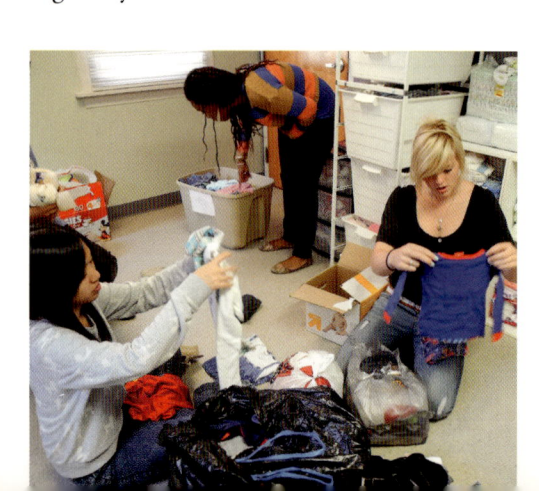

138 CHANGING OUR WORLD

Cleaning and sprucing up

Even the youngest child can wield a broom. Working together, students show respect for their surroundings and for their community by sweeping walks, cleaning windows and collecting trash. A fresh coat of paint does wonders for the spirits of those who apply the paint and those who enjoy the results. There is a special satisfaction in seeing so clearly that one can make a difference.

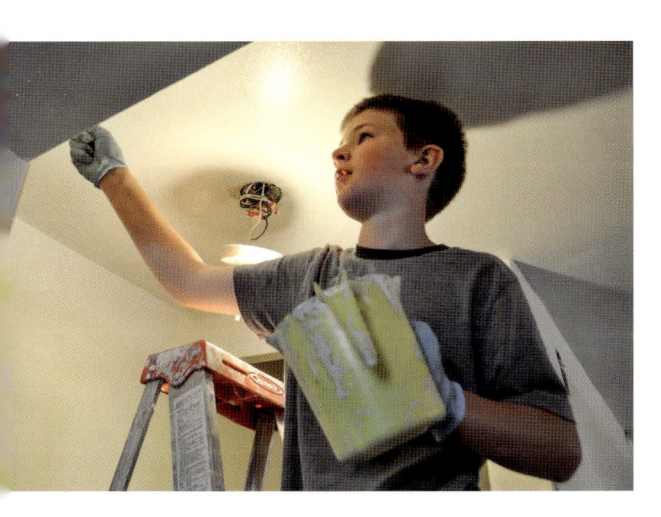

Alumni of the Year 2012

"The sense that 'to whom much is given, much is expected' has held a lot of weight with me. I feel more connected to neighbors and to God's purpose in the world when doing this sort of work."

Jessica King

Lancaster, Pennsylvania
Class of 1992

King is executive director of ASSETS Lancaster, a local economic development association. She is the former executive director of PULSE (Pittsburgh Urban Leadership Service Experience). She was founder of the Urban Project in Pittsburgh for five years before coming to Lancaster in 2007. She was assistant editor for *Gospel Herald*, now *The Mennonite*.

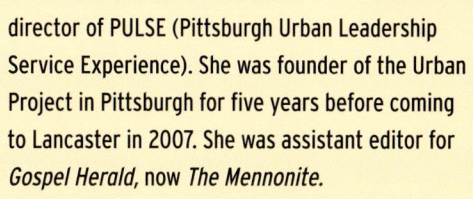

Highlights: My career started in voluntary service after college because of my pacifist beliefs. I've had the great fortune to work from the heart in all of my professional experiences since then and have been able to tie my religious and ethical beliefs directly to my vocation. Working to start and grow innovative organizations to respond to economic opportunity and racial disparities in Pittsburgh and Lancaster have been my career highlights thus far.

Education: Eastern Mennonite University, bachelor of liberal arts; Bard College, master of business administration
Spouse: Chad Martin
Family: two daughters

LMS activities: yearbook, baseball assistant manager
Church affiliation: Community Mennonite Church of Lancaster, Lancaster, Pennsylvania

CHANGING OUR WORLD   139

"Whatever you do, work at it with all your heart, as working for the Lord." –COLOSSIANS 3:23

Looking to the Future

As we close the book on Lancaster Mennonite School's first 75 years, we can't help but be inspired by the stories of the leaders who accepted the challenge of making the school what it is today. We are grateful for their vision, hard work and faithfulness. Just as important, we hope the preceding pages telling the LMS story serve to excite this generation's school leaders and supporters as they build a bridge to an even brighter future, one that honors tradition while embracing progress.

LMS has never been static. We have always crossed bridges to new opportunities.

Think about those first LMS students in 1942. Could they have imagined a school 75 years in the future? Things we take for granted—Wi-Fi, Skype, even microwaved popcorn—existed only in the realm of science fiction when Lancaster Mennonite High School opened its doors. What will the next 75 years bring?

This school has been and, we hope, will continue to be a place that prepares young minds for service and success in an unpredictable, dynamic world, a community marching into the future even as it seeks to shape it.

We can, of course, only see tomorrow dimly, but we do feel sure that the LMS of 2092 will still be true to its foundational mission of Christ-centered education.

The graduates of 2092 will have been exposed to a worldview informed by such core Anabaptist values as non-violence, reconciliation and respect for life and all creation.

We are sure, too, that our teachers will continue to instill in every student a sense of curiosity, wonder and mystery. Surely the quickening pace of communication and transportation technology will only shrink the world further, and our graduates will be ready. They will take their place in the workforce and in society in general as well-rounded global citizens who have a passion for learning, justice and service.

Will the next 75 years be easy? Has excellence in education ever been?

LMS faces challenges, and one that weighs on us presently is how to remain true to our core value of a diverse community. LMS is stronger today because students come from around the world and represent all walks of life. But that diversity is threatened by economic pressures causing more and more families to reexamine their budgets and consider whether they can afford to send their children here. About 40 percent of our students receive need-based aid. LMS has never wanted to position itself as a private school for the elite, and has worked to assure that scholarships are readily available. But as the need for tuition assistance increases, the school must begin planning today to find ways to keep the school affordable for families across the income spectrum.

Currently, we are encouraged by the response to our Bridges to the Future campaign, and we hope many more will consider supporting tomorrow's LMS students with a financial gift today. Contributions

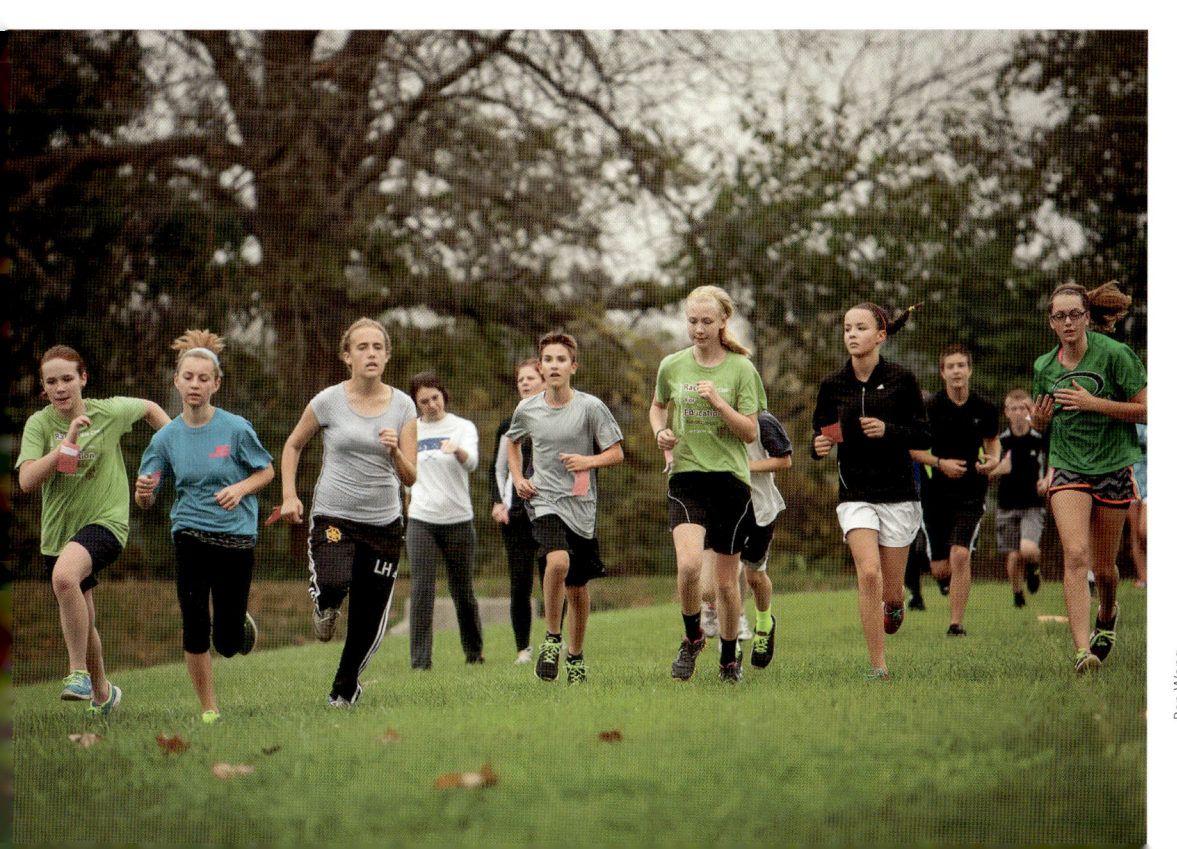

141

TRADITIONS & TRANSITIONS

Current and future leaders

The principals at LMS's elementary schools have hit on a way to help students in the higher grades develop leadership skills. They call the program Blazer Buddies. Students are chosen to perform a variety of special school tasks that help them gain confidence in social situations and boost their self-esteem.

New Danville Principal Eloy Rodriguez said Dr. Stephen R. Covey's book, *The Leader in Me*, inspired him to start Blazer Buddies. Fifth-grade New Danville students are chosen for a variety of tasks, including being helpmates in the preK and kindergarten classrooms, making morning announcements over the PA system, greeting students and visitors as they arrive in the morning, leading weekly chapel services, collecting lunch trash, and helping at school events.

Judi Mollenkof, principal of the Locust Grove and Kraybill campuses, started Blazer Buddies at her schools after learning of the program's success at New Danville.

"I've seen shy, reserved students confidently greeting kids and parents as they walk in to the school each morning," Rodriguez said. "I've seen students who would have never wanted to be up in front of an audience help to welcome a gym full of 400 adults at our Christmas programs. I've seen students who may have a hardness to them completely soften when they interact with our preK and kindergarten students. I've seen students who don't always feel comfortable reading out loud in class read our school announcements over the PA system for all the school to hear."

to an LMS endowment fund helps to assure that investment income will continue to grow to help offset rising personnel, operational and maintenance costs. Meanwhile, other friends of LMS have chosen to look to the school's future by including it in their wills and estate plans.

The financial picture, however, isn't the only challenge facing LMS. We live in polarized times, one in which people see themselves as belonging to one ideological or theological camp or another and, as a consequence, often fail to explore common ground. LMS seeks to harness the positive power of diversity and be a safe place where Christians from all perspectives are respected and feel free to express their understanding of the gospel. Indeed, that happens today, as 80 percent of our students are not affiliated with traditional Anabaptist congregations.

Going forward, as in the past, the rock that LMS stands on is Jesus Christ. We believe that Jesus is central to our faith, that community is central to our life together, and that reconciliation is central to our work.

We are celebrating our 75th year, but now is not the time for complacency. LMS has important work to do. We are educating the next generation.

The LMS story is so much more than today's curriculum, today's campuses, today's challenges. The LMS story is really about unfinished business. It's about shaping the future just over the horizon. How that story turns out will be determined by LMS graduates. They are the reason we do what we do. Our graduates have been, and always will be, thinkers, leaders, creators, advocates, healers, teachers, explorers, doers, makers, and nurturers.

We are continually surprised by the amazing things LMS graduates do. We are sure they will continue to surprise us. And we look ahead with hearts buoyed by optimism and hope as they pursue purpose-driven endeavors. They are writing the next chapter of the LMS story, and we couldn't be more excited.

Appendix

LMS Board Members, 1992–2016	144
LMS Administrators, 1992–2016	146
Lancaster-Lebanon League Athletic Titles, 1980–2016	148
LMS Graduates, 1992–2016	150
Bridge Builders for the Future	179

Board members, administrators and graduates for the years 1942–1991 are listed in the appendix of the 50th anniversary book Passing on the Faith *by Donald Kraybill.*

LMS Board Members, 1992–2016

Acosta, Moniqua Castaneda 2011–2016
Adams, Ronald W. 1997–2007
Alcantara, Antonio P. 1996–2002
Alderman, Beth Stoltzfus 2015–
Augsburger, Kristine 2006–
Baer, Rose 2006–2012
   Secretary 2006–2012
Beck, Lois K. 1991–2003
Beiler, Kathy Rutt 2015–
Breneman, Sandy E. 2001–2002
Brubaker, Robert L. 1999–2014
Burkholder, Marie L. 1995–2004
Carrasco, German 1990–1995
Charles, Jonathan 2004–
Davis, Allen 2005–2008
Denlinger, John H. 1993–2008
   Vice-Chair 2001–2006
Dich, Philip N. 1990–1993
Diffenbach, Abram W. 2003–2008
Dula, Andy 2004–
Frey, Nicholas B. 1995–2007
Garber, Shirley K. 2001–2002
Gonzalez, Juan 1996–2011
Grasse-Bachman, Carolyn 2006–2009
Groff, Mary Ellen 2001–2016
Hartzler, J. Alex 1998–2002
Hartzler, Kenneth J. 1995–1998
Heindel, James I. 1994–1997
Hershey, Nelson H. 1983–1995
Hertzler, Truman R. 1983–1992
Hess, Daniel S. 1989–1997
   Vice-Chair 1993–1997
Hess, Nancy J. 1997–2001
Hess, Paul S. 1988–1996
Hollinger, Clyde M. 2000–2003
Hollinger, Jane M. 2002–2003

Hollinger, Lloyd L. 1963–2006
   Vice-Chair 1978–1979
Hoover, Bonnie 2006–2009
Hoover, Carl L. 1987–1999
Horning, Roberta A. 1992–2001
Horst, Gerald R. 1995–
   Vice-Chair 2006–
Horst, Jeffrey S. 2003–2006
Horst, Ortho 1988–1992
Hostetter, James W. 1986–1992
Hurst, Chad G. 2011–
Hurst, George M. 1996–2008
Hurst, Nevin L. 2013–2016
Kanagy, Lamar E. 2001–2009
Kennel, Larry J. 1997–2000
King, Kyle D. 2008–2011
Kling, J. Nelson 1998–2001
Kreider, Barry R. 2000–2006
Kurtz, Kenneth D. 1999–2002
Kurtz, Paul J. 1993–2002
Lambert, Jay S. 2002–2005
Lapp, Alice W. 1988–2000;
   2003–2011
Leaman, James R. 1993–1996
Long, Cindy S. 2001–2004
Longenecker, Nelson 2008–2014
Martin, Ann L. 2012–
Martin, Barbara A. 1994–1997
Martin, Esther H. 1987–2001
   Secretary 1997–2001
Martin, Gerald E. 1991–1997
Martin, Irvin S. Jr. 1967–1988;
   1992–2006
Martin, Marilyn 2006–2010
Mast, Cindy S. 2004–
Mast, Harold R. 2000–

144 APPENDIX

Miller, Edwin Jr. 2008–2014
Miller, Larry D. 1986–1997
Mwangi, Samuel Kanyiha 2010–2016
Nafziger, Nelson C. 1990–2002
Neff, C. Melvin 1992–1998
Nell, Melanie L. 2013–
Okanya, Nelson 2015–
Poole, William 2015–
Rittenhouse, Marcia 2006–2012
Rohrer, Dwight 2008–
Roland, Rosalie Hess 2003–2009
Rudy, Daniel 2010–2013
Rutt, G. Roger 2003–2011
Rutt, John M. 1973– 2016
   Treasurer 1976–2016
Sauder, David L. 1997–2003
Sensenig, Kenneth L. 1996–2005
Sharp, Christine A. 2010–2014
Shenk, Henry G. 1990–1996
Siegrist, Joanne L. 1982–1993
Simkins, John 2006–2015
Snader, Paul E. 1997–2003
Stauffer, Connie F. 1983–2006
   Secretary 1986–1997;
   Chair 1997–2006
Stoltzfus, Isaac H. 1987–1993

Taylor, Al 2011–2015
Thomas, Vincent J. 1991–1994
Umble, Diane Z. 1999 –
   Secretary 2001–2006;
   Chair 2006–
Umble, Gerald R. 1992–1998
Watson, Blanding 2015–
Weaver, A. Earl 1976–1998
   Vice-Chair 1986–1990;
   Chair 1991–1997
Weaver, Anne Kaufman 2008–2016
   Secretary 2012–2016
Weaver, Dale M. 1987–1993
Weaver, Robert E. 1983–1995
   Vice-Chair 1990–1993
Weaver, Ronald R. 1993–2002
Wenger, Benjamin H. 1989–2001
   Vice-Chair 1997–2001
Wenger, Clifford 2003–2005
Wert, Roy E. 2001–2012
Wissler, Nancy L. 1995–2004
Yoder, Gary L. 2001–2007
Yoder, Pamela Nyce 1996–1999
Youndt, Raymond E. 1991–1994
Zeevaart, Brenda H. 2015–
Zook, Larry J. 2003–2016

APPENDIX 145

"Blessed are the peacemakers, for they will be called children of God." –MATTHEW 5:9

LMS Administrators, 1992–2016

Superintendent's Team

J. Richard Thomas, Superintendent, 1983–2016
Miles E. Yoder, Assistant Superintendent, 1983–
Marlin G. Groff, Chief Financial Officer, 1989–
Lucinda K. Petersheim, Director of Advancement, 1989–2000
Heidi E. Stoltzfus, Director of Advancement, 2001–
Joyce E. Thomas, Administrative Assistant, 1991–

TRADITIONS & TRANSITIONS
LMS Chief Administrators, 1942–2016

J. Paul Graybill, Principal 1942–1953

Amos W. Weaver, Principal 1953–1963

Clayton L. Keener, Principal 1963–1967

H. Howard Witmer, Principal 1967–1969

146 APPENDIX

Hershey Campus Principal

Albert F. Roth 2015–2015
Miles E. Yoder 2015–

Kraybill Campus Principal

John S. Weber 2006–2011
J. Daniel Martin 2011–2013
Judi U. Mollenkof 2013–

Lancaster Campus Principal

J. Richard Thomas 1983–2002
Miles E. Yoder 2002–2009
Steven J. Geyer (Acting Principal) 2009–2010
Elvin N. Kennel 2010–

Lancaster Campus Middle School Principal

David A. King 2002–2005
Elizabeth A. Landis 2015–

Locust Grove Principal

Jay L. Roth 2003–2007
Judi U. Mollenkof 2007–

New Danville Campus Principal

Judi U. Mollenkof 2002–2013
Eloy D. Rodriguez 2013–

Noah G. Good, Principal 1969–1970

J. Lester Brubaker, Principal 1970–1979, Superintendent 1979–1983

J. Richard Thomas, Principal 1983–2002, Superintendent 2002–2016

APPENDIX 147

2016 LMS Varsity Sports

FALL SPORTS
Cross Country
Field Hockey
Golf
Boys Soccer
Girls Soccer
Girls Tennis
Girls Volleyball

WINTER SPORTS
Boys Basketball
Girls Basketball
Bowling

SPRING SPORTS
Baseball
Softball
Boys Tennis
Track & Field
Boys Volleyball
Boys Lacrosse

Lancaster-Lebanon League Athletic Titles, 1980–2016

LMS has been fortunate to maintain a noteworthy winning tradition over the years, as evidenced by the number of championships and titles Blazer teams have secured.

Although the Blazer community is quite proud of its many on-the-field accomplishments, winning games and raising championship banners are not the primary emphasis of the athletic department. Instead, LMS firmly believes that athletics are a microcosm of life and that lifelong learning occurs through the rigors of competition. Values such as teamwork, discipline, selflessness, perseverance, and the importance of preparation are just a sampling of the many foundational lessons that coaches strive to impart on student-athletes throughout each season. Perhaps most importantly, the idea of living one's faith through one's athletic skill is at the core of everything the athletic department represents and teaches.

The following is a list of every section, league, district, and state title LMS teams have collected since officially joining the Lancaster-Lebanon League in the fall of 1980. The school gives the Lord due praise for blessing its programs with sustained success throughout the years.

Baseball Section Champions (1987, 2007)
Boys Basketball District Champions (1997)
Boys Basketball Section Champions
 (1991, 2003, 2014, 2015)
Girls Basketball District Champions (2008)
Girls Basketball League Champions (2009)
Girls Basketball Section Champions
 (1991, 2005, 2009, 2010)
Boys Cross Country District Champions (2007)
Boys Cross County Section Champions (2000, 2003, 2004, 2005, 2006, 2007, 2008, 2009, 2010, 2011, 2013)
Girls Cross Country District Champions (1996, 1998, 2005, 2006)
Girls Cross Country League Champions (2005)
Girls Cross Country Section Champions (1998, 1999, 2004, 2005, 2006, 2007)
Field Hockey District Champions
 (1987, 1993, 1996, 1999)
Field Hockey League Champions
 (1982, 1996, 2002, 2007)
Field Hockey Section Champions
 (1982, 1995, 1997, 1998, 1999, 2000, 2001, 2004, 2005, 2006, 2007, 2008, 2012)
Boys Golf District Champions (2005)
Boys Golf League Champions (2005)

Boys Golf Section Champions
 (2004, 2005, 2006, 2007, 2009, 2010, 2012)
Boys Soccer State Champions (2011)
Boys Soccer District Champions
 (1986, 1987, 1995, 1996, 2010, 2011, 2015)
Boys Soccer League Champions
 (1991, 1992, 1995, 1997, 1998, 2002, 2012, 2013)
Boys Soccer Section Champions
 (1981, 1982, 1984, 1986, 1987, 1988, 1995, 1998, 2000, 2002, 2005, 2006, 2007, 2008, 2009, 2010, 2011, 2013, 2014, 2015)
Girls Soccer State Champions (2008)
Girls Soccer District Champions (2005, 2006)
Girls Soccer League Champions
 (1993, 1994, 1995, 2008)
Girls Soccer Section Champions
 (1992–96, 1998, 1999, 2003, 2004, 2005, 2007–12)
Softball District Champions (1985, 1991)
Softball League Champions (1992)
Softball Section Champions (1985, 1992)
Boys Volleyball League Champions (2006)
Boys Volleyball Section Champions
 (1999, 2001, 2002, 2005, 2006, 2007, 2008, 2012)
Girls Volleyball Section Champions
 (2006, 2007, 2009, 2010, 2015)

LMS Graduates, 1992-2016

Class of 1992

Wesley Todd Allen
Steven D. Althouse
Samrawit Asrat
Kay Marie Auker
Brett J. Barton
Eric P. Beamesderfer
Reneé S. Bear
Jennifer D. (Beck) Fredrick
Noel J. (Benner) Garman
Lydia A. Blessing
Tiffany J. Book
Carol (Brubacher) Hershey
Melissa K. Brubaker
Ryan N. Brubaker
Ricardo Castaneda
Jason D. Charles
Julie L. (Charles) Nelson
Mark A. Clapper
Mark A. Collado
Jennifer L. (Conlin) Lang
Michael J. Conrad
Hilary N. Cooke
Ekutan Dannelley
Michelle L. Deller
Kendra J. Denlinger
Kirby L. Denlinger
Ronda E. (Denlinger) King
Cheryl (Diem) Davidson
Brett D. Eby
Calvin R. Eby
Monica L. English
Denise D. (Esbenshade) Oberholtzer
Eunessa J. (Esch) Lehman
Bryan L. Eshleman
Twila J. (Fisher) Shertzer
David E. Frey
Dorothy JoAnn Frey
Jason W. Garman
Bradley L. Gehman
Laurie M. Gish
Gabriel T. Gizaw
Scott E. Gochenaur
Alicia M. (Godfrey) Horst
Rebecca (Grove) Fester
Daniel A. Haile
Laura M. Hall
Amy J. (Harnish) Woods
Carla Y. (Hart) Hertzler
Maria L. (Haverstick) Fountain
Dana (Hein) Rice
Wendy J. (Heller) Hess
Kimberly (Herr) Landis
Bradley A. Hershey
Matthew R. Hershey
Caroline J. (Hess) Frey
G. Dustin Hess
Jamie P. Hess
David A. High
Daniel S. Hollinger
Richard B. Homer
Dwayne A. Hoover
Eric L. Hoover
R. Shiree (Horst) Stuart
Roger L. Hoover
Rodney C. Horst
Ronald L. Horst
Kristin E. (Hurst) Kreider
Lillian Y. Jordan
Janeen E. (Kauffman) Khul
Lori J. (Kauffman) Severein
Befekadu Kefenie
Jessica F. King
Karen (King) Wentz
Jennifer L. (Kooker) Peifer
Brian E. Kreider
Timothy L. Kreider
Bruce E. Kurtz
Jennifer N. (Kurtz) High
Thomas G. Lambert
Marvin T. Landis
Philip J. Landis
Duane R. Leaman
Tashya S. (Leaman) Dalen
Jenny N. Leasa
Adam K. Lehman
Patrick Conrad Lehman
D. Michael Longacre
Amy N. (Longenecker) Brown
Senait LouLou
Doris A. (Martin) Lehman
Jeremy L. Martin
Kendra R. (Martin) Farrow
Michelle D. (Martin) Brubaker
Timothy Z. Martin
Timothy L. Martzall
Jason L. Mercado
Sylvia I. Mercado
Marcy E. (Miller) Ebersole
Zachary R. Miller
Matthew D. Montgomery
Nissa L. (Murphy) Stoltzfus
Carl D. Myer
Mildred F. Nafziger
Randal R. Nisly

Please notify the LMS alumni office if there is an error in the graduate listing that you would like to correct.

150 APPENDIX

Lisa M. Nolt
Thomas A. Oberholtzer
Steven R. Peters
Judy E. (Petersheim) Stauffer
Laura L. Pfarr
Patricia R. (Prange) Dowd
Heather D. (Rechtsteiner) Groff
Darrel J. Reinford
Jason R. Rissler
Christina M. (Rohrer) Bonner
Coleen M. (Rohrer) Hurst
Seth A. Samuel
Candance C. (Sauder) King
Laureen J. (Sauder) Gibbel
Mary R. (Sauder) Bechtold
Sharon M. (Sauder) Muhlfeld
Mark A. Schildt
Brandon T. Seibel
John D. Sensenig
Ayalkebet Shiferaw
Obsie Shiferaw
Jeffrey S. Shirk
Valerie Y. (Shreiner) Petersheim
Brenda S. Shultz
Brian K. Snader
Corinna F. (Snyder) Herr
Jiranun Sopapong
Chad E. Stauffer
Matthew R. Stoltzfus
Timothy L. Stoltzfus
Paula M. (Stutzman) Musser
Gregory D. Swartzendruber
Calvin D. Swartzentruber
Jeremy James Temple
Fassil Teshome
Dustin B. Thomas
Eric L. Weaver
Karlene M. (Weaver) Beam
Kraig M. Weaver
Michael J. Weaver
Sally R. (Weaver) Bredeman
Sheldon R. Weaver
J. Andrew Weber
K. Anthony Weidman
Jo E. (Wenger) Fisher
Michael W. Wenger
Melody M. White
Kristin M. (Wile) Kreider
Melinda N. Williams
Jennifer D. (Wilson) Fretwell
Mekdim Yemane
Amy J. (Yutzy) Harder
Kori M. Zehr
Karl D. Zeiset
Donovan L. Zimmerman

Class of 1993

Kathi J. (Arnold) Noll
Emebet Assefa
Angela S. (Baker) Zohn
Jodi L. (Becker) Feather
Darlene F. (Beiler) Miller
Michelle L. Beiler
Sena K. (Bender) Larad
Bryan E. Beyer
Christine A. (Blake) Martin
Nevada S. (Bowman) Kirchner
David R. Brechbill
Rochelle (Breneman) Jones
Samuel B. Breneman
Chad E. Burkhart
Rochelle L. (Burkhart) Boone
Sonya J. Burkholder
Carrie L. Carbaugh
Douglas L. Charles
David A. Clapper
Tasha G. Clemmer
Andrew J. Cutting
Nathan A. Davis
Rebecca L. (DeCubellis) Brubaker
DeNise D. (Dellinger) Malanchuk
Esther Dich
Deborah S. Dick
Christopher T. Dietrich
Krista L. Dombach
Elizabeth A. (Douple) Berg
Kevin T. Ebersole
Brandon S. Edgerton
Michelle L. Engle
Shawn D. Espigh
David L. Estep
Susan E. Fair
Howard Christian Ferro
Linford D. Fisher
Brett M. Forshey
Daniel E. Frey
Naomi Jean (Fryberger) Bowers
Albert L. Fuller
Melissa J. (Garber) Hurst
Susan L. (Gascho) Cooke
Judy K. Gerber
Rodney W. Gingrich
Timothy L. Gingrich
Dawn R. (Gochnauer) Harnish
Crystal D. (Good) Trost
Chad P. Groff
Jonathan N. Groff
Marcia A. (Groff) Ritrovato
Renee M. (Groff) Dennis
Melody A. Habecker
Jennifer J. (Harrison) Martin
Rhonda C. (Hartzler) Zook
Andrew N. Heisey
Jansen M. Herr
Keith B. Hershey
Wendy J. (Hershey) Kleinschmidt
Christine L. Hess
Melissa Faye (Hess) Blair
Jolyn R. (Hoover) Nolt
Kevin L. Hoover
Ryan L. Hoover
Jonathan M. Horning
J. Andrew Hostetler
James W. Hostetter
Christa R. (Huber) Reuel
Susan D. Hughes
Jeremy D. Hutson
Daniel Jordan
Christopher S. Kauffman
Ryan W. Kauffman
Fran Kathleen (Kennel) Kratz
David L. King
Jonathan R. King
Kenneth A. Kline
Galen D. Kraybill
Peter J. Kraybill
Bradley J. Kreider
Valerie L. (Lahr) Greco
Kristine Dawn Lantz
Joshua B. Leaman
Alexis V. (Lefever) Trout
Christopher Mark Lehman
Jeffrey S. Lehman
Emily Maria Leister
Linda J. (Livengood) Brenneman
Todd D. Lockard
Andre L. Martin

APPENDIX 151

Alumni of the Year 2013

"LMS played a large part in who I am today. I was more influenced than I realized by the culture of not just academic rigor, but of classes taught with investment and involvement."

Linford Fisher

Cranston, Rhode Island
Class of 1993

Fisher is an associate professor of history at Brown University and the author of *The Indian Great Awakening* and *Decoding Roger Williams*.

Highlight: One of the many highlights of my career so far has been the opportunity to recover aspects of American history that have been overlooked or minimized, particularly that of Native Americans. My current book project has taken me to archives in Bermuda, Barbados, Jamaica, the Bahamas and the United Kingdom as I try to piece together the intertwining of Native American and African slavery in the wider English Atlantic world between 1600 and 1800. It is rewarding to feel like I am helping in some small way to give a voice to these difficult elements in our shared histories.

Education: Lancaster Bible College, bachelor's degree in religion; Gordon-Conwell Theological Seminary, master's degrees in church history and religion; Harvard University, doctorate in American religious history
Spouse: Jo Evonne (Wenger) Fisher, Class of 1992
Family: four children

Activities at LMS: soccer, senior class vice president
Church affiliation: Providence Presbyterian Church, Providence, Rhode Island

---

Jeffrey A. Martin
Jeffrey C. Martin
Thomas W. Martin
Shawn B. Marvin
Alex R. Mast
Ryan C. Meck
Joel A. Metzler
Annette C. (Milich) Frey
Jeffrey M. Miller
Kristina J. (Miller) Horning
Rhea D. Miller
Wendell S. Epp Miller
Bryan Z. Morris
Jebessa Mosissa
Lisa D. (Moyer) Pinchak
Kayoko Murata
Andrew M. Musser
Anthony S. Musser
Curtis L. Musser
Debra J. (Musser) Kraybill
Timothy L. Musser
John M. Myers
E. Ray Nafziger
Natalie J. (Neff) Henry
Maria R. Otto
Heather L. (Patton) Rosario
Ann M. (Prichard) Gehman
Hans E. Rauch
Stephen M. Rhinehart
Timothy J. Rice
Kendra N. (Risser) Ice
Amy Catharine (Rissler) Shultz
Juan Marcos Rodriguez
Janine K. Rohrer
Brent W. Roland
Laura I. Rosado
David Scott Rosenberry
Angela R. Ruhl
Ann Louise (Ruhl) Shultz
Marla M. Schnupp
Jared G. Seibel
Michael C. Seymour
Jordan A. Shaub
Tiffany N. (Shellenberger) Porter
Regina G. (Shenk) Canete
Beverly Jo (Shirk) Wilson
Heidi Ann (Shultz) Pence
J. Philip Siegrist
Holly Carol Simmons
Joshua V. Sinopoli
Jennifer L. (Smoker) Rogers
Gwenyth L. (Stambaugh) Eyler
Christina S. (Stauffer) Conover
Kimberly G. Stauffer
Dorcas I. (Steckbeck) Landis
Dawn M. (Stoltzfus) Fisher
Douglas R. Stoltzfus
Marlin G. Stoltzfus
Timothy C. Stoltzfus
Dana N. (Stoner) Beiler
Gerald D. Swanger
Hailu Tilahun
Valerie A. (Todd) Ehst
Addy L. (Trager) Dangler
Karin D. Tursack
Luanne M. (Tyson) Hershey
Chad M. Umble
J. Randal Umble
Jon R. Umble
Sarah E. Vizcarrondo
Kyoko Wakamatsu
J. Matthew Weaver
Jill N. (Weaver) Houck
Kreg R. Weaver
Margaret L. (Weaver) High
Sheldon S. Wenger
Mary L. (Wenrich) Phillips
Derek Andre Wissler
Matthew T. Wissler
Donovan Shawn Witmer
Jason D. Wolgemuth
Gordon James Yoder
Heather S. (Yoder) Weaver
Melissa D. (Yoder) Wissler
Bethlehem G. Yohannes
Hamelmal G. Yohannes
Thomas C. Zak
Paula J. Zimmerman

Class of 1994

Abdirisaq Hersi Ahmed
SooJung Ahn
Mikiyas Alemu
Yonatan Alemu
Timothy Ryan Althouse
Jonelle Marie Anderson
Tricia L. (Bare) Stoltzfus
Ryan P. Beiler
Hope A. Bender
Wendy J. (Bender) Brister
Richard C. Benites
Denise Yvonne Black
Glen R. Blessing
Jennifer R. (Boll) Leaman
Krystal Joy Boll
Elizabeth W. (Brewer) Broughton
Hans C. Brubaker
Rachel M. (Buckwalter) Witmer
Robert Willis Byers
Alison D. (Carpenter) Hollis
Moniqua M. (Castaneda) Acosta
Guillermo De Novais
Regina Mae (Denlinger) Romanucci
Carla R. (DePasquale) Smoker
Fadi V. Diab
Joyce Nhac An Dich
Chad Anthony Diller
Eyob M. Dimberu
Jeremiah D. Eastep
Kendra G. (Eberly) Sustrisna
Krista D. (Ebersole) Sensenig
Kevin M. Eisenberger
Benjamin L. Eller
Joel D. Ernst
Jeffrey D. Eshleman
Timothy S. Everett
Lisa A. (Fahnestock) Dyck
Michael Fantahun
Henok Ferede
Gloria J. (Fisher) Eby
P. Michael Freed
M. Rosanne (Frey) Horst
Joaquin J. Garcia
Brenda D. (Garges) Reinford
David Jamil George
Julie Anne (Gish) Gingrich
Thomas V. Glick
Karen B. (Gochnauer) Kreider
Jamey C. Groff
Jennifer K. (Groff) Metzler
Michael C. Groff
Pamela Dawn Groff
Rodney D. Groff
Elsabet Assefa Haile
Jolene R. (Harnish) Wehmer
Patricia J. (Haverstick) Weaver
Jolynn R. (Heisey) Wickmann
Naomi A. (Heisey) Myer
Douglas M. Hershey
Erica Joy (Hershey) Herr
Jason E. Hershey
Marilyn L. (Hershey) Richardson
Ryan M. (Hess) Linder-Hess
Timothy M. Hess
Troy M. Hess
Jonathan L. High
Jennifer B. (Hoover) Lambert
Sharon J. (Hoover) Eshleman
David C. Horning
Ted Douglas Houser
Jeremy E. Hurst
Ilene H. Huynh
Allyson R. Kauffman
Brian Eugene Kauffman
J. Marvin Kauffman
Christel Annette Kautz
Jessica Dianne (Keirn) Engle
Obsitu A. Kelifa
Carlotta M. (Kopczynski) DeVoll

Deanna E. (Kurtz) Dickson
Kendall D. Kurtz
Nathan M. Landis
Wendall M. Landis
Seth Alan Laninga
Jodi Lynn (Lapp) Fahnestock
D. Aaron Latsha
Maria B. (Leaman) Bowman
Mark C. Leaman
Brian E. Longenecker
B. James Madonna
Angela J. Martin
Juanita Joy (Martin) Fox
Lew K. Martin
Lisa D. (Martin) Garcia
Michael L. Martin
Neal Roy Martin
Robert Anthony Martin
Sara Kathryn Martin
Timothy I. McGinnis
Michael H. McGowan
Dawn N. (Mellinger) Meck
Laura B. (Mellinger) Beach
Philip G. Metzler
Frances E. Miller
Karen L. (Miller) Rauch
Kaylene R. (Miller) Brubaker
Sarah R. (Miller) Butler
Wendell S. Miller
Jessica M. (Moyer) Echogoyen
Melodi R. (Mumma) Miller
Aya Nagano
Rebecca M. Neff
Evette Negrón Cortes
Lara N. (Nissley) Longenecker
Kevin R. Noll
Jeffrey S. Nolt
Melody D. (Nolt) Althouse
Emma-Lisa B. Öberg
Christopher L. Ochs
Ryan M. Olah
Mary C. Peltzer

Michele R. (Petersheim) Book
Caren A. Place
Derek Christopher Plank
Daniel James Ristenbatt
Gisela Rivera
Eric Nathan Roberts
Douglas Alan Rohrer
Jennifer L. (Rohrer) Gallinaugh
David G. Roth
Rachel B. (Roth) Sawatsky
Leonard D. Royal
Angi Dorene (Russ) Frederick
Megan N. (Rutt) Clapper
Arlin Robert Sauder
Daryn L. Sauder
Matthew L. Sauder
Carmen J. (Sensenig) Martin
Ruth Elizabeth Sensenig
Timothy L. Shirk
Jennifer E. (Simmers) Tweed
Rebecca L. Skrabak
Chad E. Smoker
Greg L. Smoker
Stephanie A. (Smoker) Yoder
Jessica Lynn (Smucker) George
Sheila J. (Stauffer) Aukerman
Angela D. (Stoltzfus) Conrad
Jesse R. Stoltzfus
Jonathan L. Stoltzfus
Melissa (Stoltzfus) Beamesderfer
Andrea E. (Stoner) Leaman
Richard Tessema Tefferi
Lungile Pride Tembe
Carrie Lynelle Thomas
Lori M. (Thomas) Heitland
Marlisa J. Thomas
Rebecca A. (Thomas) Staskel
Shana D. Thomas
Denis Lynn Todd

APPENDIX 153

Tara J. Tomlinson Hess
Veniamin V. Vysotsky
James W. Wagner
Michelle L. (Weaver) Stoltzfus
Timothy V. Weaver
Wanda L. (Weaver) Stauffer
F. Adam Weidman
Delinda L. Whiting
Teressa L. Wiker
Keith D. Wilson
Laura E. (Worme) Venters
Bantiwossen B. Yemane
Andrew E. Yoder
Gale C. (Youndt) Weaver
Melissa (Young) Michels
Steven C. Yutzy Burkey
Meshesha Zaudou
David R. Zimmerman
Jared Matthew Zimmerman
Jennifer L. Zimmerman
Jeremy L. Zimmerman
Yvonne Chérie Zimmerman
Johann R. Zwally

Class of 1995

Tyrone L. Bair
Elizabeth (Barley) Leaman
Sarah M. Barley
Melissa J. Beamesderfer
Susan R. Beiler
Elaine Marie Blake
Andrea (Blank) Good
Karen M. Braun
Joel D. Breneman
Kirsten N. (Brubaker) Fuhr
Jeffrey G. Bruner
Jenelle E. (Burkhart) Kauffman
Ryan S. Burkhart
Christine F. (Burkholder) Nolt
Misty D. Caldwell
Joy (Cann) Delevieleuse
Jewel (Charles) Czaja
Lawrence A. Chiles
Jodi K. Cole
Jerry E. Coleman
Mark J. Cote
Salvatore Curto
J. Matthew Davis
G. Toby Delevieleuse
Brian M. Denlinger
Rosella R. Denlinger
Steven B. Denlinger
Rachel M. Dick
Tiffanee M. Dimitris
Angela (Erb) Weidman
Gregory K. Erb
Evan L. Esch
Douglas S. Estep
Leah May (Everett) Frey
Shannon R. (Fausnacht) Karl
Michael W. Fennell
Jason P. Forshey
Kristine Lisa (Fralich) Shaw
Leslie M. Fritz
Joanna R. (Gentry) Pfarr
William R. Giersch
Paul Timothy Gierschick II
Dustin S. Gingrich
Timothy N. Godshall
Danita R. Good
Kate E. Good
Philip H. Good
Colin C. Greene
Kevin R. Groff
Seth T. Hankee
Michael A. Harder
Angela Tyson (Harnish) Posey
Sonya M. Harnish
Claudia S. (Hartzler) Patrick
Suzanne L. Hauber
Megan (Heisey) Fleming
Daniel C. Heller
Timothy E. Heller
Joleen (Herbert) Reiff
Crystal B. (Hershey) Wenger
Crystal M. Hershey
Jenelle R. (Hershey) Gerlach
Joshua Kirkum Hershey
Matthew G. Hershey
David S. Hess
Deanna (Hess) Martin
Doretta (Hess) Giersch
Eric P. Hess
Jennifer M. Hess
Mark J. Hess
Matthew E. Hess
Matthew J. Hess
Wendy Jo Hess
Jonathan E. Hollinger
Kristina A. Hoober
Troy N. Hoover
Craig J. Horlacher
Joshua J. Horning
Clifford R. Horst
Kendall N. Horst
Mindi (Horst) Bruckhart
I. Bradley Hostetter
Shauna M. Houser
Jewel B. (Huber) Ruhland
John P. Humphreys
Tia R. (Hurst) Straub
Rebecca (Interrante) Carroll
Wakako Ito
Kimberly G. (Johns) Horst
Joe E. Johnson
Natsuko Kaneoka
Johanna B. (Keefer) Fisher
Jeryl A. Keener
Reuben L. Kennel
Ruth C. Kilgore
Mark R. King
Jeremy J. Kratz
Sarah L. (Kraybill) Lind
Heidi R. Krieg
Laura A. (Kukich) Dawson
Amanda Kathryn Lake
Jessica E. (Landes) Spieser Landes
Barry L. Landis
Brendon J. Landis
Douglas A. Landis
Elizabeth A. Landis
Joel D. Landis
Brett A. Larson
Eric L. Leaman
Adrienne K. Leasa
Beth A. Leatherman
Jason D. Leister
Kyle J. Levengood
Scott Lingo
Jodie D. Magill
Courtney Elizabeth Maines
Adonica J. Martin
Keith R. Martin
Melinda F. (Martin) Eisenberger
Melody M. Mast
Amy N. (Miller) Knutsen
Felisa G. Miller
Jason D. Miller
Reuben Z. Miller

Daniel R. Mongeau
Amy L. (Moquin) Strunk
Brian Todd Myers
Kenneth C. Noll
Joshua G. Pfarr
Jennifer L. Puckett
Rachel K. Rauch
Henry Redmond, IV
Kendall S. Reiff
Sherrie (Reinford)
   Johndrow
James E. Renno
Emilie (Replogle) Hoffert
Jodi (Rohrer) Brubaker
Ryan C. Rohrer
Heather J. Salfrank
Nasser A. Salim
Jacquelyne F. (Samuel)
   Rudy
Kimberly J. (Sauder)
   Stoeckel
Timothy R. Sauder
Laura A. Schildt
Marisa J. Schnupp
Alexandra Sey
Diana R. Sharp
Kevin M. Sharp
Kimberly J. Shellenberger
Sarah D. Shepherd

Matthew A. Smith
Carmela D. (Smoker)
   Hershey
Julie (Smoker) Watterson
Dustin E. Smucker
Renita (Snader)
   Denlinger
Marilyn J. Snyder
Nathaniel A. Stauffer
April Y. (Stoltzfus)
   Dendler
Christina B. Stoltzfus
Jonathan Clemmer
   Stoltzfus
Michael G. Stoltzfus
Nessa R. (Stoltzfus)
   Stoltzfus Barge
S. Justin Stoltzfus
Tania M. (Stover) Rush
David J. Strite
Rie Takayama
Garey T. Thomas
Jody L. (Thomas) Arnold
Leon Anthony Trager
Wendy L. Trail
Khiet Le Tu
Douglas M. Umble
Jennifer M. (Umble)
   Heller

Emeka O. Unonu
David J. Van Horn
Nathaniel J. Van Hekken
Bryan K. Weaver
David J. Weaver
Jennie D. (Weaver) Groff
Matthew L. Weaver
Wesley A. Wenger
Michael T. Wissler
Anne M. Witmer
Denison S. Witmer
Nao (Yamamoto) Kim
Christopher G. Yerkes
Matthew G. Yoder
William J. Young
Tonya S. (Zehr) Eberly
Karen (Zeiset) Short

Class of 1996

Fasil Aynu Abdu
Dawit K. Alemayehu
Yonas Alemayehu
Heather J. (Allgyer)
   McEneaney
Heidi J. (Allgyer) Kurtz
Tara Dawn (Bare)
   Kenkelen

Krista N. (Bechtold)
   Garner
Sheena L. (Bechtold) Erb
Stephanie M. (Behmer)
   Kimani
Arlan R. Beiler
Christopher E. Beiler
Surafel Mesfin Belew
Reagan M. Bender
Joshua D. Benjamin
Dana B. Bingaman
Thatcher F. Book
Neil A. Breneman
Ryan K. Brenner
Randall R. Brubaker
Jason L. Buckwalter
Darin T. Burkholder
Diana R. (Carpenter)
   Zimmerman
Craig E. Carver
Kimberly A. (Charles)
   Stoltzfus
Talita N. Chiles
Mandy D. Clark
Rebecca L. Clunan
Elizabeth (Correll) Sisler
Mary E. (Coté) Weaver
Silas R. Crews
Marla E. Depew

Kristen J. (Derck)
   Nafziger
Corie Ann (Deshong)
   Welsh
Mahlet Dessalegn
Paul B. Diala
Irene A. Dich
Doreen J. (Ebersole)
   Bishop
Douglas C. Eby
Jeremy R. Erb
Lauren A. Fahnestock
Kent D. Fellenbaum
Chad A. Fisher
J. Randall Fisher
Reginald J. Fisher
Andrea M. (Forrey)
   Metzler
Shawn D. Forry
Mark E. Forshey
Kimberly Lynn (Garrett)
   Martin
Sean M. Garvey
Jeffrey L. Gingrich
Jay E. Glick
Ryan Mathias Good
Gerald E. Groff
Jennifer D. Groff
Nebiyu Y. Haileselassie

Yemesrach Y.
   (Haileselassie)
   Daugherty
Stephanie K. (Hanna)
   Knudsen
Andrew M. Harnish
Kimberly (Harnish)
   Forry
Bradley D. Hartzler
Rebecca A. Hazell
Neil P. Heisey
Daniel H. Heller
Matthew D. Hersey
Alison J. Hershey
Jessica A. Hershey
Kurt E. Hershey
Rachel E. (Hershey)
   Hershey
Brigette D. Hess
James O. Hess
Konrad A. Hess
Kristine M. (Hess)
   Larison
Laura Beth (Hess) King
Laura J. (Hess) Gehris
David F. High, IV
Angela R. (Hiller) Myers
Christina L. Hofmann

Keith Nisly

Elizabeth M. (Hollinger) Kellum
Jamie S. Hoover
Keith J. Hoover
Kristine (Hoover) Miller
L. Luray Horst
Jill (Hostetler) Brenner
Gemma (Hostetter) Bruner
Derrick M. Hudson
Tonia M. Huete
L. Maria (Hurst) Forry
Lawanda Rose (Hurst) McKay
Troy Dean Hurst
Kelly E. (Huston) Sheaffer
Miki Ito
Yoshiro Ito
Steven P. Johns
Carly J. Kauffman
Hawi D. Kejela
Kristin E. (Kennedy) Slevim
Andrea (King) Smoker
Bonnie Lynn King
Karla B. (King) Gibson
Karyn L. Koenig
Jonathan A. Kooker
Jonathan A. Kratz
Brent M. Kreider
Glenn E. Kurtz
Ryan M. Kurtz
Leslie M. Lahr
Michael W. Lambert
Deborah J. Landis
Gary E. Landis
Joseph P. Landis
Sara A. Laninga
Po P. Lao
Hans B. Leaman
Joel M. Leaman
Debra M. Lefever
Theodore H. Lehman
Matthew D. Long
Amanda J. (Luther) McGhee
Carey (Martin) Bender
Courtlyn S. Martin
Jill R. (Martin) Hayes
Kelly J. McFadden
Krista (Metzler) Kauffman

Jennifer L. (Milich) Redding
Melinda Joy (Miller) Landis
Sheldon D. Miller
Ryan K. Moquin
Justus T. Moyer
Gwendolyn (Musser) Kurtz
Joyce J. Muthoga
Loren P. Nafziger
Milka Negatu
Felix Paul Negron
Tram N. Nguyen
Regina K. (Noll) Fleager
Michael L. Nolt
Mindy C. (Nolt) Hankee
Rita D. Nolt
Erick E. Ochs
Erick R. Oehme
Eun-Young Yool Park
Rebecca J. Peifer
Shawn W. Petersheim
Michael G. Poirier
R. Brian Posey
Petrina J. (Ranck) Westfall
Krystal Joy (Replogle) Yoder
Jason A. Rhoads
Thomas L. Rice
A. Cheree (Risser) Chetan
Justin J. Risser
Renee C. (Rohrbaugh) Slaymaker
Anthony P. Rohrer
Jason L. Rohrer
Monica R. (Rohrer) Lederman
Nathan K. Rohrer
Mindi R. Roland
Bronson T. Ruth
Anthony S. Rutt
Eric J. Rutt
John L. Rutt
Kengo Saito
Stephen M. Sarro
Amy E. (Sauder) Lehman
Kara (Sauder) Kurtz
Kristal J. Sauder
Matthew A. Sauder
Dustin D. Schlenbaker

Angela L. Sharp
Danelle L. (Sharp) Bare
Shannon (Shultz) Ebersole
Reuben J. Sinopoli
Kholekile Skosana
Laura Ann (Smoker) McDonald
Lisa (Smoker) Underwood
J. Matthew Smucker
Rodney L. Smucker
Travis J. Snavely
Gerald W. Stauffer
Elisabeth A. (Steckbeck) Moyer
Jeffrey Lee Stoltzfoos
A. Wilmer Stoltzfus
Clark A. Stoltzfus
Colleen R. (Stoltzfus) Staley
Daryl E. Stoltzfus
Michelle (Stoltzfus) Caruso
Nevin E. Stoltzfus
E. Melissa (Stott) Moyer
Angela (Stutzman) Stoltzfus
Youngeun Suh
Jodi M. Thomas
Fikir Tilahun
Maria (Troncale) Buck
Lisa (Velez) Rutt
Franklin L. Wagner
Thomas H. Wagner
Alicia K. Wann
Jennifer (Weaver) Burkholder
Kendra S. (Weaver) Martin
Konrad L. Weaver
Lyn M. (Weaver) Chartowich
Mitchell S. Weaver
Ronald R. Weaver, Jr.
J. Anthony Weber
Jonathan W. Wenrich
Joanna M. (Worme) Rhodes
Kenneth L. Yoder
Kendra L. Yost
Bryan S. Zimmerman
Dain M. Zimmerman

Holly N. (Zimmerman) Steffy
Justin D. Zimmerman
Nathan A. Zimmerman
Patrick R. Zimmerman
Ryan C. Zimmerman
Roxine K. (Zook) Riehl

Class of 1997

Mahlet (Aklu) Rutt
William Gordon Allen
Akihisa Arakawa
Matthew F. Barley
Douglas F. Bear
Dawn M. (Beiler) Coleman
N. Janelle (Beiler) Stoltzfus
Anthony N. Beyer
John S. Blake
Heather S. (Boll) Burkey
Janelle C. (Boll) Jacobs
Jamie (Bradley) Johnson
Angela S. (Brechbill) Martin
Myron L. Brubacher
J. Andrew Brubaker
Jesse D. Brubaker
Phoebe A. Brubaker
Pamela G. Bruce
Kristopher T. Bucher
Aaron C. Buckwalter
Nathan R. Buckwalter
Seth H. Buckwalter
Carmalita Carelse
Jill M. (Charles) Stoltzfoos
Carmen M. Chiles
Anita R. Clark
Joshua A. Cole
Darien J. Covelens
Christopher M. Cox
Edisa A. Curto
Carla J. (Denlinger) Shirk
Kathryn J. (Denlinger) Willard
Prisca A. Diala
Brenton D. Ebersole
Rosalyn J. (Ebersole) Gehman
Philip C. Eby

156 APPENDIX

Susan L. Eisenberger
Hamilton H. Emery
Jeremy V. Ernest
Patricia L. (Esbenshade) Clark
Cheri R. (Forry) O'Donnell
Abigail M. Fretz
Emily J. Friesen
Joseph C. Fuller
Derrick B. Garber
Regina (Garges) Yeakel
Seth D. Gehman
Michael E. George
Jason D. Gerlach
Alicia J. Gierschick
Janette L. Gockley
Adianez Gonzalez
Beth Ann Good
Heather L. (Good) Nyce
Rebecca R. (Good) Fennimore
Lisa M. Gouge
Rebecca L. Gramm
Candice W. Griffin
Kristen (Gross) Cline
Anthony A. Harnish
Steven J. Harnish
Jonathan P. Hartman
Rebecca Hass
Jan M. Heindel
Tiffany D. (Hershey) Betz
Amy K. Hess
Gregory D. Hess
Jeremy J. Hess
Jonathan M. Hess
Todd A. Hess
Kristin E. Hines
Yukari Hiroyama
Jena C. (Hoellwarth) Miller
Laurie L. (Hollinger) Weitzel
Bradley J. Hoover
Brian D. Horn
Joseph P. Horning
Matthew F. Horst
Nelson R. Horst
Ryan E. Horst
Adrienne (Hostetter) Neff
Winona S. Houser

JoAnna S. (Hursh) Hess
Yumie Ito
Aaron M. Kauffman
Darren L. Kauffman
Gary A. Keirn
K. Evan Kennedy
David M. King
Jennifer A. (Kratz) Stancliff
Philip A. Kratz
Matthew D. Kreider
Debra S. (Kunkel) Fisher
Olivia (Lake) Verrillo
Evan S. Landes
Ryan D. Landis
Jin Woo Lee
Jason R. Lehman
Karen E. (Long) Maddox
Bradley S. Longenecker
Joseph L. Lusby, Jr.
Andrew L. Martin
Carl A. Martin
Chad D. Martin
Cindy R. (Martin) Metcalf
Darren P. Martin
Dustin R. Martin
Kendra R. (Martin) Tanner
Kurtis R. Martin
Wayne L. Martin
Rodney D. Mast
Lindsay A. (Mattox) Shertzer
Tara (McFadden) Welch
Robert N. Meck
Curtis L. Miller
E. Matthew Miller
Kristina J. (Miller) Shirk
Yoshie Miyazaki
Summar F. Monte
Jill K. (Musselman) Siegrist
Sherri (Musser) Weinhold
Kimberly B. Myers
Nicole R. (Nafziger) Erickson
Christopher Ryan Neff
Sara B. (Nissley) Peifer
Junichi Ogawa
Danielle Ormerod
Jason T. Peifer

Elisabeth (Penner) Bontrager
Erica J. (Petersheim) Lewis
Elvita Quiñones
Liza C. Ramirez
Jason E. Redmond
Joshua M. Reich
Krista (Reiff) Weaver
Jennifer R. (Reitz) Kratz
David H. Rhine
Lynelle J. (Risser) Kreider
Rachelle M. Roberts
Zachary T. Roberts
Abbey N. (Rohrer) High
Julie Reneé (Rohrer) Martin
Scott R. Rohrer
David A. Salfrank
Meghann E. (Sanders) Horst
Desiree L. Sarro
Jeremy L. Sauder
Jacob M. Scandrett
Jesica R. Schluter
Jonathan A. Sellers
Douglas C. Seymour
Melissa J. (Shellenberger) Jeanes
Lelayitu Shiferaw
Anthony G. Siegrist
D. Marc Siegrist
Richard S. Siegrist
Rosemary S. (Siegrist) Blessing
Ryan A. Siegrist
Christopher D. Simpson
Kevin G. Smoker
Randall W. Smoker
Sherry L. Smoker
Josi Ann (Smucker) Hershey
David D. Sonne
Erin L. Southwick
Theodore S. Spangler
L. Patrick Stauffer
Carrie N. Stoltzfus
Nathan R. Stoltzfus
Scott D. Stoltzfus
Thomas L. Stoltzfus
Benjamin A. Stone
Karalyn M. Stoner
Erica (Strong) Mancuso

Lila Sue Swearingen
Mathaus Q. Trager
Hang H. Tu
Daniel R. Tursack
Agwu O. Ukwa
Angela J. (Umble) McComsey
Ryan E. Umble
Ndidi C. Unonu
Nathan E. Varner
Adrian H. Wallace
Kristen L. (Weatherlow) Buckwalter
Janina (Weaver) Knowles
Jeryl M. Weaver
Keith R. Weaver
Kent R. Weaver
Marlene (Weaver) Martin
Anthony L. Wenger
Mitchell T. Wissler
Yodith Woldu
C. Aisha Wolfe
Heather M. Wolgemuth
Kristen L. Yecker
Kyle H. Yerkes
Heather (Yocum) Buckwalter
Heidi J. (Yoder) Pixley
Jennifer B. (Yoder) Ames
Chad M. Zackowski
Devon J. Zehr
Benji R. Zeiset
Randall J. Zimmerman
T. Nicole (Zurin) Flora

Class of 1998

Nelson Aguilera
Jill S. Alexander
Christopher Lee Allgyer
Gregory W. Atencio
Amanda J. Aungst
Nebiyu Ayele-Gulte
Steven Bamberger
Amy J. (Barndt) Duerr
Courtney L. (Bechtold) Brubacher
LaReta Joy (Beiler) Smucker
Darren Bender
Rachel Candice Berkman
Benjamin David Bixler
Joshua Bomberger

Alumni of the Year 2013

"Peacebuilding is not only for diplomats, politicians or activists, but also for artists, architects, musicians and poets."

Tashya Leaman Dalen

Lancaster, Pennsylvania
Class of 1992

Dalen practices landscape architecture and urban design, founding the Good Land Collaborative in 2012 as a means for designing spaces, communities and cities that promote public engagement, ecological health, and cultural flourishing for all segments of society. She has been an adjunct professor in urban ecology and ethnography and coordinated community-based art projects at the Center for Public Humanities at Messiah College and The Philadelphia Alumni Writers House at Franklin & Marshall College.

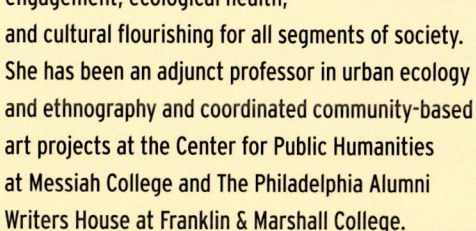

Highlight: In graduate school, I researched cities divided by war—Beirut, Lebanon; Sarajevo, Bosnia-Herzegovina; and Rijeka, Croatia—asking how public space might help knit together polarized populations. I've had the honor of listening to accounts of both hope and despair, and all that lies between, beginning to learn about the complex process of peacebuilding.

Education: Messiah College, bachelor's degree in history; Cornell University, master's degree in landscape architecture
Spouse: Craig Dalen
Family: two children

Activities at LMS: student council, field hockey, Campus Chorale
Church affiliation: East Chestnut Street Mennonite Church, Lancaster, Pennsylvania

Sarah (Bowers) Bloom
Jodi L. (Brechbill) Lapp
Angie Elaine Breneman
Abel A. Brook
Benjamin K. Browand
Debra L. (Brubaker)
  Weaver
Melissa Ann Brubaker
Jill M. Buch
Christopher R. Burkhart
Jessica L. (Burkholder)
  Martin
Michelle R. (Charles)
  Esh
Nathan R. Charles
Timothy N. Charles
Brandon C. Clark
Andrew G. Cote
Tara L. Covelens
Daniel Shank Cruz
Jessica (Cueto) Riehl
Annette Lynn (Darity)
  Garber
Sarah W. (Dean)
  Sizemore
Mitchell S. Denlinger
Rodney L. Denlinger
Shannon R. (Denlinger)
  Meck
Kidest Dessalegn
Nebyou Desta
Krystal Yvonne Eberly

Craig A. Ebersole
Andrew R. Engle
Claudia P. (Everett)
  Good
S. Robert Ferenczy
Aida Fisseha
Belen Fisseha
Amanda Elizabeth Flores
Laura Marie Forshey
Shelley Ann Francis
Sonya J. (Frey) Bayley
Timothy A. Fulmer
Javier M. Garcia
Rodney Gehman
Sarah Ann (Gehman)
  Bixler
Chad B. Glick
Shauna (Glick) Miller
Deborah A. Good
Kevin M. Good
Kimberly K. Green
Michael J. Greene
Andrew R. Greenwald
Bethanie W. Gross
Jared Seth Hankee
Andrew L. Harnish
Peter J. Hart
Alysia A. Herr
Timothy R. Hershey
Brad A. Hertzler
J. Daniel Hess
L. Douglas Hess

Michael B. Hess
Julie M. (Hines) Ramsey
David P. Hofmann
Denise K. (Hoover)
  Olmstead
Laura R. Horning
Jonathan L. Horst
Kyle B. Horst
Nathan J. Hostetter
Wendy Joy (Hostetter)
  Davis
Mindi Jo Huber
Heather R. Hulshart
Uk-Jin (Jack) Jeong
Ruth Johnson
Susannah C. Keiser
Sarah (Kennel) Haines
Crystal B. (King) Johns
Jonathan L. King
Sharon L. King
K. Scott Kreider
Daniel P. Kurtz
Joshua Benjamin Kurtz
Angela Jo Lambert
Blake Charles Lambert
Christopher Lin Landis
Melissa (Landis)
  Eilenberger
Regina A. (Landis)
  Martin
Sarah C. Lantz
Cynthia Ann Lapp

Dustin R. Lapp
Ryan D. Lapp
Joseph Paul Leaman
Sung Woo Lee
Krista M. Lehman
Vanessa G. (Lehman)
  Crowl
Wesley L. Longacre
William L. Longacre
Audrey L. Martin
Eric R. Martin
Heather Jo Martin
Heather Nicole Martin
Holly J. Martin
Janell M. (Martin)
  Almodovar-Cora
Justin R. Martin
Kristina (Martin)
  Flewelling
Melita Rose Martin
Kimberly A. (Metzler)
  Stauffer
Anita D. Miller
Jared A. Miller
Maria B. (Miller) Wulin
Roger L. Miller
Mimie Moipone
  Mokwana
Reiko Moriya
Vania L. (Moskal) Frey
Jason L. Moyer
Faith Mwaura

I. Grace Mwaura
Robert E. Myers, III
Danielle L. Nickle
Jeffrey M. Nissley
Geoffrey S. Nolt
Janelle R. Nolt
Jeane L. (Nolt)
  Bowerman
Jodi M. (Nolt) Burkepile
Katharina Nuss
Ayodeji Oladeji
Fumi Ono
Nathanael J. Overly
Jairo N. Paulino
Jared R. Peifer
Kari (Pennell) Yarnall
Anthony Lee Petersheim
Kristin C. Peterson
Jennifer L. Pittman
M. Brooke Posey
Russell James Pyle
Derek L. Ramsey
Erin E. Reci
Jessica M. Reynolds
Shawn J. Rice
Sheldon J. Rice
Debra L. Ristenbatt
Rachel N. Rodriguez
Geoffrey W. Rohrer
Jessica (Rohrer) Weaver
Rebecca (Rohrer)
  Waynick

Megan C. (Rutt)
  Rosenwink
Michael A. Sauder
Frederic F. Scandrett
Paul M. Scotten
Tonya R. (Shaub)
  Anderson
Kristy J. Shellenberger
Mitchell L. Shellenberger
Charity G. (Shenk) Zook
Gary S. Shepherd, Jr.
Loretta J. (Shertzer)
  Zook
Lois (Shirk) Martin
Ryan M. Showalter
Jillian R. (Simmers)
  Diffenderfer
Jonathan P. Smith
Crystal D. Smoker
Kyle T. Smoker
P. David Smoker, Jr.
Burnell D. Smucker
Kristen (Smucker) Dice
Hope L. Sone
Isaiah B. Stauffer
Matthew T. Steffy
Teresa D. (Stoltzfoos)
  Smoker
Alanna M. Stoltzfus
Amy J. Stoltzfus
Derek L. Stoltzfus
Suzanna Jill Stoltzfus

158 APPENDIX

Rebecca J. Strite
Jessica L. Strong
Sara Michelle Stutzman
Emnet Tilahun
Oleg Tkachenko
Nneka N. Unonu
James A. VanHekken
Joshua R. Vanderplate
G. Alexandro Vargas
Andrew S. Weaver
Kerri B. Weaver
Melanie R. Weaver
Erin K. Weidman
Chandra N. Wenger
Robin John Wenger
Elizabeth L. (Wenrich) Clark
Susan J. Wenrich
Shannon N. Windle
Elizabeth A. (Wisk) Witmer
Marta S. (Wissler) Hoear
David S. Witmer
Betelihem Wodajie
Sarah B. Wolf
Travis L. Yoder
Dustin S. Zechman
Amy S. Zeiset
Kristy Ann (Zeiset) Weaver
Jared A. Zimmerman
R. Mikhael Zurin

Class of 1999

Jamilla A. Afrane
Sinedengle Assefa
Maame A. Atiase
Juliet H. (Aungst) Nyce
Eric M. Baker
Travis R. Bare
Luke R. Barley
Nickolas R. Beamesderfer
Daniel G. Beauchamp
Andre M. Beiler
Justin R. Beiler
Kirubeil M. Belew
Jonathan M. Benner
Heidi D. (Bixler) Sell
Laura K. (Boll) Peifer
Angela D. (Brenneman) Wood
Crystal D. Brubaker
David J. Brubaker
Debra J. Brubaker
Jeremy R. Brubaker
Regina D. (Burkholder) Acker
Amanda K. Byers
Brenda M. Carrasco
Valerie E. Chandler
Debra M. (Charles) Bearden
Jacob R. Charlton
Kristina R. Clark
Steven H. Cliff
Christine R. (Cochrane) Halliday
Kate E. Cole
Matthew J. Correll
Sara R. (Cox) Kauffman
Laura C. (Dale) Geib
Byrone A. Davis
Michael A. Deitrich
Laura S. Deller
Carrie (Denlinger) Warner
Jeremiah C. Denlinger
Joanna F. Doyle
Joshua A. Eastep
Jared I. Easton
Jason T. Eberly
Eric Kent Eby
Charis B. (Eckert) Gramm
Spencer E. Embley
Karisten (Emery) Buckwalter
Rebecca D. Ernest
Kristen M. (Eshelman) Enck
Enanga Daisy Fale
Rhonda M. Felpel
Erica Dene (Fisher) Allain
Lee S. Forshey
Derek Q. Frey
Jerel L. Frey
Jeffrey D. Gantz
Cheryl L. (Gehman) Horst
Evan M. Gentry
Yonatan Getachew
Michelle L. (Gingrich) Wenden
Brian R. Gochnauer
Gievanne M. (Gonzalez) Garcia
Andrea M. (Good) Leaman
Michael M. Good
Melissa D. Gorick
Hans S. Groff
Stacy L. (Groff) Burkholder
Wayne E. Groff
Gabriel P. Hagy
Biruk Y. Haileselassie
Joel D. Harnish
Renee L. (Harnish) Frey
Jeffrey M. Hartenstine
Katherine E. (Hass) Goree
Richard A. Hellings
Ryan B. Herr
Alisa K. Hershey
Laura B. (Hershey) Brubaker
Sarah E. (Hershey) Rohrer
Timothy K. Hershey
Joel M. Herzog
Jill (Hess) Beamesderfer
Katie S. Hess
Kelly J. Hess
Laura J. Hess
Shana J. (Hess) Stauffer
Mami Hino
Jason L. Hock
Rachel A. (Holmes) Wenger
Drew T. Hoober
Marcia B. Horn
Jennifer M. (Horst) Riment
Joshua D. Hostetter
Robert A. Hostetter
M. Leann (Huber) Brown
Shane C. Ingram
Jessica R. (Johns) Mast
Joshua R. Johnson
Kassandra M. (Kane) Paulino
Kevin M. Kauffman
Kristen S. (Kauffman) Lusby
Stephen C. Kauffman
Emily B. Kautz
Kandace R. Kautz
Shelly J. Keagy
Megan R. Keefer
Michael A. Keener
Eric Scott Kennel
Jesse L. Kilgore
Jandee Kim
Derek A. King
Kerwin M. King
Rachel E. King
Theresa L. (King) Gamber
Benjamin D. Klassen
Megan E. Kraybill
Brianna M. Kube
Justin L. Kurtz
Margaret L. Kurtz
Tamara N. Kurtz
Daniel T. LaFauci
Jerome A. Landis
Nathan P. Landis
Rebecca L. (Landis) McLarty
Stephen D. Leaman
Aelee Lee
Jeung (Anna) Yon Lee
Darrell E. Lehman
Sarah C. (Lehman) Schrock
Jung Mi Lim
Jesse E. Lopez
Daniel P. Lyne
Danielle M. Mangiro

Keith Nisly

APPENDIX 159

Alumni of the Year 2013

"I found LMS was a place where many of the faculty cared about me and that caring, mentoring and role modeling shaped me more than just the content of the classes."

J. Nelson Kraybill

Elkhart, Indiana | Class of 1972

Kraybill is a pastor, author and president of Mennonite World Conference. He currently is a pastor at Prairie Street Mennonite Church in Elkhart, Indiana. Kraybill was president of Associated Mennonite Biblical Seminary from 1996 to 2008. He was program director at the London Mennonite Center in England from 1991 to 1996. He was first ordained as a pastor at Taftsville Chapel Mennonite Church in Vermont.

Highlight: My 2010 book, *Apocalypse and Allegiance,* is an introduction to the book of Revelation for non-specialists, and it has been translated into several languages. Also, Mennonite World Conference work has shown me the vitality of the church in many parts of the world. I lead tours to the Holy Land, and blog about biblical sites at www.peace-pilgrim.com.

Education: Goshen College, bachelor's degree in history; Princeton Theological Seminary, master of divinity; Union Theological Seminary, doctorate in New Testament
Spouse: Ellen Graber Kraybill
Family: two daughters
Activities at LMS: Wrote "Still at Large," a humor column for the *Millstream*
Church affiliation: Prairie Street Mennonite Church, Elkhart, Indiana

---

Robert E. Martens
Amy R. (Martin) Stoltzfus
Dana M. Martin
Jeffrey L. Martin
Jordan C. Martin
Michael J. Martin
Ryan L. Martin
Shane T. Martin
Jennifer E. Miller
Theresa M. Miller
Erin Mizukane
Randall M. Moate
Robert E. Mohler
Jordan D. Moyer
Bonaya J. Mudda
Benjamin J. Myers
Jessica L. (Neely) Burkhart
Brad D. Newland
Craig A. Nissley
Christopher D. Noll
Andrea J. (Nolt) Hackman
Theresa J. (Nolt) McNear
Jana L. (Oberholtzer) MacKay
Aaron M. O'Brien
Toyin O. Oladeji
Jared L. Peifer
Jeremy R. Peifer
Matthew M. Pellman
Heather M. (Pfrommer) Crosby
D. Brent Posey
Nathan B. Ray
Matthew C. Ressler
Daniel S. Risser
Esther (Rogers) Pujol
Michelle A. Romano
J. Denise (Ruhl) Strausbaugh
Martin P. Rundle
Maria J. (Sauder) Beiler
Kristine J. Sensenig
Kevin L. Shenk
Kathy I. (Shiley) Abele
Sarah E. Shirk
Harim Shon
Janine N. (Siegrist) Mason
Megan Smoker (Beiler)
Yvonne J. (Smoker) Rivera
Eric K. Smucker
Joshua L. Smucker
Samuel S. Sonne
Gregory P. Steffy
Bradley D. Stoltzfus
Glenn M. Stoltzfus
Keith A. Stoltzfus
Rachel L. Stott
Jayne E. (Thomas) Kennel
Amy C. (Transue) Hartenstine
Anna C. (Troncale) Martin
Brandon M. Umble
Jessica L. Vanderplate
Julian T. Walker
Kelly L. Walraven
Ryan K. Weaver
Dayna Marie (Weinhold) Reidenouer
Matthew B. Werner
Paul D. Williams
Anita J. (Wingard) Jerva
Darin L. Wright
Holly S. Yerkes
André M. Yoder
Julie A. Yost
Nichole (Younger) Dysput
Dwight R. Zimmerman
Monica L. Zimmerman
Justin M. Zook
Ian B. Zubaly

Class of 2000

Joshua M. Adams
C. Ryan Albrecht
Eyob Alemu
Bradley M. Alexander
Susan M. Altland
Luke Austin Anderson
James I. Artz
Mesgana Berhanu Ayele
Ryan C. Bannon
Young Woong Bark
Colleen Joann Barker
Christopher Philip Barley
Jonathan E. Beck
Emnet Befekadu
Justin P. Bellone
Kirk R. Benner
Ryan J. Bertz
Michelle L. (Bogedain) Moser
Tricia L. (Bollinger) Buckwalter
Jason L. Breneman
Courtney J. Buchen
Joel A. Buckwalter
Justin L. Buckwalter
Kristi Lynn Burkholder
Alexis Kirsten Byrd
Daniel A. Carpenter
David O. Chryst
Ryan M. Ciaccia
Audrey L. (Clark) Troop
Timothy B. Cochran
Anne Marie Coté
Crissa L. (Cox) Gehr
Michelle L. Cozzone
Christina Joy Cruz
Nathan Roy Darity
Megan (Dehmey) Yost
Cory C. Deist
Karina K. Derksen-Schrock
Heidi Natasha Derstine
Joseph H. Dietrich
Andrew Daniel Dietzel
Christina S. (Doe) Bagley
Randall J. Ebersole
James B. Eby
Jessica S. (Eby) Eby
Trevor J. Eby
Heather A. Ely
Jocelyn R. Engle
Daniel Mason English
Diana Romaine Erb
Karinda Joy Erb
Mali Allyn Evearitt
Betelehem Fekade
Benjamin P. Fields
Kevin J. Forry
Natasha M. Frantz
Ryan Emerson Frey
Matthew James Fulmer
Jared K. Garber
Gregory S. Gehman
Shiekuma Terhemen Gemade
Matthew L. Gierschick
Angela M. (Gingrich) Horst
Lili Girma
Yafet Girma
Joshua Samuel Gish
Steven T. Glick
Kelli J. (Godshall) Martin
Robert Lee Goeke
Robert A. Good
Travis D. Good
Rustin R. Gramm
Mark M. Graybill
Kimberly A. (Griffin) Maines
Anthony David Groff
Josiah Aeschliman Groff
Michael S. Habte
Lauren N. (Hamlin) Uhrich
Jason M. Harnish
Sherry L. Harnish
Nora Ashley Helmus
Mark Andrew Herd
B. Lloyd Herr
Evan J. Ross Hershey
Greta L. (Hertzler) Stoner
Philip B. Hess
Trent C. Hess
Valerie K. (Hess) Darity
Naomi S. (Heyburn) Ross
Melanie A. Hilton
Rachel Elizabeth Hoover
Valerie Joy Hoover
Travis Hornberger
Eric Lee Horst
Jeffrey L. Horst
Sheldon A. Horst
Stephanie Anne Horst
Jacob Andrew Hostetler
Benjamin Charles Hostetter
Chad Ellis Hurst
Christopher Stephen Ide
Derek Adam Jenkins
Scott L. Jenks
Matthew Neil Johns
Laura Ann (Kautz) Nguyen
Heather K. (Kessler) Hairhoger

160 APPENDIX

Joshua David Kiehl
Hyun Jin Kim
Eileen R. Kinch
Taylor Kinney
David Ashby Kirkland
Grace Klemmer
Sarah A. Kolp
Jessee L. Kopczynski
Rebekah J. (Kratz)
   Brubaker
Megan Mariah LaFauci
Kirk Andrew Rutt
   Landes
Kimberly Joy Landis
Craig S. Lapp
Tina M. Lapp
Bryan A. Leaman
Janine E. Leaman
Kari Ann (Lefever)
   Burkhart
Hee Dae Lim
Macy E. (Linde)
   Ketcham
M. Laura (Livengood)
   Stoner
Dirk W. Logan
Jessica S. (Lusby)
   Buckwalter
Nicholas Ngumo Maina
Andrew Owens Maines
Admas Makonnen
Angelina Maldonado
Jessica A. Maley
Carrie L. (Martin)
   Beachy
Kathy Ann (Martin)
   Horst
Tiffanie Shanelle Martin
James A. Mast
Tamara L. Mast
Tonya R. (Mast) Johns
Brandon S. Maust
Candace Nicole
   McCauley
Jeanette Yvonne Meck
G. Kent Metzler
George Donald Miller
Kyle N. Miller
Michael J. Minnich
Deborah A. Mulugeta
Jenelle S. (Musselman)
   Roynon
Ruth R. W. Muthoga

Kabulo Blanche
   Mwilambwe
Inl Yeong Na
Joo Yeong Na
Laura B. (Nafziger)
   Roman
Rachel L. (Nauman)
   Walsh
Elizabeth Ann Neff
Dina Negatu
Jason M. Nissley
Brent Douglas Nolt
Funke O. Ojo
Bolaji O. Oladeji
Sung Hyun "Sunny" Park
Shannon S. Pascal
Jana M. (Petersheim)
   Troyer
D. Brent Posey
Bethany L. Rainal
Shawn M. Ramsey
Andrew D. Ranck
Nicholas E. Reeser II
Rebecca B. Reich
Emelene K. Reist
Benjamin Yo Risser
Amy Marie Rohrer
Jason B. Rohrer
Kelly L. (Rohrer) Smith
Nicole Alison (Rose)
   Ober
John Patrick Sauder
Valerie D. Sauder
Andrew Fischer Scandrett
Brent A. Schildt
Andrew J. Derksen-
   Schrock
Amber N.
   (Shellenberger)
   Bitterman
Timothy Jacob Shenk
Daryl J. Shirk
Jonathan Lynn Shue
Jeffrey L. Siegrist
Luke Clayton Sinopoli
Alisha R. (Smith) Heller
Cloyd Robert Smith II
Jeffrey Allen Smoker
Michael J. Smoker
Ryan Daniel Smoker
Sheldon J. Smoker
Lori J. (Snader) Lehman
Evan A. Southwick

Joshua David Stafford
Gerald D. Stoltzfoos
Evangelyn P. (Stoltzfus)
   Rodriguez
Todd Randall Stoltzfus
Michael J. Stoner
Bozho Todorich
Mark Anthony
   Tomassetti
Jesúa Berenice Tomé
Kevin A. Tullos
Heather R. (Umble)
   Yoder
Salim Taha Wagaw
Abraham Peter Walters
Jewel M. (Weaver)
   Martin
Justin Lyn Weaver
Nelson Randall Weaver
Erica Lynn Weber
Rachel E. (Webster)
   Duteriez
Michael Allen Weisser
Joel T. Welch
Kimberly J. Wenger
Kirsten N. (Wenger)
   Cooper
Jessica L. (Westcott)
   Stafford
Duane A. White
Caleb J. Wilde
Adam Edward Woge
Daniel A. Yocom
Dorothy L. Yoder
Jeremy B. Yoder
Julie A. Yoder
Kenneth W. Yost
Elizabeth Anne (Young)
   Miller
Joshua D. Younger
Wudasse Zaudou
Rebecca Kay
   Zimmerman
Theresa L. (Zimmerman)
   Oswald

Class of 2001

Habeeb Abiola
Kabir Abiola
Thaddeus G. Acosta-
   Davis
Sameia M. Ahmed

Elone Alemayehu
Jeffrey W. Anderson
Justin Paul Anderson
Henok Bahru
Jeremy Reginald Banks
Rebekah R. (Barnhart)
   Crouse
Jeremy T. Basom
Emily Dawn Bauman
Ryan M. Bechtold
Fiker Befekadu
R. Alburn Binkley
Brandon M. Boll
Jason T. Boll
Kevin M. Brandt
Joel Scott Breneman
Daniel R. Brubaker
Joseph R. Brubaker
Peter M. Brubaker
Chad R. Burkholder
Jeffrey L. Butler
Tony G. Carrasco
Derrick R. Charles
Michael D. Day
Peniel Dimberu
Christina N. (Dimitris)
   Schoffstall
Ryan K. Dissinger
Jeffrey L. Dombach
Sara A. (Duling)
   Ferenczy
Ryan J. Ebersole
Joelle Marcia Eckert
Karin D. (Esh) Gemeda
Russ Fedarinenko
Virginia A. Ferenczy
Samuel David Ferguson
Wanda O. Fletes
Amanda Ruth Forry
Christopher D. Fretz
Joel Mark Gimmi
Matthew R. Gish
John W. Glick
Daren E. Good
Jason Lloyd Good
Kristopher D. Good
Eric R. Goodman
Rachel Elizabeth Gotwalt
Christopher D. Grant
Elizabeth Joy Graugh
Angela Y. (Groff)
   Williams

Keith Nisly

APPENDIX **161**

Biniam Y. Haileselassie
Junko Harada
Karla M. (Harnish) Stauffer
Krista J. (Harnish) Cruz
Philip J. Hartshorne
Sanae Hasegawa
Josh E. Heindel
Bryan C. Hershey
David A. Hess
Douglas S. Hess
Jered M. Hess
Aaron R.C. Hines
Nathaniel Lee Holmes
Melinda Jane Hoover
Sheila D. (Hoover) Burkholder
C. Nicole (Horn) Adeladel
Cheryl Megan Horn
Cicely D. (Horst) Berkey
David A. Horst
Ryan C. Horst
Sherri R. (Horst) Read
Audrey J. Hostetter
Megan L. (Hostetter) Kennel
Paul W. Hostetter
Sarah R. Humbert-Martin
Joshua R. Hunt
Mark S. Ingram
Terah L. (Jacobs) Kennel
Jung Yoon Jang
Joon Jeong
Allison E. (Jerchau) Liz
Gordon L. Kautz
Jun Kawamura
Joshua D. Keefer
Laurie Nicole Keener
Timothy A. Keener
Carly E. (Keirn) Koehn
Nathan L. Kennel
Zachary Brian Kennel
Jared M. Kosakoski
Jeanne E. (Kreider) Allegret
Melanie L. Kreider
Derric R. Krout
Joseph J. Lalli
Stephen C. Lambert
Jill P. (Leaman) Milton
Shawn D. Lehman
Mesgana Lemma
Karl R. Linde, Jr.
Gerald N. Livengood
Katharine M. (Lombardi) Rodriguez
Richard E. Longenecker
Samuel C. Lopez
Ethan Timothy Lyne
Joel B. Martin
Joel M. Martin
Keith R. Martin
Kimberly S. (Martin) King
Ryan Henry Meinzer
Ranae Yvette Miller
Stephanie L. (Miller) Lehman
Andrejs Misulovins
Ryan M. Moate
Bilal J. Mudda
Timothy Adin Mumma
Hannah Y. (Negron) Smith
Stefanie Mae Neikam
Rachelle A. (Newcomer) Vriend
Matthew Newman
Cameron D. Nolt
Kevin J. Nolt
Joshua David Northeimer
Nathan Evan Ormerod
Steven E. Pauly
Nathaniel Richard Pellman
Brandon Ewing Pfrommer
Jeremy A. Ranck
Matthew J. Rannels
Jeremy C. Redcay
Derek L. Redmond
Brynn Marie Reeser
Erika L. (Reitz) Good
Maigen E. (Ressler) Winegardener
Tiffany N. (Rohrer) Myers
Adam Brandt Roth
Janelle M. (Rutt) Young
Paul Ian Sadaphal
Meron Sahelu
Sarah E. (Saunders) DiFilippo
Kurtis A. Sensenig
Michael Sensenig
Michael Elliott Shaub
Doreen G. (Shirk) Nicholas
Peter M. Shirk
Aaron L. Smith
Megan Deanne (Smith) Allen
Kelly N. (Smoker) Lapp
Natalie H. (Smyth) Wright
Timothy W. Spiegel
Zachary Tobias Stehman
Michael D. Stockin
Amanda R. (Stoltzfus) Thomas
Justin D. Stoltzfus
Justin M. Stoltzfus
Zel J. Stoltzfus
Sabrina L. Strong
Alazar G. Tekalinge
Regina K. (Thomas) Risser
Bethany N. (Toews) Wong
Matthew Todd Transue
Arsene Mukendi Tshidimu
Rodney Allen Umble
Meredith W. (Wallin) Steidler
Evangelene Niki Walters
Nathan C. Weiler
Joel D. Weinhold
Susan Marie Wenger
Adam E. Whitlatch
Becky (Yoder) Boll
Janae A. (Yoder) Hostetter
Yohannes Yosef
Holly A. Young
Rebecca S. (Young) Miller
Christian J. Zimmerman
Julie A. (Zimmerman) Fridley
J. Robert Zook

Class of 2002

Sonya J. Abreu
Sylvia J. Abreu
Amanda Leigh Adams
Jennifer M. Adams
Mekdelawit Ayalew
Selam B. Ayele
Erik Leroy Baker
Matthew Joel Stoesz Bauman
Justine E. (Beiler) Weber
Robel Mesfin Belew
William Douglas Blair
Chase E. Boian
Kendra S. (Bollinger) Martin
Nathan N. Bontrager
Mark Bui Breneman
Isaac Ethan Brown
Joel A. Brubaker
Jonathan L. Brubaker
Laura A. (Buchen) Breneman
Jed D. Burkholder
Lisa N. Burkholder
Ryan Charles Byler
Shirlyn A. Byrd
Brandon Kelley Canty
Twila Dawn Charles
Namwoong Cho

Jin Ho Choi
Jin-Man Chung
Jenna Bryn Ciaccia
Ashleigh Michelle Clark
Peter K. Connelly
Rebecca Joy (Coté) Erb
Lindsay M. (Dale)
 Schrock
Derek L. Denlinger
Jonalyn C. (Denlinger)
 Risser
Nathan K. Denlinger
Yemeserach A. Dessalegn
Ivonne Emilie Diaz
Justin Matthew
 DiNunzio
Andrew Paul Eby
Janelle C. (Engle) Benner
Belen Eshetu
Rebecca M. Esposito
Jennifer J. Evans
Benjamin Roy Everett
Jeremy C. Felpel
Jonathan D. Fretz
Takako Furuta
Zachary John Garber
Erika Rose Garvey
Dwight A. Gehman
Jacob J. Gehman
Julie L. (Gingrich) Horst
David Samuel Gish

Sherri Ann Glick
Ryan R. Goeke
Juan Carlos Gonzalez
Jonathan Jacob Good
Trisha Y. Good
Shannon Louise Gray
Anna Marie Groff
Matthew Ryan Groff
Ryan S. Groff
Monica Joy Habecker
William Hope Handy
Jessica Lynn Heaps
Jason David Heil
Kristen E. (Herr)
 Petersheim
Brent D. Hershey
Eric Eugene Hess
Nathan Scott Hoover
Timothy Robert Hoover
Brent Lyndon Horst
Michael S. Horst
W. Christopher Horst
Dustin A. Hostetter
Katrina Joy Hughes
Margaret Mae Ingram
Laura S. (Jackson)
 Burkholder
Chioke O. Jefferson
Maria Smucker Kanagy
Luella Marie Kauffman
Joshua Michael Kautz

Stephanie Joy Kautz
Carrie Joy Keagy
Daniel R. Keener
Dilnesa Kifle Eshete
Clair Lamar King
Ryan D. King
Jennifer R. (Kopp) Miller
Hellina Korajian
Jessica M. Kreider
Adrienne Kathleen
 Kuhlengel
Amy Joy Kurtz
Wendy C. Kurtz
Adam Christopher Lake
Howard Thomas Lake
Adrienne L. Landis
Jason Dwight Landis
Emily S. Lantz
Duane L. Lapp
Gregory Kyle Lapp
Kelley J. Lapp
Kristin R. Lapp
Rodney L. Lapp
Austin LaVon Leaman
Sangshin Lee
D. Andrew Lehman
Joel C. Lehman
David W. Lim
Clarissa Carr Linde
Darrel S. Martin

Janelle M. (Martin)
 Yoder
Jere A. Martin
Jolynn Beth Martin
Neal L. Martin
Bethany H. McKenney
James G. Mickley
Matthew C. Miller
Joseph Cline Mitrani
Jena R. (Moyer) Umbrell
Herold Robert Mugabi
Stephen M. Mulvenna
Shelby L. (Mummau)
 Heim
Alfie Esther Njeri
 Muthama
Amanda S. (Nelson)
 Stoltzfus
George William Ngobi
Mary C. Nickle
Renee N. (Nissley)
 Gruber
Sherrie M. (Nolt) Good
Eun Young Park
Ian H. Phillips
Mikel P. Pojani
Rebecca Lynn Raczka
Colin M. Reci
Brandon B. Reeser
Bryce J. Ressler
Megan Elise Ressler

Mark S. Rineer
Lauren E. Rodriguez
Bradley S. Rohrer
Christen R. Rohrer
Jason M. Rohrer
Laura Beth Rohrer
Melissa S. Root
Daniel Evan Rose
John C. Rowe
Jason M. Rutt
David A. Sadaphal
Justin Adam Sauder
Nicole H. Schober
David A. Schrock
Bethlehem Hailu
Michael Hailu Sebsibe
Justin M. Shenk
Meba Shimelis
Angela Marie Shirk
Marilee R. Smeltzer
Tonya Dee Smoker
Wayne Clayton Smoker
John E. Smucker
Justin L. Smucker
Arlin J. Snyder
Austin Jared Steffy
Jonathan David Steffy
Calvin B. Steidler
Carlee B. Stoltzfus
Caroline Marie Stoltzfus
Douglas Ryan Stoltzfus

Lynn A. Stoner
Emily J. (Stott) Patterson
Kebebush Telahun
John Michael Thomas
Jonathan David Thomas
Fesseha Moges Tilahun
Hiyab Tilahun
Penn Anthony
 Tomassetti
Lydia C. Troncale
Jordan M. Umble
Kathryn E. Umble
 Smucker
Chrystal S. Vible
Gina M. (Weaver) Lusk
Kevin Scott Weaver
Renae Alicia Weaver
Shannon D. Weaver
Andrew J. Weber
Eric J. Weber
Darcy A. Weinhold
Alissa Marie Wendland
David M. Wenrich
J. Grant Wissler
Meba Yeshitela
Alison Dorit Yoder
Krista R. Yoder Latortue
Tiffany Nicole Yoder
Heung Seuk Yoon
Mathewos Yosef
Linford N. Zeiset

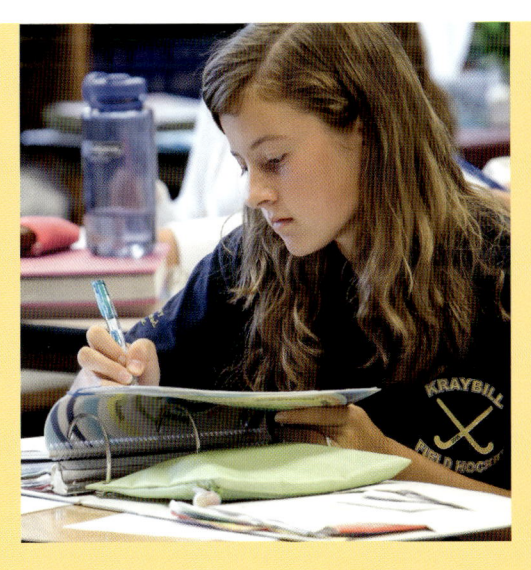

APPENDIX 163

Steven M. Ziegler
Patrick Dorsey Zielinski
Amy Grace Zimmerman
John H. Zimmerman

Class of 2003

Joshua David Addington
Daniel Joseph Allia
Benjamin S. Anderson
L. Beau Baker
Trevor S. Bare
Timothy Lawrence
  Basom
Kelsey A. Beach
Samantha Jean Beam
Joel W. Benner
Janessa Lynn Beyer
John Eldon Blank
Andrew K. Bogedain
Lindsey M. Boll
Daniel Josiah Brown
Amy Laurene Brubaker
Duane Mark Brubaker
Michelle J. Brubaker
Allison Gail Cattell
Chieh-ru Cheng
Kristi Leigh Connelly
J. Kyle Denlinger

Jeremiah Jesse Derksen
Vincent M. DiGuardi
Kimberly Dyan Dilworth
Jeffrey Allen Dise
Erika Helen Doe
Lonita Rose Dueck
Adam D. Durst
Dustin Timothy Ebersole
Joanna Renee Ebersole
Matthew L. Eby
Stephen James Edwards
Kendra E. Emery
Jeffrey Robert Erb
Lenita Renee Esh
Kelsey Marie Feerrar
Jeremy Reed Ferenczy
Neil L. Forshey
Nicholas H. Frantz
P. Joy Gehman
Nathan Robert Geiger
Bilen Getachew
Devon R. Geyer
Ashley Elizabeth Gieg
Cynthia Renée Gingrich
Shannon Joy Gish
Sarah Louise Graybill
Adrian DeVon Groff
Tonya Marie Groff
Ji Hoon Ha

Nathanael G. Haile
Ronald W. Hall
Christina Nicole
  Handwerk
Heather Brydie Harris
Jonathan David Heinly
Joy R. Heisey
Douglas A. Herr
J. Kyle Hershey
Joel C. Hess
Kristen Leigh Hess
Tiffany Ruth Hess
Colin A. Hines
Brian A. Hollinger
J. Andrew Hoover
Alicia Renee Horning
Elizabeth Anne Horst
Matthew Thomas Horst
Andrew Scott Hostetter
Jodie Khetsiwe Hostetter
Brian David Humbert
David C. Hunt
Brandyn J. Hurst
Joshua Michael Hykes
Jessica Ann Kasper
Douglas Charles
  Kauffman
Melissa Kaye Kauffman
Jonathan David Keener

Randal Harold Keener
Sheri Lynn Keener
Carmen Joy Kennel
Rebecca N. Kilgore
Matthew Mack Kinard
John Paul Klemmer
Kevin R. Kreider
Tammi Kumpf
Stephen D. Kurtz
Katie Joy Landis
Joel M. Lapp
Jonathan C. Larson
Jonathan Michael Lausch
Rachel Elaine Lefever
Jay M. Lehman
Toni Diane Lehman
Christine Bernhard
  Letsch
Megan Elizabeth
  Lombardi
Jennifer Ann Lopez
Cory Nicholas Maestle
Adrienne Renée Mansker
Amanda Rae Martin
Dustin Lee Martin
Kelly Renee Martin
Nancy Marie Martin
Nicole E. Martin
P. Daniel Mast

Ryan Gary McCauley
Julie A. Meck
Megan E. Mellinger
Dara Lynn Melrath
Andrew John Metzinger
J. Karl Metzler
Daniel V. Miller
Dianna M. Miller
Natasha Joy Miller
Christine M. Minnich
Marie Elaine Moyer
Hiywete Mulugeta
Sarah Jade Mumma
Kelly A. Mummau
Sammy Mwaura
Se-lim Na
Jamie Lauren Nash
Laura E. Newcomer
Austin Kaylor Nick
Jared Alan Nissley
Rebecca Lynn Olinger
Angélica M. Pagán
Felicia Marie Pagán
Emily Margaret
  Parmarter
Jesse Thomas Pellman
Amber C. Pierce
Amy Elizabeth Porter
Alexander James Ranck

Trevor Ryan Ranck
Anne Elizabeth Rauch
Travis G. Redmond
Brian M. Z. Reece
Jennie Patricia Reed
Sara Elizabeth Reitz
Vanessa Joy Rice
Amy Rosa
Tadios Tafese Samuel
Mary Kate Sanoski
John William Schroeder
Konrad Lee Sensenig
Joy Yvonne Shaiebly
Kevin Eugene Shaiebly
Philip Leon Shirk
Jonathan Edward Shoff
Clinton Mark Simmons
Geraldine C. Smith
Jonathan A. Smith
Ji-won Son
Matthew Herbert Speck
Benjamin Aaron
  Stoltzfoos
Keith Lamar Stoltzfoos
E. Zachary Stoltzfus
Sara Jacobs Stoltzfus
Rachel Lynn Straus
Alef N. Tadesse
Luladey M. Tilahun

Derek L. Umble
Mikaela E. Villalobos
Michael A. Vizcarrondo
Matthew S. Walker
Kara Rose Warfel
Jan Lawrence Watson
Justin Scot Weaver
Matthew Aaron Weaver
Leah Janne Wilde
Tyrae Dean Williams
Darrin Ray Wingard
David L. Witmer
Matthew James Woge
Emily Elizabeth
 Wolgemuth
Magidellawit Worku
Yohannes Worku
Elizabeth Anne Yocom
Jared A. Yoder
Jesse Weaver Yoder
Jonathan Blake Yoder
J. Andrew Young
Joy Linette Zimmerman
Tiffany Lynn
 Zimmerman
Paul Andrew
 Zimmerman-Clayton
Jeremy L. Zook

Class of 2004

Nebiyu Ambachew
 Abraha
James Allen Acosta-Davis
Wesley Adam Addington
Kiera Ren Andersen
Emmanuel M. Arriaga
Christopher Steven
 Atencio
Bernard Addo Atiase
Heather Joy Aument
Joshua Everett Baker
Priya Janelle Banks
Alicia Jo Beiler
Michael Raymond
 Binkley
Karra Beth Black
Jesse J. Blank
Harrison G. Blom
Mark Andrew Brandt
Brett J. W. Brenner
Joshua M. Brubaker
Matthew R. Brubaker

Adam Richard
 Buckwalter
Luis Bunda
Ashley Nicole Burkhart
Cynthia Ann Burkholder
Kara Ann Burkholder
Jacob Norris Chapman
G. Catherine Cherono
Brittany Danielle
 Clemmer
Davina Mary Cody
Meredith Laura Cole
Gregory Anderson
 Collins
Stephanie L. Coolbaugh
Jonathan P. Coté
Lane Philip Crouse
Benjamin Bryan Davis
Lewam Dawit
Gutu Birri Debela
J. Curtis Dehmey
Marco Raymond
 Deitrick
Sophia Marie DeJesus
Todd Bradley Denlinger
Sunil R. Dick
Angela M. Dietzel
Suesan Downes
Jeremiah R. Ely
Nathan John Emerson
Zachary S. Figard
Martha Lynn Fisher
Craig Nathaniel Forshey
Erin Nicole Frederick
Faith L. Frey
Rebecca Joy Fulmer
Joella Shalom Garber
Adey Lemma
 Gebregiorgis
Samson Getachew
Randy Joel Gingrich
Daniel Joel Gish
Erin K. Gish
Esther M. Good
Grant Michael Good
Sheldon R. Good
W. Michael Good
Shannon Marie Griffith
Eric Michael Grosh
Bartholomew S. Hain
Natalie Carlyn Hanna
Alisa Joy Hardin
Janae Lynn Harnish

Andrew T. Heil
Jesse Lynn Heindel
Kimberly Anne
 Hernandez
Jonathan David Herr
Justin D. Hershberger
Cheryl Lynn Hershey
Kristina Beth Hershey
Loren F. Hershey
Austin W. Hess
Jeremy Michael Horning
Mattie Suzanne Horning
Andrew Lynn Horst
Drew Edward Horst
Joshua Barton Horst
Nathan C. Horst
Mitchell Scott Hostetter
Ramona Ana Hurst
Peter Timothy Ingram
Joong-Gil Jang
Annie Elizabeth Johnson
Rebecca Ann Kane
Shaun Matthew
 Kauffman
Bethlhem Tenna Kebede
Megan E. Keener
Jennifer Lynne Kelly
Sean David Kerr
Sang Mi Kim
Lisa Nicole King
Ashley Marie Kreider
Whitney Moriah Kulp
Jason Graham Ladley
Stephanie Diane Landis
J. Nicole Lapp
S. Jay Lapp
Jonathan K. Layman
Brandon Michael
 Leaman
Megan Alysha Leaman
Ji Hoon Lee
Jung Min Lee
Joel Daniel Lehman
R. Matthew Lehman
Patience M. Livermore
Gail Elizabeth
 Longenecker
Kirsten Joy Madea
Shailar Wesley Maines
Karena J. Martin
Nicole J. Martin
Gretchen K. Mast
Kurtis H. Mast

Amanda Michelle
 Matthews
Kristopher Ryan
 McWilliams
Jon Michael Mease
Kirubel Abebe
 Mekonnen
Shawn Allen Mellinger
Gregory Allan Miller
Suzanne Joy Miller
Christina Mockus
Marlese Alexandria
 Moonitz
Angela N. Moyer
Felicia Rae Mozloom
AnnRuth Njoki
 Muthama
Rebecca Leigh Nash
Krystal Joy Neff
Rebecca Anne Nelson
Laura Elizabeth Nissley
Janetta Ranae (Nolt)
 Hibshman
Marcus J. Norman
Kaitlyn B. Northeimer
Jonathan Ray Peachey
Alessandro L. Pizzini
Nathaniel Steven Potter
Todd S. Pyle
Sharyn K. Ranck
Tyler Austin Ranck
Sarah Juanita Raush
Adam Scott Reeser
Abigail Joy Ressler
Ariel Claire Ressler
Douglass Eugene
 Rexroad
Matthew Paul Rhinehart
Courtney Rebecca Ridley
Jessica J. Rohrer
Wendi Elizabeth Rowand
Jalisa Michele Rutt
Selamawit Tafese Samuel
Tedros Santungwana
Matthew Christian
 Sauder
Lauren Ann Schmid
Emily Elizabeth
 Schonewetter
Daniel Paul Sclafani
Jan R. Sensenig
Matthew Todd Shank

Alumni of the Year 2014

"I'm a Blazer through and through, and getting an award helps to send the message out that I'm doing what I think God put me on the earth to do. If you're not helping others, I think you're just wasting time."

Ty Bair

Lancaster, Pennsylvania
Class of 1995

Bair is a social studies teacher in the School District of Lancaster, Pennsylvania. He was Wal-Mart Regional Teacher of the Year, Coca-Cola Teacher of the Year, and Dell Teacher of the Year. He received the 2013 Essence of Humanity Award for his work with Exit Lancaster.

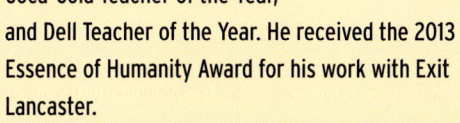

Highlight: God is great and he has placed me in situations where I could recognize the love from others, as well as the ability to see how people have helped me but did not have to. Therefore, I felt that God has wanted me to help others and I co-founded an educational nonprofit called Exit Lancaster that mentors disadvantaged youth.

Education: West Chester University, bachelor's
 degree
Spouse: Carrie Thomas Bair, Class of 1994
Family: two sons

Activities at LMS: basketball
Church affiliation: Grace Ubuntu Fellowship,
 Lancaster, Pennsylvania

Andrea Noel Shellenberger
J. Andre Shenk
Tara Marie Shenk
Jonathan Robert Shirk
Amanda N. Sipe
Allyssa Renee Smoker
Andrew K. Smoker
Joanne Elizabeth Smucker
Ellilta T. Solomon
Jared D. Spence
Jason M. Spence
Matthew Bryant Steffy
Jesse Daniel Stoepker
Bethany Jo Stoltzfus
James Daniel Stoltzfus
Malinda Beth Stoner
Joseph Daniel Straughan
Fukiko Sugimoto
Richard Scott Sweger
Meredith Leanne Talbert
Katelyn Elizabeth Talbott
Donovan E. Tann
Tiffany Jayne Taylor
Ryan Ray Troyer
Kevin Michael Vreeland
Danette Elizabeth Wann
K. Grant Weaber
Trisha Nicole Weaver
James Nelson Weber
Philip E. Weiler
Luke Thomas Weinhold
Melissa Jo Weinhold
DeVon Tyler Wenger
Jennifer Lynn Wenrich
Amber Lynn Wiker
Jordan L. Wissler
Elizabeth B. Yearsley
Ryan Lawrence Yerkes
Joshua Dale Yoder
Tyler J. Yoder
Ruth Yosef Yohannes
Adrienne Beth Zimmerman
Amanda Sue Zimmerman
Tony Lynn Zimmerman

Class of 2005

Joshua Luke Adams
Michael Andrew Alexander
Wesley P. Anderson
Todd Elliott Aukamp
Elizabeth Anne Basom
Maria Joy Bendit
Scott Robert Bertz
Lisa Nicole Bollinger
N. Samuel Brown
Abby Elizabeth Brubaker
Valerie S. Brubaker
Brittany Rae Burkholder
Courtney Lee Burkholder
Alora D. Canty
Steven Nathanael Carpenter
Laura Catherine Cattell
Lindsay Frances Cattell
Michael Reinford Charles
Brittany Kay Collazo
Jennifer Lynne Cousar
Melitza Cruz
Julie Corrin Denlinger
Rebecca Mae Dickinson
Jack Brandon Diffendarfer
Dustin Scott Diller
Lindsay Jean Dilworth
Kyle Craig Dimitris
Leandro Ryne Dueck
Heather Sue Dunlap
Charles A. Engle
Erin Suzanne Esbenshade
Jessica Lynn Esh
Sarah A. Esposito
Elizabeth A. Evearitt
Meredith Olive Everett
Blandine Fée
Chelsey Lee Felpel
Rebekah Anne Fiscus
Alexandria D. Frauman
Kate Marie Gamber
Jennica Kathleen Garber
Jennifer Lynn Garber
Josiah Carl Garber
Matthew David Gehman
Alexis Nicole Gessner
Joseph Patterson Gibson
Christine Wanjiku Gitonga
Scott E. Glick
Hee Jung Go
Christopher David Godshall
Charissa Sue Good
Mary Anna Good
Robert S. Gotshall
Abigail Aeschliman Groff
Kristen Janae Groff
Kristen Jo Groff
Amanda J. Grove
P. Mitchell Gyger
Janelle L. Harnish
Matthew Ian Hartshorne
Meghan Yvonne Hershey
Alicia D. Hertzler
Benjamin R. Hess
Rachel Elizabeth Hess
Ryan Lee Hess
Scott M. Hess
Katharine May Hoffer
Jonathan Tyler Hollinger
Christopher G. Holter
Meghan E. Hoover
Rachel Eileen Horning
Kyle Aaron Horst
Melissa Ashlin Horst
Nicholas Timothy Horst
Shawn Allen Horvath
Justine Renee Hostetter
Bryan D. Hurst
Ben Hess Jackson
Ha Young Jang
Hyo Jin Jang
Yohannes Teshome Jarso
Christine Lynn Jerchau
Johanna Josephian
Jordan R. Kauffman
Rodney William Kauffman
Joshua M. Keener
Christie Nicole Keller
Christina Marie Kelly
Rose Elizabeth Kilgore
Eun Ae Kim
Kyung Rim Kim
Caitlin Marie King
Jennifer Joy King
Jennifer Nicole King
Mary Joy King
Elizabeth Ann Kirby
Christopher Micheal Kowalski
Danae A. Krout
Michael Steven Kuhns
Alexander Phillip Lake
Jason R. Landis
Joanna Laws Landis
Ryan Matthew Lapp
Karen Louise Layman
Carolyn Alicia Leber-Eyrich
Jae Ik Lee
Won Joon Lee
Adam John Lefever
Rachel M. Lehman
Benjamin J. Lesher
Adam Daniel Lever
Cooper Wilhelm Linde
Brindha Lingan

166 APPENDIX

Rachel Lynette Lusby
Kristen Michelle
 Mansker
Ariel Celeste Marquet
Eric N. Martin
Jared Lee Martin
Keith Ryan Martin
Ryan Andrew Martin
Rachel Swartley Mast
Ellen Headrick McCrae
Colin Charlie
 McCullough
Astin J. Melhorn
Julia Ruth Mickley
Carlton E. Miller
Julie Ann Miller
Rachel Maurine Moffett
Felicia Shere Moore
Bisrat Mulugeta
Seung-min Na
Dennis M. Ngumo
Justin Andrew Nickle
Kimberly Malaika Nissly
Benjamin Mark Noll
Derek R. O'Melko
Jin Chun Park
Kendra Janette Parmarter
Sara Jayne Poole
Shanyn Leigh Radtke

Amber Nicole Reed
Adrian C. Reeser
Aaron Joshua Reist
Rebecca Erin Reitzel
Stefanie Marie Reitzel
Elizabeth Renee Rogers
Colette M. Root
Kimberly Jo Roth
Leah Elizabeth Ruth
Elizabeth Thanh Rutt
Katelyn Joy Rutt
Megan Suzanne Sauder
Joyce Lauren Scandrett
Mara E. Shank
Whitney N. Sharp
Andrea Robyn Shaw
Weston Paul Shertzer
Dong Eun Shin
Danita Ruth Shirk
Jillian Lynn Snader
Olga Socotuhova
Katie Helen Sollenberger
Heather L. Speck
Christina Joy Stipe
Jennifer Lorraine
 Stoltzfus
Kimberly R. Stoltzfus
Todd A. Stoltzfus
Wesley Elliot Sweigart

Estel Franklin Taylor
R. William Thomas
Jonathan Wesley Thorn
Hanna Gezahegn Tokon
Lee Anthony Tomassetti
M. Aaron Trimble
Joshua Edwards
 Villalobos
Rachel Esther Ward
Rita Kay Weaver
Sarah Jane Weaver
Deanne M. Weber
Emily Joy Weber
Danelle Renee Weinhold
Alana R. Wenger
Clark Alan Wenger
Nathan E. Whatmore
Vincent Whitman
David Michael
 Whittemore
Brittany R. Wilkinson
Brandon Dannarr
 Williams
Penni Anne Wissler
Daniel Paul Witter
Ji Reh Won
Hee Sun Woo
Senait Fekadu Worku
Jacob Alexander Wright

Sarah Margaret Yearsley
Zerubbabel Getachew
 Yeshaneh
Kevin Darryl Yoder
P. Nicholas Zamora
Joseph H. Zimmerman

Class of 2006

Keren Marie Acosta-
 Davis
Crystal N. Albrecht
Hannah Marika
 Andersson
Rachel Ellen Anschuetz
Courtney Elise
 Augsburger
Marion Rose Bair
Jodi Elynn Baliles
Tyler Magann Barker
Cassandra Jean Beam
Apryl J. Becker
Blen Giday Berhane
Alyssia Nicole Beverly
Kelly Amanda Boltz
Leah Ann Bomberger
Ibsitu Boyer
Benjamin Richard Brown
Kelly A. Brown

Jasmine Kathleen
 Brubaker
Vanessa Gail Brubaker
J. Michael Burkhart
Alexandra Marie Bybel
Robert Lee Carlson
Sarah Isabella Carlson
Kaitlyn Amanda Charles
Desireé Annette Collazo
Timothy S. Coté
Brent Matthew
 Daugherty
Amy Kathryn Denlinger
Paula Sue Dirks
Bradley Keith Ditzler
Amy S. Ebersole
Jesse Wood Edwards
Dietrich Benjamin Eitzen
Thomas Handy
 Ellsworth
Lauren Joy Fairfull
Tingting Fan
Vincent M. Ferenczy
Sara Elizabeth Foster
Asher Friedrich Garber
Brianna Brooke Garber
Sarah Jane Garraty
Phillip Charles Gehman
Thomas M. Gish

Megeara Louise Glah
Rebecca Joy Graybill
Katharine N. Griffith
Alecia Nicole Groff
Debra L. Groff
Lindsey June Grosh
Sarah Michelle Grosh
Faith Allison Hall
Austin Charles Haller
Hyejin Ham
Jae Bum Han
Marissa Elizabeth
 Handwerk
J. Michael Harnish
Kevin Lee Harnish
J. Kate Hershey
Linford Aaron Hershey
Mitchell Drew Hershey
Allison Jenae Hess
Philip J. Hess
Christine Elizabeth
 Hewitt
David Sanford High
Stephen C. Hlavacek
Eun Jee Hong
Cody A. Hoover
Amy Elizabeth Horst
Benjamin William Horst
Trevor Bryan Horst

APPENDIX 167

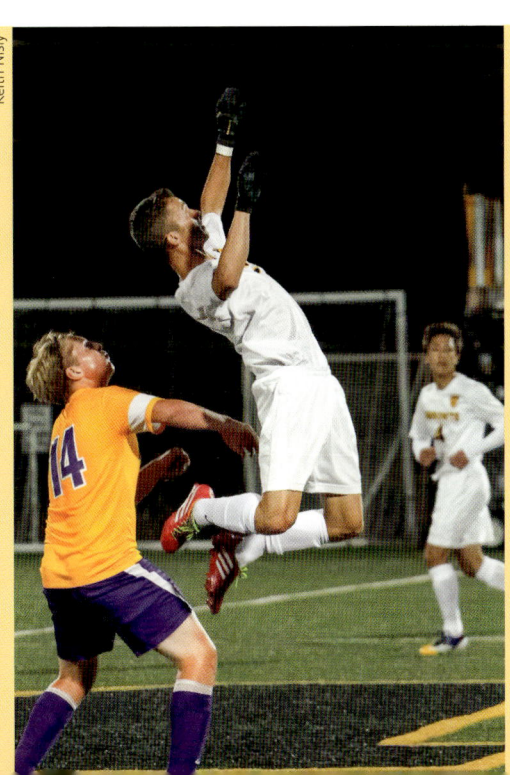

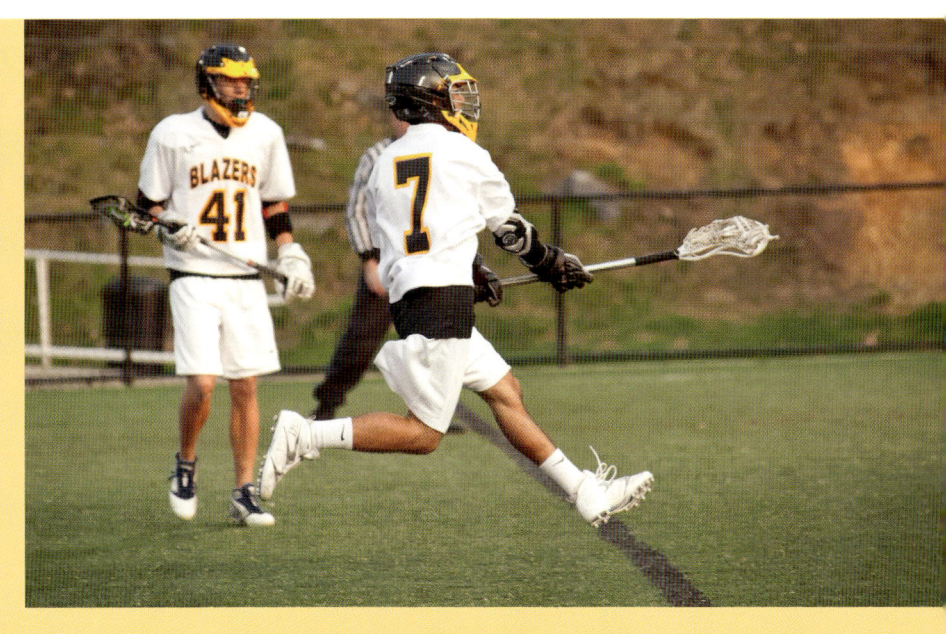

Alumni of the Year 2014

"Lancaster Mennonite School has provided my parents, my wife and me, and our four children the foundation of Christian education that in turn has given us countless opportunities to impact others. For this, I am eternally grateful."

"All four of our children have different gifts and skills. The school was really able to emphasize each of their own gifts. I feel it is a place they can be encouraged by classmates, which makes them feel safe to be who they are."

J. Michael Eby

Gordonville, Pennsylvania | Class of 1990

A seventh-generation farmer, Eby founded and is president of Dairy Farms LLC. He is a sales representative for WDAC radio. Owner of White Gold Milk, he is chairman of the National Dairy Producers Organization, which he helped start.

Highlight: To be able to raise my children on my seventh-generation family dairy farm is my biggest accomplishment. I have also been able to impact the dairy industry through a grassroots effort in Lancaster County. It has taken me all over the United States and continues to be an ongoing example of how the Lord can work in your life above and beyond your expectations. Starting the White Gold Milk label was a dream come true and to see it in grocery stores and nonprofits across Pennsylvania is humbling.

Spouse: Lynette J. Eby
Family: four children

Activities at LMS: Future Farmers of America, Campus Chorale
Church affiliation: Calvary Church, Lancaster, Pennsylvania

Lynette J. Eby

Gordonville, Pennsylvania | Class of 1991

Eby owns and operates Eby Farm Bed & Breakfast. She is a volunteer pre-kindergarten aide at LMS' Locust Grove Campus.

Highlights: My children will always be the most important life experience and being able to be at home with them is my greatest accomplishment. I also thoroughly enjoy meeting and serving thousands of people from all over the United States and the world who spend time at our farm bed and breakfast. The relationships I have developed continue to broaden my Christian worldview and my compassion for others. I also have been able to perform music in many different ways and places to glorify the Lord.

Spouse: J. Michael Eby
Family: four children

Activities at LMS: Campus Chorale, softball, orchestra, piano accompaniment
Church affiliation: Calvary Church, Lancaster, Pennsylvania

Luis David Hostetter
Mikaela Ann Hostetter
Bryant Andrew Houseal
Sarah Michelle Hunt
Sheldon Earl Hurst
SukJay Jeong
Sydney E. Jones
Jacqueline A. Juma
Mo Se Jung
Meagan A. Kanagy
David Andrew Kautz
Joshua Paul Keagy
Ryan Paul Keagy
Monica Lynn Keeney
Caitlin Ann Kerr
Goeun Kim
Kunyhong Kim
Joanne R. Kinch
Ashley Elizabeth King
Sammy Martin Kiptoo
Jacob Scott Kraybill
Tyler Anthony Kreider
Joel Andrew Lambert
Daniel Martin Landis
Katelyn Elizabeth Lapp
Kevin J. Lapp
T. Joshua Lapp
Kendall Anthony Leaman
Ross Michael Lehman
Rebecca Ann Lever
Jeffrey Roy Long
Ashlee M. Martin
Erika Yvonne Martin
Karen Emily Martin
Paige L. Martin
Sabrina F. Martin
Joshua D. Mast
Kari Lynn Mast
Kent Alexander McCauley
Meghan E. McEvoy
Christopher Daniel McIntosh
Joel Larnell Meck
Brittany Lynn Mellinger
Rebekah Lauren Mentzer
Jacqueline Miller
Laura Marie (Miller) Risser
Tsion Zewdu Minas
Kathleen Mockus
Benjamin David Moore
Jenna Elizabeth Moyer
Allison Marie Nafziger
Stephen Anthony Natale
Jaclyn Louise Neikam
Donald Jarod Nelson
Jeremy Michael Nissley
Lance E. Nissley
Trevor Jon Nissley
Brian Richard Olinger
Katelyn Corrine Pierce
Derrin L. Ranck
Rachael Eve Ranck
Michael A. Raush
Trevor W. Reddig
Emily Elizabeth Rhinehart
Terrence Rosario
Sarah Brandt Roth
Peter Jonathan Rutt
Karla R. Santiago
Eric William Sather
Karissa J. Sauder
Amy Grace Schilthuis
Carissa Marie Schutz
Amanda Ruth Shank
Chelsea Lynn Shank
Brianna Nicole Shenk
Jordan Hans Shenk
Stephanie Nicole Sherick
Jared Scott Shirk
Rhoda Elnora Shirk
Jeannette L. Siegrist
Theodore C. Simmons
David A. Simpson
Daniel B. Sipe
Annali Rempel Smucker
Joseph Paul Smucker
Christopher G. Snader
Jonathan Michael Spicher
Jonathan Alan Stoeckle
Emily Hannah Stoepker
Kyle D. Stoltzfoos
Scott Michael Stoltzfoos
Kelly Lynne Stoltzfus
Abel Neguisse Tadesse
Valerie Naomi Talbott
Marie Sophie Fahkeh Tawe
Matthew D. Taylor
Naomi Tsegaye

168 APPENDIX

Michael Jordon Umble
Scott Marshall Umble
Jared Robert Vanderhoff
Benjamin C. Vible
Rosanna Edwards
 Villalobos
Andrew Robert Wagner
Alisha Michelle Walker
Joel William Warfel
Allison Joy Weaver
Ethan Michael Weaver
Renita J. Weaver
Stephanie Marie Weaver
Chanea Brooke Wenger
Jessica Ann Wheeler
Brook Fekadu Worku
Sarah Elizabeth Wright
Chloe Yocum
Craig Steven Yoder
Jamie A. Yoder
Petros Yosef Yohannes
Jordan Lee Zimmerman
Joshua Lee Zimmerman
Elizabeth Katherine
 Zimmerman-Clayton
Crystal Marie Zook

Class of 2007

Zachariah Blaine Acosta-
 Davis
Benjamin J. Adams
Hyowon Ahn
Ryan Matthew Andricks
Sarah Elizabeth Atkinson
Obed Ayala
Kenton Winfield Baer
Heidi Anne Baker
Rodley R. Barlet
Jonathan D. Beltz
Benjamin T. Benner
Luke A. Bingaman
Kaitlin Sue Black
Gisèle Rosine Bogoto
Briana Joy Bollinger
Jessi Lynn Bowman
Tyler J. Breneman
Christian Douglas Brown
Reneé E. Buckwalter
Sarah Ruth Buckwalter
Chad A. Burkholder
Kara Janine Burkholder

Victoria Ann Bybel
Sharon Marie Byrne
Hye Ryun Cho
You Mi Choi
Jin Ho Chung
Kwan Mi Chung
Kristen H. Ciaccia
Tiffany D. Clark
Daniel Brinton Collins
Gregory Coolbaugh
Michael C. Cousar
Adriane Beth Crouse
Elizabeth J. Cummings
Adrienne Nichole
 DeJesus
Salem Girma Desta
Sanjay R. K. Dick
Abigale W. Diffenbach
Brittany H. Dougherty
Lawrence James Dunlap
Kirsten Nicole Eldredge
Travis James Esh
Kristina E. Fenninger
Carolyn Sue Fisher
David G. Fite
Joseph Patrick Flanagan
Susanna Veronica
 Fortuna
Dabney Gantz
Julia Elizabeth Garber
Lyle Nicholaus Garvey
Lindsay Rose Gehman
Michael Gedle Gessesse
Samuel Andrew Gibbs
Jonathan Mutisya
 Gichure
Brianne Noelle Good
Derek Chesare Good
Hannah E. Good
Nicholas Alexander
 Good
Adam Courtland Hall
Sharon R. Hall
Janae Lynelle Haller
Richard Thomas
 Hannum
Kersten Marie Harnly
Maria Leticia Hartzler
Jin Renee Heindel
William J. Heiser
Allison Birnie Henke
Neal A. Hershey

Joshua M. Hertzler
Kalah Renee Hess
Devin D. Hiestand
Taylor Malin Hofford
Justin D. Hollinger
Angela R. Hoover
Abigail C. Horst
Curtis Lee Horst
Peter Voth Horst
Zachary Allen Horst
Melinda Sue Hughes
Brent A. Hurst
Leah J. Ingram
Mark H. Jackson
Kyung Chan Jang
Jenisa Shelby Jeblee
Bethany Joy Johnson
Peter Joseph Kachnycz
Idris Imurana Kamara
Jacob Lee Kanagy
Kyung Chul Kang
Christie Alison Kelly
Hye Jin Kim
Yun Sik Kim
Zachary S. Kindrew
J. Sarah Kleintop
Joseph Scott Klinger
Brandon E. Kopp
Buruktawit Challa
 Koricho
Charles T. Korir
Christine Faye Kreider
Cheri N. Kropf
Trevor Keith Kuhlengel
Micah Corydon Kulp
Jung Eun Kwak
Heun Woo Kwun
Leà A. Lambert
Audrey Rebecca Landis
Jessica Leigh Lapp
Jihyung Lee
Eric David Lefever
Daniel P. Lehman
Josh A. Lehman
Kendall Raymond
 Lehman
Dietrich Elmon Linde
Han Ju Liu
Kuei Cheng Liu
Elizabeth Margaret
 Livermore
Caitlin Marie Lizotte

Allysn Noelle
 Longenecker
Robert James
 Longenecker
Breann Elizabeth Lyle
Ashlee Nicole Martin
Brian Jacob Martin
Keith Andrew Martin
Nathaniel C. Martin
Elizabeth Noel Mast
Kenton Robert Mast
Bethany Anne
 McClearen
Kendra Lynn McGinnis
Analicia L. Medina
Molly Brittany Mellinger
James Lamar Metzler
Darin M. Miller
Michael A. Miller
Timothy Michael Miller
Natalie P. Mitrani
Hannah R. Moffett
Benjamin Mark
 Morrison
Mireille Mujinga-
 Citundu
Andrew David Mumma
Eric Ray Mylin
Nicholas J. Nendel
Jonathan Horst Nofziger
Hyoung-Keun Park
Eli B. Passage
David Hamilton Peck
Franklin R. J. Peiffer
Allen Scott Petersheim
Kelly Rae Pitman
Timothy Scott Plack
David W. Porter
Brent A. Ranck
Kevin C. J. Reece
Drason Michael Reece
Patrick Drew Ressler
Benjamin David
 Rittenhouse
Addison T. Root
Courtney Elizabeth Ross
Wilson E. Roth
Elizabeth Ann Ashley
 Sadaphal
Daniel Lee Sauder
Jacquelyn Danielle
 Sauder

Rebecca Lynn Sauder
Audrey Monique Secker
S. Amanda Shank
Sarah R. Shank
Desireé Marie Sheppard
Ian Keith Sheppard
Lindsey Erin Shertzer
Jason William Siegfried
Theresa M. Siegrist
Eric S. Smoker
K. Heidi Smucker
Charlene Joy Snader
Bethany Sommerfeld
Ashley Nicole Soto
Jason Alan Sprunger
Annette Rose Stoltzfus
Danielle Avis Stoltzfus
Jeffrey Wayne Stoltzfus
Tomoaki Sugiyama
Riza Miksch Sukman
Peter Charles Talbert
Doris Ann Taylor
Taj Marie Taylor
Kevin Michael Thomas
Esther Marie Trimble
Larissa B. Trimble
Joseph C. Troncale
Yu Lan Tsai
Arielle Elyce Turner
Morgan A. Umble
Aimy Joan Valentin
Nathan Vincent Vecchiarelli
Kristopher Michael Walter
Mark Andrew Way
D. John Weaver
J. Matthew Weaver
Jenessa M. Weaver
Mandi Lynn Weaver
Dean Melvin Weinhold
Charlotte Joy Wenger
Louis A. Wenger
Sara Marie Wenrich
Andrew Thomas Whitlatch
John C. Williams
Jonathan Darnell Williams
Paige Nicole Wissler
Mesgana Petros Wontamo
Patrick Avery Yerkes
Eric B. Yoder
Megan D. Yoder
Zachary D. Yoder
Chu Wei Yuan
David V. Zayas
Nebiyat Getachew Zena
Kara Cynthia Zimmerman

Class of 2008

Brett H. Albert
J. Eric Albrecht
Mario Josue Araya
Hyunji Baek
G. Michael Baer
Shana Elane Baliles
Carson Lyle Bechtold
Angela R. Becker
Samantha Joy Beiler
Daniel J. Bendit
Frantz Luther Benjamin
Laura L. Benkendorf
Mbongeni Sydney Bhembe
Kyle E. Bomgardner
Veronica Erin Bonner
Stephen C. Bortsalas
Erica Lynn Brossman
Keilor D. Brown
Alex Matthew Brubaker
Gina Marie Burkholder
Jillian R. Burkholder
Justine E. Burkholder
Joshua Nathan Byler
Seth E. Charles
Erika L. Christopher
Julie Ann Collins
Joanna R. Coté
Ashley L. Dagen
Gregory Ross Davis
Daniel C. F. Dellinger
Amber Diane Dennis
Benjamin R. Detwiler
Sarah E. Dickinson
Fikeveni Khulekani Dlamini
Jessica Nichole Ebersol
Audrey B. Ebersole
Jenna Lee Ebersole
Bethany L. Engle
Racheal N. Erb
Tyler David Esh
Laura A. Estep
Phylicia Lee Fasnacht
Erin Lyn Fisher
Drew Thomas Fleager
Jessie Lee Floyd
Clay Kyle Tyler Forshey
Lauren Kathleen Frey
John A. Fueyo
Charise J. Garber
Kendall J. Garber
Nebiyou Gebeyehu
Kidus Lemma Gebregiorgis
Kari Karlene Gehman
Samuel Antonio Genoese
Joshua Adam Gingerich
Nathan Paul Gish
Tanner Harrison Gochenaur
Laura E. Gochnauer
Cara Marie Good
Kyle Edward Gordon
Kelsey Jo Gorman
Alyssa Joy Groff
Hana Elise Grosh
Ji Hoon Han
Victoria Leanne Heisey
J. Kandace Hershey
Justin Andrew Hershey
Lisa Michelle Hershey
Mary E. High
Alanna Ruth Hiller
Jordan Alex Hollinger
Rebecca Ann Horning
Collin Ray Horst
Hamilton J. Horst
Melody Hunt
Kelsey Shana Hurst
Serena F. Jeblee
William Roger Josephian
Yu Chul Jung
Byungwan Kang
Jong Chul Kang
Brittany Jayne Kauffman
G. Kyle Kauffman
Moses M. Keener
Jessica Lauren Kerr
Ey Jae Kim
Hyun Suk Kim
Jung Gu (Liam) Kim
Kyung Yong Kim
Nam Ho Kim
John Mark King
Austin R. Kling
Katelyn E. Kreider
Kelly N. Kreider
Laura Marie Kretz
Joseph A. Lab
Katie Elisabeth Landis
Katrina Elizabeth Landis
Janae Sharene Lapp
Lindsay Michele Lapp
Andrew William Leaman
Benjamin Michael Leaman
Geonho (Brandon) Lee
Jisoo Lee
Seungbum Lee

John R. Leed
Kaitlin E. Leeking
Sara J. Lefever
Patrick A. Legutko
Brianna Danae Lehman
Ryan M. Lehman
Kush P. Lengacher
Katherine Ann Lesher
Jason Matthew Long
Jonathon Andrew Martin
Matthew J. Mast
Geoffrey Allen Matthews
Theodore Jacob Maust
Meghan H. McNeill
Sarah Grace Mellinger
Katia Elizabeth Merzilus
Peter Marcel Mickley
Trent D. Miller
Dorothy C. Mozloom
Alyssa B. Mylin
Michael C. Nathan
Chad Newcomer
Derek Joel Nissley
Ann Ntari
Rachel Marie Olinger
Kyle Steven Pfautz
Mary E. Poole
Bradley J. Raush
Brigetta Marie Reeser

E. Michael Rios
Crystal Joy Rodriquez
Christopher D. Root
Calvin Glick Ruth
Catherine Fern Ruth
Sarah M. Rutt
Joselyn Santiago
Melissa Joy Sauder
Mark D. Schilthuis
J. Luke Schlosser
Jung Eun Shin
Christopher Mark Shoff
Josiah James Shuman
Teddy S. Shumbusho
Austin D. Siegrist
Hannah B. Siegrist
David B. Sioma
Nathaniel W. Tann
Stella Joy Taylor
Timothy John Taylor
Paul Matthew Thomas
Rachael Lauren Thorn
Josiah Jacob Toews
Chelsea Rae Vecchiarelli
Micah Donald Warfel
Corey Scott Weaver
Lori Lee Weaver
Margaret W. Weaver
Darren L. Weinhold

Jonathan Tyler Weinhold
Emily J. Wenger
Kira NiKae Wenger
Joshua Edward Wheeler
Lisa Ann Wingard
Belane Belayhun Wondimu
Nathan Owen Wright
Suzanne Marie Yocom
Emily Lauren Yoder
Henok Yosef Yohannes
Danielle N. Zeamer
Samrawit Getachew Zena
Ashley B. Zimmerman
M. Kathryn Zimmerman
Anya K. Zook

Class of 2009

David W. Adams
Salina Mayloni Almanzar
Jared Daniel Althouse
Nigel B. Anjiri
Eric J. Augsburger
Erika Babikow
Camille Mari Batts
Austin Shane Benner
Kaitlyn G. Beyer

Alana Michelle Bingeman
Michael George Bodner
Joseph Allen Bomberger
Krista J. Breneman
Allison M. Brown
Alicia J. Buckwalter
Matthew E. Burkhart
Ji Su Choi
Sang Han Choo
Elizabeth A. Cleaves
Valerie Colon
Andrew D. Cousar
Eileen K. Darby
Damian Fernando Delgado
Crista J. Deller
David Lon Denlinger
Rebecca J. Detwiler
J. Carlos Devers
Alexandra Emilia Diamantoni
Jason Keith Diller
Kirsti Allison Dimitris
Brandon Matthew Dimmig
Jasmine Nicole Dorsey
Erich Rainer Eitzen
Ashley Marie Engle

Dean Robert Engle
Ryan T. Fisher
Amber Christina Beth Forshey
Lauren M. Fueyo
Quentin James Geib
Chance McLemore Glover
Lucas Kyle Good
Kate R. Grosh
Rebecca Joy Grosh
Jaclyn Grace Gyger
Blene Hailu
Addison W. Haller
Ji Sook Han
Darian Adam Harnish
Ellen Marie Hartshorne
Alexandra Marie Hauck
Devin James Hawthorne
Julie Marie Heinly
Sa-Rang Her
Jay Robert Hernley
Jenna M. Hershberger
Juliana K. Hershey
Abigail R. Hertzler
Emily Katherine Hess
Dana Elizabeth Hiestand
Elizabeth M. Hoffer

Thomas Christopher Hollis
Jody R. Hoover
Jonathan Hoover
Kristin Arielle Horn
Andrew Cordell Horning
Brandon D. Horst
Evan W. Horst
Ryan L. Horst
Sarah L. Horst
Matthew J. Hostetter
Emily R. Hursh
Suhwan In
Christopher B. Jarrett
SoYoung Kang
Sung Hoon Kang
Jordan Matthew Keener
Mary Elizabeth Keeney
Ashley B. Kemp
LeAnne Marie Kile
Hansol Kim
Jungkwan Kim
Sunjin Kim
Lindsay Marie King
Darshika Kirubaaharan
Bria M. Klase
Stephanie Rae Knowles
Tyler James Koontz
Joshua William Kopp

Emily Hannah Kraybill
Molly Caroline Kraybill
Rebecca Hope Kraybill
Andrew Nathan Kreider
April Cherié Kreider
Kyle A. Kreider
Katie Beth Kurtz
Brett Alexander Ladley
Carrie Amanda Lambert
Desirae K. Landis
Kaela S. Landis
Tyler Scott Landis
Katelyn A. Leaman
DaBin Lee
Seehyung Lee
Lauren Kate Longenecker
Troy William Losey
Matthew Angelo
   Mallozzi
Amie L. Martin
Andrew Bryce Martin
Scott Mathew Martin
Ian S. Mast
Saralyn Kay Mast
Emma Margaret
   McCaskey
Megan E. McGinty
Allory A. Melhorn
Jennifer Nicole Mellinger
Yenegeta Assefa Mengistu
Sarah Joy Mentzer
Ashley Renee Milburn
Bryan A. Miller
Jordan S. Miller
Stephanie Lynn Miller
Deanna Reneé Moore
Nathanael Paul Morrison
Emily E. Nejmeh
Rachel R. Nendel
Margaret Young Nicholas
Joel Horst Nofziger
Rebecca K. Noll
Connor Olney
Eun Bin Park
Geo Young Park
Kelsey D. Patterson
Michael Crist Peachey
Andrew W. Reddig
HyunJi Rho
Katelyn J. Rittenhouse
Brittany Renee Rohrer
Josiah Kyle Rohrer
Monica J. Root

Solomon James Rudy
Lilianna M. Santos
Jordan D. Schultz
Luke Edward Schutz
Elliott R. Seavey
Isaac Michael Sharp
Jamila Rose Shenk
Jennifer Beth Shenk
Sharon E. Sheppard
Morganrae Sherick
Nicole M. Simpson
David Craig Skiles
Kami Marie Skoloda
Ryan David Smoker
Caroline L. Smucker
Jordon Paul Smucker
Alison Elizabeth Snader
Nathan Andrew Snyder
Jeeyun Song
Benjamin Cronin
   Sprunger
Katherine Victoria
   Stapleton
Dalton John Stauffer
Timothy Nathaniel
   Stoepker
Rachel L. Stoltzfoos
Austin Michael Stoltzfus
Joy Michelle Stoltzfus
Kiersten Louise Stoltzfus
Lauren Elizabeth Nolt
   Stoltzfus
Benjamin Jack Stoner
Lena Marie Strickler
Sheila Grace Talbott
Kourtney Joy Thalheimer
Phillip Robert Thomas
Maria Antoinette
   Tomassetti
Karianne Torres
John D. Trimble
Devin Kenna Troy
Ryan Thomas Turley
Eric Christian Umble
Franklin Antonio
   Valentin
Katelyn N. Vanderhoff
Seth George Warfel
Matthew Lawrence
   Wassall
Hans J. Weaver
Heidi Nicole Weaver
Jannelle K. Weaver

Thea Rose Weaver
V. Scott Weaver
Korinne J. Wenger
Matthew Wier
Michelle K. Witmer
Yun Sun Won
Kelsey Elizabeth Yeingst
Rebecca Weaver Yoder
Thomas Eric
   Zimmerman

Class of 2010

Mattilde Frances Abel
Sameh Alobwede
Louise Babikow
Christine Rose Baer
Andrea J. Beck
Michael D. Becker
Matthew S. Beltz
Samuel Berhanu
Bryant Daniel
   Betancourt
Matthew Samuel Blank
John Ryan Bomgardner
Matthew Aaron Boronow
Carli S. Bowman
Samantha L. Brubaker
Abby L. Burger
Joseph R. Byler
Keith Campbell
Shane Cantrell
Inhak Choi
Shinik Choi
Arisa Chon
Galie Darwich
Austin Tyler daSilva
Jordan Antonio daSilva
Dawit Getachew
   Delnesaw
Kari Joy Denlinger
Joseph Nicholas Dennis
Gregory Shayn Ebersol
Derek Lynn Ebersole
Tyler Martin Eckman
Mark H. Ellsworth
Erica Lynne Engle
Micah Charles Everett
Kendra Louise Felpel
Douglas P. Frauman
Jordan Christopher Frey
Todd Donald Funk
Jeremy Lee Garber

Travis Scott Gehman
Aaron Martin Gish
Heather Gochnauer
Nicole L. Godfrey
Adam Hamilton Gooch
Falicia Lynn Good
J. Austin Good
Austin Nicholas Groff
Elliot M. Groff
Amanda Elizabeth Haller
Kathryn Elise Harris
Gabriela Andrea Hartzler
J. Tyler Hawkes
Jonathan Miller
   Hershberger
Derek Abram Hershey
Jacob Glen Hollinger
Eric Anthony Hoober
Aaron James Hostetter
Day Hser
Erin R. Ipsen
Noah E. Jemison
Beya Kabambi
Alyssa Kachnycz
Chelsea R. Kanagy
Casey Patrick Kelly
Rachel Elizabeth Kennel
Doyeon Kim
JinSoo Kim
Kyua Kim
Sungho Kim
Yeji Kim
Joshua H. King
Kayla M. Klase
Kimberly Lynne Knowles
Yuna Kobayashi
Karina Janelle Kreider
Charlotte Kruis
Jonathan Michael Lapp
Justin Daniel Lapp
Erin Rebecca LaVenice
Nicole E. Leaman
Nicole R. Leaman
ChangHee Lee
Gi Hoon Lee
Hee Lim Lee
Mollie Sharie Lehman
Tae Young Lim
Emma J. Lindsey
Kara Lofton
Heidi Marie Long
Nathan John
   Longenecker

Trent A. Losey
Jin Soo Ma
Michael J. Madea
Brett E. Martin
Elliot T. Martin
Kevin Paul Martin
Morgan Lauré Marzulli
Andrea L. Mast
Joel Mast
Keith W. Mast
Kristopher D. Mast
Nathan Frank Mast
Lauren Michelle McMullen
Christian George Merzilus
Mekias Mesfen
Garrett D. Miller
Gi Eun Min
Seth David Moffett
Lillian Ruth Mozloom
Beza Mulugeta
Celina Renee Nissley
Pambi Nzunga
Martha Erin Osborne
Stephanie Lyn Palazzo
Danielle Nicole Peirson
Elizabeth Brooke Phipps
Caroline R. Poole
Logan P. Ressler
Stephanie Nicole Rheinheimer
Jonathan Rojas
Dean A. Royal
Bethany N. Rudy
Ho Yoon Ryu
Annie Cristina Sanchez
Josué Santiago
Ryan Craig Schloneger
Levi K. Schlosser
Jessica P. Schroeder
Erin Felice Secker
Ryan Lawson Seibert
Benjamin P. Seldomridge
Jae Young Shim
Nathaniel Herbert Shuman
Amanda Kente Shumbusho
Emma R. Siegfried
Kyle E. Siegfried
Zachariah L. Smith
Ann Marie Soper
Eliot D. Staikos
Mindy J. Stipe
Jamal Stokes
Joshua D. Stoltzfoos
Andrea Jo Stoltzfus
Angela Stoltzfus
Courtney Alexandra Stoltzfus
Kristen M. Stoltzfus
Emerald Boka Tawe
Talya Keturah Taylor
Juan Diego Torres
Ricardo Enrique Torres
Marisa L. Umble
Christian Tyler Vincent
Jasmine N. Walker
Kristofer L. Watson
Lisa Janelle Weaver
Melissa Rose Weaver
Taylor M. Wenger
Lamar Fenelon Whitman
Thomas Charles Witthoft
Benjamin D. Yoder
Philip Timothy Yoder
Katherine A. Zell
Yordnos Zewdie Teffera
Jordan L. Zimmerman
Melissa Chantel Zimmerman
Jessica R. Zook

Class of 2011

Juliet J. Abel
Seok Ahn
Katherine Lee Andrews
Keshon Jared Archey
Sofonias Abaye Assefa
Caroline Joy Augsburger
Daniel S. Baker
Janell K. Baliles
Keira Lynae Batts
Benjamin A. Bauman
Tyler R. Beaston
Christopher P. Beiler
Jonathan Lee Bender
Michelle C. Bendit
Yves Larry Benjamin
Donald J. Benkendorf
Grant L. Benner
Dominik Ryan Berthold
Isaiah Frederick Bornman
Meghan Rae Brady
Grace Elizabeth Broderick
Kaitlin Brubaker
Hilary L. Burkholder
Yu-Sheng Chen
Donald Granville Clark
Kelsey L. Clemens
Amy Elizabeth Collins
Sean Timothy Criswell
Danielys E. Cubilete
Jason daSilva
Samuel F. Dawit
Hannah Deland
Eric C. Denlinger
Rachel L. Dickinson
Joseph L. Diller
Brent Dimmig
Danielle Dimon
Nicholas Patrick Donnelly
Emily A. Ebaugh
Biniam Estifanos
Jonathon Ryan Eutsey
Natasha Shana Fearnow
Isaac S. Flood
Rebekah Delene Foultz
Ariel M. Francis
Jared Nicholas Frey
Nikaela Elizabeth Frey
Anita G. Garber
Bonita C. Garber
Kristen J. Garber
Benjamin Russell Gardinier
Lanjiabao Ge
Ryan Paul Gehman
Zachary S. Gish
Sebastian Gobat
Melina Elise Godshall
Kelsey A. Good
Naomi Irene Good
Jasmine P. Graybill
Carissa K. Harnish
Valerie B. Heisey
Travis D. Hernley
Katelyn A. (Hoover) Ragsdale
Emily K. Horst
Tanner G. Horst
Brandon Paul Houck
Thomas Jefferson Huber
Kaitlyn Luana Hurst
Harrison W. Jarrett
Caleb G. Kaylor
Yen Elizabeth Keener
Caitlyn Autumn Kelly
Eric L. Kemp
Gahye Kim
Hyun Soo Kim
Sang Eun Kim
Seung Jun Kim
Song Yeon Kim
Janae E. King
Michael Tyrone Kiser
Benjamin D. Klinger
Barrie R. Koonce-Frederick
Emily Koup
Brandon R. Kratz
David Allen Krauss
Kyle Anthony Kreider
Richard Steven Kreiser
Rachel Lauren Kurtz
Ye Jin Kwon
Kelley M. Landers
Tasha J. Landis
Daniel Lankford
Leigh Anne Lapp
Zachary Ryan Lare
Matthew David Lauver
Zachary J. Leaman
SeHee Lee
Yongsun Lee
Yubin Lee
Yuijae Lee
Corey Matthew Leonard
Caroline Marie Linde
Ajantha Lingan
Luis Lopez
Keilah M. Maldonado
Savannah M. Marks
Amanda M. McCoy
Tara Kathryn McGinty
Nathaniel Thomas McKnight
Andrew David McMullen
Erik Anthony Scarlotta Meinzer
Bethany D. Miller
Jared Scott Miller
Jeffrey S. Miller
Gustave Cornelius Mozloom
Guiying Mu

Alumni of the Year 2015

"I support LMS because I care about Christ-centered education that encourages students to develop their gifts to be shared as followers of Jesus. I like that the LMS graduate profile includes academic, spiritual and lifestyle components."

Rhoda Reinford Charles

Lancaster County, Pennsylvania
Class of 1972

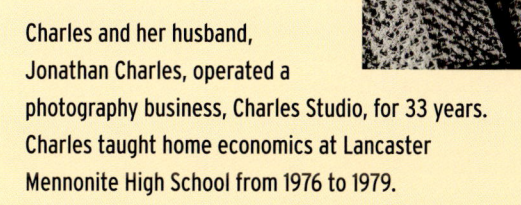

Charles and her husband, Jonathan Charles, operated a photography business, Charles Studio, for 33 years. Charles taught home economics at Lancaster Mennonite High School from 1976 to 1979.

Highlight: While I taught in the classroom at LMH for only three years after college, I have always enjoyed teaching in women's groups since then. For the past seven years, our congregation at Habecker Mennonite Church has been blessed by the arrival of Karen refugees who fled Burma to Thailand refugee camps. Now as they resettle in Lancaster, it has been a special joy for me to walk with the women as they learn life skills in this new country. I am returning to my home economics teaching days to most eager students.

Education: Eastern Mennonite University, bachelor's degree in home economics education
Spouse: Jonathan Charles, Class of 1970
Family: three children, four grandchildren

LMS activities: Campus Chorale, feature editor for the *Millstream*
Church affiliation: Habecker Mennonite Church, Lancaster, Pennsylvania

APPENDIX 173

Kaitlyn M. Nafziger
Christopher Dwane Newswanger
Eric Ngumi
Truc Vo Thanh Nguyen
Alexandria O'Connell
Seho Oh
So Youn Oh
Young Hyeon Oh
Adriana Faye Ortega
Michelle Peachey
Katherine M. Peck
Stephanie N. (Peifer) King
Chance Joseph Piazza
Nicholas Piraino
Alexandra M. Poff
Curtis L. Ranck
Shelby Geneva Auer Rhodes
Jeremy Rittenhouse
Isaiah Rivera
Emily Rodriguez
Andrea M. Rohrer
Janae Rohrer
Kyle L. Ruder
David Paul Rudy
Hannah Aube Sauder
Jason D. Sauder
McKenzie L. Sauder
Rachel Saunders
Alexa R. Schreier
Julia Noelle Scott
Tiffany Seda
Brittany Sehenuk
Emily V. Shank
Yoo Seung Shin
Benjamin P. Shoff
Hans Shuman
Patrick Lee Siegfried
Jenna J. Smerdon
Austin Lee Smucker
Jason Thomas Spicher
Christina E. Springer
Molly G. Stapleton
Jillana Danielle Stauffer
Alexis Rose Steckel
Dawon Suh
Sarah Terlizzi
Nicholas Richard Thalheimer
Hollis Elizabeth Thorbahn

Yeniakal Tilaye
Angel Vasquez
Jacob James Wanner
Charleen Waters
Keri Jane Weaver
Peter Thomas Weida
Luke S. Weierbach
Yu Kai Wen
Sally Anne Wenger
Roger S. Wenk
Mary Ona Wheeler
Joseph Witmer
Kaitlyn May Witmer
Isaah Woods
Hyun Jung Yang
Saier Zeng
Yixin Zhang
C. Timothy Zimmerman
Jillian E. Zook
Zachary Gordon Zook

Class of 2012

Rebekah E. Adams
DaeSoo Ahn
Madison Ali Alley
Lesley Anne Andricks
Anne Marie Baer
Eileen C. Barker
Abigail Lynn Basom
Robert Michael Beauchemin
Berkeley Smucker Beidler
Kidus Kibebew Belay
Jonathan Maxwell Bodner
Christi Boronow
Rebecca Bowers
John W. Brabazon
Natalie Emma Brubaker
Chengqi Cai
Danielle Campbell
Hyobin Chung
Emily Jayne Clouser
Alex Thomas Craley
Christopher Curet
Jaclyn N. Dagen
William Dejesus
Elizabeth Rose Derstine
Mariangelis Diaz
Aaron Eckman
Olivia Grace Edwards
Mark Engle

Caitlin B. Erb
Kari Evans
Linsheng Fan
Jamila Flores
Amanda Jean Forte
Rachel E. Fueyo
Tsegamihret Getahun Gebru
Christle Gehman
Sawyer M. Gochenaur
Kristen M. Gochnauer
Jorgy Gonzalez
John David Good
Brandon A. Gordon
Toshanne K. Greenawalt
Shen Gu
Charlie Hargrove
Alejandra J. Hartzler
Natasha R. Hartzler
Luke E. Hershey
Meghan Hershey
William P. Hoffer
Connor Reid Malin Hofford
Elizabeth J. Horst
Jordan Michael Hostetter
Yaxu Hu
Luke J. Hursh
E. Ellyce Hurst
Gray Price Irwin
Grace Sarah Jemison
Kassandra Dakneel Jensen
Peiyao Jian
Katherine Johnson
Da Eun Jung
Andrew Scott Kauffman
Christopher Alden Keener
Benjamin G. Kennel
Chung Kyu Kim
Anya Rachelle Kreider
Logan Mitchell Kreider
Olivia Kruis
Peter Aaron Landis
Ariane Dominique LaRue
Kyle Leaman
James Hyun Woo Lee
Yongwoo Lee
Megan E. (Lehman) Kreider
Micah Daniel Lehman

Taylor Lindsey
Wenbin Luo
Karisa Martin
Isaac K. Mast
Olivia Georgette Mast
Hurubie Kenno Meko
DeAnna Lanay Mercado
Analies Miller
Benjamin Michael Miller
Devon J. Miller
Keri L. Miller
Rachel M. Miller
Amy Sophia Mishler
Joshua John Morales
Christina Louise Mulé
Audra F. Mylin
Vy Thuy Yen Nguyen
Leigh Young Nicholas
Alex Nissley
Austin Nissley
Joon Young Oh
Dylan Zachary Palmer
Joonhong Park
Nemecis Perez
Brittany Pollard
D. Haley Probst
Connor Markus Ream
David Aaron Reist
Maria Catherine Reitmeyer
Jessica L. Rheinheimer
Lydia Rittenhouse
Jose A. Rodriguez
Keegan James Rosenberry
Luis A. Santiago
John David Satriale
Lauren J. Sauder
Jared Schatz
Dustin E. Schroeder
Rebekah Louise Sharp
Beckah Rose Shenk
Stephen Philip Shenk
Esther HaeMin Shin
Taylor B. Smith
Jihye Son
Morgan Ashley Steffy
Allen Stoltzfus
Samuel Roy Stoner
Lara Kay Strickler
Kathryn J. Swiontek
Ethel-Ruth Lokeh Tawe
Emily Terlizzi

174 APPENDIX

Steven Travis
Trisha Tshudy
Kaitlyn Elizabeth Valan
Leo L. Valmonte
Jon Ryan Wagner
Elisabeth Riane Walker
James Wallace
Maria J. Wanner
Steven D. Wasilewski
Danielle R. Weaver
Patrick Christopher Whalen
Andrew Phillip Whittaker
Tayler Shawn Wilson
Ian M. Wolman
CiLiang Yang
Andrew A. Yoder
Yue Yu
Xiaoqing Zhang
Zhipei Zhang
Sara Tang Yen Zhao
Drew Elizabeth Zimmerman

Class of 2013

Skyler W. Adams
Do Hyun Ahn
Mihyang An
Colleen Ann Andrews
Adam Kenneth Anthony
Megan Baak
Wendell Baer
Monica Joy Beiler
Merykokeb Kibebew Belay
Heran Tensae Berhanu
Katelyn A. Blest
Nina Bodner
Laurel Irene Bornman
Victoria Bostwick
Amy Brown
Madison Elizabeth Brubaker
Elizabeth Joy Byler
Yue Chang
Lillie Kathryn Cheuvront
Elora Cook
Stifanos Mesfin Daniel
Brandon Dasilva
Gordon Dimmig
Huy Duc Dinh

Liban Abraham Dinka
Kimberly J. Dohner
Nicole Drawbaugh
Yue Du
Katey A. Ebaugh
George Anton Eitzen
Lia Feleke
Giovanny X. Figueroa
Nikole E. Fisher
Aaron Flanders
Carsen Mitchell Frey
Heather Fry
Christina Gantt
Francesca Mica Genoese
Benjamin John Gibbs
Caleb Gish
Madelyn L. Gish
Danielle L. Godfrey
Xingyin Gong
Meghan C. Good
Andre Groff
Fikire Ashenafi Haile
Ji Hye Han
Caleb Kaufman Harnish
Songda He
Olya Natalia Hershey
J. Ian Hertzler
Jacob M. Hertzler
Jedidiah Joshua Hess
Rachel Hoober
Cole R. Hoover
Jessica L. Hoover
Emanuel Paul Horst
Marshall C. Horst
Xuanyi Hu
Zachary D. Hummel
J. Gabriel Imhof
A-Shanti D. T. Jenkins
Mingyue Jiang
Jenelle Lyric Johns
Andre M. Kalend
Sarah Kalend
Viktor Kaltenstein
David M. Kerr
Deok-Hoon Kim
Isaac J. King
Katelyn E. King
Spencer P. Kling
Caleb M. Kopp
Nathaniel Kratz
Yanpeng Lai
Anson Tsz Chun Lam
Ketura L. Landis

Jacob D. Leaman
Kristen J. Leaman
Namkyu Lee
Yu Sung Lee
Alexis Marie (Lehman) Snyder
Michael S. Leiby
Jingwen Li
Brandon M. Litten
David Longenecker
Caroline Nicole Lynch
Courtney Martin
Chloe M. Mattilio
Malcolm Joshua McGill
Nebiyou Meshesha
Christina Miller
Ethan K. Miller
Christopher D. Milligan
Seyed K. Mojtabaei
Lacie Nicole Mosteller
Collin Nafziger
Elizabeth M. Nendel
Jared Mark Nisly
Sindi Johanna Nolt
William James Noonan
Christopher Cuyler O'Brien
Woo Youn Oh
Seo Jun Park
Andrew Elliot Pauls
Emily Marie Pautler
Lydia Peachey
Robert Barkley Poff
Nathan Ranck
Colims Dall Reserve
Abigail Lyn Rineer
Oliver Henry Robins
Mitchell Rohrer
David Rojas
Julian Rojas
Ralph A. Rossi
Thomas Joseph Ambrose Ryan
Jonathan Sauder
Kaitlin R. Sauder
Sara A. Schlosser
Nathan J. Schnupp
Geoffrey Ian Scott
Jerel K. Sensenig
Minghao Shang
Tyler Shertzer
Andrew John Shesko
Jeshurun O. Shuman

Jessica Simpson
Jon David Snader
Emily A. Snyder
Kristin Spalding
Caron Scott Stephen
Caitlin Quinn Stewart
Sandra Uvon Stewart
Brandon Joseph Stream
Carl John Sturges
Laura Katherine Thomas
Yankai Tong
Christian O. Vázquez
Anthony M. Vega
Connor J. Vincent
Andrew J. Wassall
Nicholas E. Weaver
Angela Joy Weiler
Juo Yu Wen
Chantél B. (Wenger) Gish
Raquel Wenk
Timothy Peter White
Bohao Xie
Langyi Xie
Yi-Hsun Yang
Yibin Yang
Ying Yang
Mengjie Ying
Trentin Yoder
Seungmo Yu
Zhouchunyu Yu
Hang Zhang
Jin Zhang
Yilin Zhang
Xinhao Zhang
Pengju Zhao
Qiansui Zhou

Class of 2014

Fabienne Abel
Kayla V. Abel
Kathleen Michelle Adams
Helina Roman Andargie
Karah B. Ashley
Emily Augsburger
Alexander R. Baer
Kezhi Bai
Darris Jamael Bair
Alpha Nirvana Balencio-Polanco
Rediate Befekadu

Alumni of the Year 2015

"The biggest compliment I can give LMS is that we entrusted the school with educating and helping us raise our three girls. Each one was provided a solid education grounded in Christ, which is evident in their lives today."

William K. Poole

Lancaster, Pennsylvania
Class of 1979

Poole is executive vice president for S&T Bank and a partner with GreenLeaf Financial Group. He was the founding president of Hometowne Heritage Bank. Poole is chairman of the board of directors of Sight and Sound Theatres.

Highlights: I served as the assistant girls varsity basketball coach for six years when my daughters were on the team. In 2008 the team won the district championship played at Giant Center in Hershey. Helping LMS during the acquisition of Hershey Christian School was very rewarding. The merger brought together two high-quality schools with a common mission of serving students and impacting their lives.

Education: Millersville University, bachelor's degree in business management
Spouse: Diane K. Lehman Poole, Class of 1980
Family: three daughters

Activities at LMS: basketball, soccer
Church affiliation: LCBC Church, Manheim, Pennsylvania

Olivia Beiler
Christy L. Bender
Donald Rend Bender
Biruk Moges Beyene
Emily Rebecca Blank
Sheila Brooke Bollinger
Nina Mae Brasten
Emily Anne Breneman
Graydon Gstaad Briguglio
Rachel Dianne Bronkema
Daniel W. Brubaker
Jung Bin Cheok
Wanje Cho
Dae Han Choi
Wootaeck Chung
Carlos Eduardo Colón
Tyler James Constein
Emily Ann Crane
Jewan L. Dawkins
Day Day
Tia Dennis
Caleb Christian Derstine
Joel Daniel Diller
Maxwell W. Dimon
Joseph J. Eberly
Bethany L. Eby
Ashlyn Nichole Ellis
Tianyi Fan
Xinyuan Fan
Lesly E. Fernandez
Kyara Figueroa
Krista Fisher
Keyla Flores
David Joseph Forte
Lucas C. Forte
Hannah Elizabeth Forwood
Paul Jeffrey Fredericksen
Xin Fu
Logan J. Garber
Madeline Garber
Rylee Gardinier
Carissa Brooke Gehman
Sierra R. Gibble
Autumn Ginder
Kailah E. Ginder
Renae J. Gochnauer
Juan David Gómez Penagos
Christopher Javier Gomez Diaz
Deanna A. Good
Cameron S. Graybill
Samuel Habbershon
Aubrey Haller
Zane Alexander Harnish
Grace Elizabeth Hernquist
Jonathan A. Hess
Matthew Robert Hess
Vy Tra Truc Ho
Natalie Hoober
Chunhao Hu
Heyao Huang
Wanqi Huang
Yi Huang
Namhee Hyun
Marcus O'neil Irwin
Ji-Won Jang
Jeff Jean
Yokabed Wubishet Jekale
Feihang Jia
Allison Kachel
Jinghan Kang
Kellie Michelle Keener
Anika Keys-Ludwig
Kenedy Marie Kieffer
Ashley Kilhefner
Hyun Joong Kim
Daniel P. King
Jordan Klase
Carolyn Elizabeth Krasley
Mia Elisabeth Kuniholm
Jeho Lee
Zachary Lehman
Kexin Li
Hantao Liang
Hsin-nan Lin
Wai Laam Ling
Christian D. Lopez
Timothy Paul Markovits
Cassidy Ann Martin
Janessa Martin
Gregory Martinez
Sophia M. Mast
Adaria Ímaní McGill
Alex Zander Michael
Bersabeh Miliard
Hope Miller
Aaron Mishler
Joseph Michael Montalbano
Shanshan Nai
Tyler Newman
Heidi D. Newswanger
Esteban Nieves
Krista Leigh Olonovich
John Conor O'Sullivan
Andres David Polanco Guevara
Caleb Joseph Daniel Prescott
Buqing Qian
Madison Rae Reeser
Isaac Howard Robins
Alan Grant Rockwell
Fransesca Daniella Rosario-Melo
Heather E. Rudy
Elaine Miyoko Sahm-Terada
Bryan Jose Santos
Uriah Aron Sauder
Jesse Schatz
Tristan Wade Schmitt
Brian Shenk
Kirsten May Sherick
Heidi Shuman
Domenik Siedenbuehl
Pascal Siedenbuehl
Skylar Sims
Benjamin Michael Smith
Brandon Soto
Mitchell Thomas Steffy
Hadassah Stoltzfus
Madeline Page Stoltzfus
Amber M. Trimble
Armando Santo Tyson
Ethan Vincent
Andrew David Walker
Carrie M. Walker
Madalyn R. Waller
Yudan Wang
Greta Wanner
M. Thomas Wanner
Eric Matthew Weaver
Lara Madalyn Weaver
Melanie Weinhold
Melinda R. Wenger
Alexander Sandri West
John S. Witmer
Henry Steffy Wolfe
Jingyuan Wu
Jiayi Xiao
Botao Xu
Jingzhe Xu
Ke Xu
Qiguang Yang
Zihan Yang
Alyse G. Yoder
Tong Zhang
Yimeng Zhang
Xiaoyi Zhao
Huiyu Zheng
Andre E. Zimmerman
Hannah J. Zimmerman
Joshua A. Zimmerman
Daniel Zook

Class of 2015

Hershey Campus

Sarah Boadi
Kate Clark
Josiah Eckert
Rachel Felty
Bryce Fisher
Kristen Haldeman
Zachary Hoyt
Jonathan Hyatt
Sang Yun Hyon
John Kase
Margaret Keller
Maddison Kern
Esther Kumi
Colin Leidich
Kortney Marvel
Sarah Miller
Sarah Moore
Ivan Moynihan
Destiny Shaffer
Courtney Shaw
Bradford Whitson

Lancaster Campus

Noel Abebe
Naomi Z. Abraham
Amy Y. Adams
Zachary Evan Alderman
David Antonio Alejos Acosta
Cameron G. Andrews
Jaycie Armelle Augustin
Eric Scott Bailey

Micaiah Marie Barley
Jeffrey A. Becker
Jeremy Alexander
  Berthold
Yoel DeJesus Bobadilla
Matthew Christian
  Bomberger
Caleb Henry Bornman
Emily N. Brabazon
John Gerald Breisinger
Morgan Olivia Brubaker
Kiah Lee Bucher
Judah Benjamin
  Buckwalter
Orlando Burgos
Ian Timothy Burkhart
Mana
  Chawalitsuphaserani
Po-Hua Chen
Yulim Cheon
Dylan M. Coleman
Julian Angel Collazo
Anisha Lizz Colon
Ivo Giovanni Colon
Katelyn Marie Coryell
Sparford DeVon
  Crawford
Jazmin Ivellis Cruz
Khup Khen Dal
Alexandra Frances Davis
Angelyn Denise Dawkins
Helena Marie Derksen
Shunong Diao
Victoria Ann Diller
Alec Ryan Drawbaugh
Timothy DuBoe
Evan Patrick Dunn
Mikayla Joy Eby
Allison Paige Elliott
Matthew Brandt
  Eshleman
Alexa Joy Evans
H Kordell Fisher
Megan Leigh Fletcher
Jabril Richard Frescatore
Takahiro Fukuhara
Jingyuan Gao
Kaleigh Kristine
  Gerringer
Anna Christine Gibbs
Jacob Gish
Aleana Hannah Glah

Alexa Nikelle Gochenaur
Devin Edward Goff
Erin Nichole Groff
Johnathan Patrick Harker
Adam Kaufman Harnish
Mengya He
Graham Hunt Heindel
Zachary L. Horst
John Isaac Hursh
Luke Benjamin
  Husbands
Aymari-Khadesia
  Di-Naye Jenkins
Minyan Jia
Daniel Seth Kachnycz
James Mwangi Kanyiha
Ethan Jess Keen
Elinor Grace Weber
  Keener
Christian C. Kemp
Kyeongji Kim
Cierra Noel King
Lindsey Anne Kreider
John Paul Kruis
Lauren Elizabeth Lanas
Shayna Rae Landis
Mengran Li
Xiang Li
Zhengcheng Li
Justin Michael Lilly
Yanan Lin
Jeffrey Ling
Pamela Nicole Lozano
Ashley Corina Lynch
Stergos Aris Marinos
Deion Jordan Marks
Garyd Erik Martin
Isaac Roth Martin
Joshua Peifer Martin
Kara Deanne Mast
Mackenzie Lynn
  McBride
Olivia Marie McDowell
Tieagra Chantél McNeil
Emma Charlotte Millar
Anna Angelica Miller
Skylin Blu Miller
Andrew S. Milligan
Abimael F. Montanez
Josue Morales
Katie Elizabeth Muckel
Sarah Ann Myers

Mika Dang Nguyen
Zihui Ni
Josiah Kurt Nisly
Trenton Montgomery
  Ortiz
Hillary Paula-Gil
A'sia Monyé Payne
Erik I. Peachey
Cohen Grant Peifer
Brad J. J. Pinkerton
Karina Veronica Prins-
  Acosta
Boyuan Qiu
Madeleiny Jisselle
  Ramirez
Travis Cedric Replogle
Rudolph Francis Rigano
Benjamin Todd
  Rittenhouse
Daniel Grant
  Rittenhouse
Sonya Lynae Rohrer
Maraly Idalyn Rosario
Kaylor Bret Rosenberry
Emily Jean Miriam
  Rosenfeld
Katherine Anna Rutt
Jarred Daniel Sands
Austin Jay Sauder
Brett Daniel Sauder
Brianna M. Scheidt
Grace Lynn Schnabel
Jesse Lynn Schnupp
Charlotte Elizabeth
  Schreyer
Jonathan R. Schultz
Ian James Schwabe
Jamie Nicole Sensenich
Songyan Shi
Xander Bodie Silva
Taylor Jeanne Smith
Mason Taylor Stoltzfus
Noah Kane Sturges
Jiaming Sui
Maria Iveth Swartley
Kelsey Sue Troyer
Phong Ba Truong
Yokabell Legesse Tsehaye
Thomas James
  Underwood
Fernando Leonel Urena
Katerine Urena

Kimberly Syn Hwi Vun
Alaina Nicole Walker
Meijie Wang
Zhonghong Wang
Ziyue Leslie Wang
Chelsea Nicole Weaver
Eric Michael Weaver
Jonathan Tyler Weaver
Alexa René Weidman
Tiffany R. Weiler
Landon B. Wenger
Haleigh Autumn
  Whitney
Jennifer Renée Winters
Haemoon Won
Brittany Nicole Worthy
Siyuan Wu
Yinxuan Xu
Cesia Odallys Yanez
Jincheng Yang
Yushi Yang
Zachary David Yoder
Zhengting Yu
Diyang Zhu
Benjamin Jaycob Zook

Class of 2016

Hershey Campus

Christy Rae Ammons
Brandon Breindel
Andrew Furjanic
Sarah Hennigh
Zara Kaleem
Joshua Kirman
Madalyn Koach
Connor Mills
Natalee Nelson
LeAnna Ramos
Teresa Rogers
Kyle Salter
Jared Shireman
Robert Tyler Warthman
Cody Whitman
Brig Wilson

Lancaster Campus

Salem Abebe
Bethel Biniam
  Alemayehu
Jeisha M. Arroyo Acosta
Katie Ashley

"We will never forget the 2011 LMH boys soccer season. Our son, Keegan, was led by godly coaches, supportive upperclassmen and classmates that would become forever friends. To witness this team of friends become state champions was a great experience. Everyone rallied around them and celebrated their success." —Rob and Candy Rosenberry, parents

Evan Augsburger
Andrew Baak
Ryan Andrew Bailey
Alexander James Baker
Abigail Katherine Beiler
Natnail Getachew Belete
Judah Blumbergs
Alex Bollinger
Drew Bollinger
Rebekah Renee Boone
Benjamin James
    Breisinger
Naomi Bronkema
Hannah Lea Brubaker
Julian Samuel Brubaker
Breanna Blaize Buckner
Anyi Cai
Lauren Elizabeth Cairns
Kehang Chang
Vanessa Rose Charles
Ting Hon Cheung
Bora Choi
Isabella B. Clair
Hadassah Sara Colbert
Isreali David Colon
Annika Cook
Joshua Daniel Davenport
James Bradley Davidson
Sophia Mei-Rong
    Deibert
Madison Elizabeth
    Dietrich
Faith Erin Dinger
James Weber Duncan
John E. Ebaugh
Emma Eitzen
Kenni Ellen Farrar
Nathan Flanders
Tsz Wing Fong
Maia Garber
Marshall Quinn Gehman
Trenton A. Good
Collin Thomas Green
Marc Anthony Hall
Nathaniel Harnish
Kathryn Thyra Hernquist
Faith Hershey
Alexandra Brianne Hill
Ruohan Hu
Cody Brendon Hurst
Joshua Imhof

Anna Jackson
Victoria Estelle Jarvis
Nathanael Jean-Philippe
Lucas C. Jemison
Alexis Michelle Jones
Mariah Kaltenstein
Hyunwoo Kang
Erin Melissa Kauffman
Kyle Joseph Kerr
Kaden Kieffer
Ryan T. Kindelberger
Abigail M. King
Jack Kintigh
Josiah Kratz
Ivan Kuliashou
Alexa Rae Kurtz
Rebecca A. Lauver
Cheuk Lam Law
Emily A. Leaman
Kara Marie Leaman
Tsz Ching Lee
Heather Rose Leiby
Jiayi Li
Wei Lin
Yang Liu
Qiaodan Lou
Alex Yaniel Malave
Seth Mann
Holly Gabrielle Martin
Sophia Martin
Madeline H. Mast
Michael McAnany
Katherine Marie McCoy
Madison Marie
    Monschein
Elijah Montanez
Jared Mosteller
Victor Amos Muhagachi
Su Youn Na
Jeremy Newswanger
Duc Tri Nguyen
Khai Macq Nguyen
Michael O'Brien
Sanghyun Park
Madison V. Peck
Emily Caris Peifer
Kate E. Phillips
Ezra D. Prescott
Noelle Rae Price
Damyan Reserve
Kyle Richards

Beardsley Bertrand
    Rimpel
Keven J. Rios
Nelson Rivera
Raven Rita Rodriguez
Briana Chantel Romero
Charles Hackman Ross
Sarah Wyman Rundle
Brian Alexis Sanvicente
Alison P. Sauder
Jeremy Sauder
Changyu Shi
Isaac Troyer Sommers
Rachel Joy Steckbeck
Monica Steffy
Rachel Stone
Benjamin Robert
    Stutzman
Chenxuan Sun
Sarah Noelle Taylor
Tatyana Anita Taylor
Edna Eyob Tesfaye
V. Halsey Thompson
Obse M. Tolla
Ky An Tran
Luke J. Trimble
Madeleine Ruth
    Trompeter
Malena C. Tyson
Rajen Upreti
Nguyen Thao Van
Thuy Tien Ho Van
Stephanie A. Vazquez
Terrill Jordan Verling
Nicholas Steven Roth
    Walter
Mingyang Wang
WenYuan Wang
Seth Jaron Weaver
Katelyn Elizabeth
    Wenger
Lindsey Nicole White
Ekshesh Abebe Wurwur
Jiawei Xu
Bryce Yoder
Lea Quinn Zangari
Jingjing Zhang
Haoyuan Zheng
Linxuan Zhu
Siwei Zhu
Xinlei Zhu

178 APPENDIX

Bridge Builders for the Future

Founder's Circle

As long time friends, alumni and parents of LMS alumni and students we recognize the gracious generosity of our Founder's Circle. Members of the Founder's Circle have invested in the 75th Anniversary celebration and made a significant gift to the LMS endowment. Their endowment gifts will ensure that LMS can continue its vision and mission as a leader in affordable Christian education that changes lives and transforms our world.

Harold R. and Ruth E. A. Mast

Named Endowments

Endowments are legacy gifts that exist in perpetuity. These gifts, representing the vision of the donor, are carefully managed by Lancaster Mennonite School to provide permanent, ongoing support for our students and programs. Endowments are managed to provide annual income and also to grow the corpus (the body of the endowment) so that the gift does not lose purchasing power over time. Endowment gifts may be made from current income, planned giving and estates.

Named Student Aid Endowments

Danny Wenger Memorial Scholarship
Betty Hershey Newswanger Memorial Early Education Endowment
Burnell E. & Eunice Harbold Luckenbaugh Endowed Scholarship Fund
John H. and Thelma Wolgemuth Family Endowment
Gladys Mellinger Endowment
Glen D. Lapp Memorial Endowment for Student Aid
Ivan M. Martin Scholarship Endowment
J. Burnell Denlinger Memorial Scholarship
Kim Weaver Memorial Endowment
Martin Limestone Endowment
Selah Art Scholarship Endowment
Student Council Scholarship Fund
Richard and Janet Frey Endowment

Named Program Endowments

Advanced Biology Endowment
Clarence and Elva Rutt Memorial Music Endowment
Connie H. Stauffer Early Childhood Education Innovation Endowment
Daniel Glick Endowment
David & Edith Thomas Endowment
FFA Endowment
Ivan & Irene Martin Endowment
Joyce E. & J. Richard Thomas Superintendent's Office Endowment
Kraybill Campus Endowment
Kristin Palazzo Memorial Visual Arts Endowment
Learning Support Endowment
Music Endowment
Noah G. Good Endowment for Science Education
Vi Bender Memorial Fund
Victoria Heisey Memorial Learning Support Center Endowment
Wellness Program Endowment

Named Athletic Endowments

Brent Nauman Memorial Endowment for Intramurals and Athletic Programming at LMH
Jodi Byers Memorial Endowment
Lacrosse Endowment Fund
Hoober Haller Athletic Leadership Endowment
LMS Blazer Baseball Endowment

Campus Endowments

Hershey Campus Endowment
Kraybill Campus Endowment
Locust Grove Campus Endowment
New Danville Endowment for Excellence

APPENDIX 179

Iron Bridge Society

The Iron Bridge Society is a group of persons who are passionate about leaving a legacy of Christian education for generations to come. These friends have included LMS in their planned giving and/or estate plan. Members are invited to select school events and receive estate and planned giving tips. You too can join them by including LMS in your estate plan thereby leaving a legacy of Christian education for generations of students yet to come!

Gerald R. '72 & Rose Ann Baer
E. Robert & Elva Bare
George M. & Lois Beck
Benuel S. '60 & Janet Beiler
Katie B. Beiler
Mark B. & Roseanna Boll
Lena '52 & Michael R. Brown
Robert L. '65 & F. Lois '64 Brubaker
John R. '56 & Miriam '55 Buckwalter
J. Paul '57 & Esther '57 Clymer
John H. & Debbie Denlinger
Daniel L. & Joanne Dietzel
Peter A. & Marian Dimmig
John W. Eby '58
Charles F. & Beulah M. Frey
Jay Richard '64 & Janet Landis Frey
Elaine W. '62 & Leon W. Good '60
Lois M. '59 & Carl L. Good
Dale B. & Joyce E. Graybill
Florence Beiler Groff '53
Marlin G. '74 & Sue A. Groff
Mary Ellen '65 & Harold M. '62 Groff
Joyce E. '78 & J. Richard Haller
David M. '49 & Florence Harnish
J. Alex Hartzler '86
Daryl F. '88 & Charlene Heller
J. Eby & Kathryn Hershey
Marlin R. '67 & Barbara '67 Hershey
Noah L. & Parmalle C. Hershey
Ernest M. '60 & Lois E. '60 Hess
Mervin W. & Nora L. Hess
Marcy & Rick High
Virginia O. Hoover
Erma L. '59 & Carl Horning
Lorene '65 & Earl Horst
Gerald R. '65 & Linda Horst
Pluma Y. Hostetter '48
Miriam M. Housman

Chad G. '91 & Coleen M. '92 Hurst
George M. & Lois Jean Hurst
Louetta W. Hurst '62
Naomi W. Keiper '56
Lois R. Kennel '50
Dorothy J. King '53
Laurence S. '49 & Shirley A. King
Nathan '56 & Melba '57 King
Simon P. & Mary Jean Kraybill
Gail M. & Raymond D. Lanas
Ivan B. '50 & Mary E. '54 Leaman
Patricia '66 & J. Harold Leaman
Allon H. '64 & Doris E. '64 Lefever
Lola M. Lehman '59
Ray A. '71 & Teresa E. Long
Esther H. '66 & Lewis M. Martin
Irvin S. '63 & Rachel G. Martin '64
Laverne M. '54 & J. Elvin Martin
Lew K. '94 & Kayleen Martin
Barbara Mast
Ernest S. '59 & Esther J. '59 Mast
Harold R. '65 & Ruth E. A. '66 Mast
Katie B. & Albert Mast
Robert S. & Barbara Mathews
James E. '53 & Rachel G. Metzler
Lorraine Murphy '60
Emerson R. Newswanger
Richard J. & Lynne H. Palazzo
Robert L. '73 & Lucinda Petersheim
William K. '79 & Diane '80 Poole
Alta M. Ranck
Reba '60 & J. Ray Ranck
Merle R. & Ruth Ann Reinford
Clarence H. Rutt '49
G. Roger & Pamela Rutt
John M. '55 & Rebecca C. Rutt
John D. & Lisa M. Sands
Norman G. '50 & Jean Shenk '50

John C. Simkins
Connie Heisey Stauffer '55
Edgar Stoesz
Harvey Z. & Lillian M. Stoltzfus
Heidi '89 & Rodney Stoltzfus
Joyce E. '69 & J. Richard Thomas
A. Richard '56 & Ruth S. Weaver
R. Todd '83 & Anne Kaufman Weaver
Matthew A. '03 & Lindsay '05 Weaver
John S. & Janet F. Weber
Clifford R. '79 & Carol A. Wenger
Daniel L. Wenger '56
Roy E. '55 & Esther S. '56 Wert
Clyde B. & Nancy L. Wissler
Robert R. '61 & Naomi Wyble
Dale R. & Joanne Z. Yoder
Julia M. Yoder '47
Miles E. & Dawnell F. Yoder
Loren L. '65 & Helen '65 Zimmerman
Mark B. '59 & Karene Zimmerman
Larry J. '80 & Dawn '79 Zook

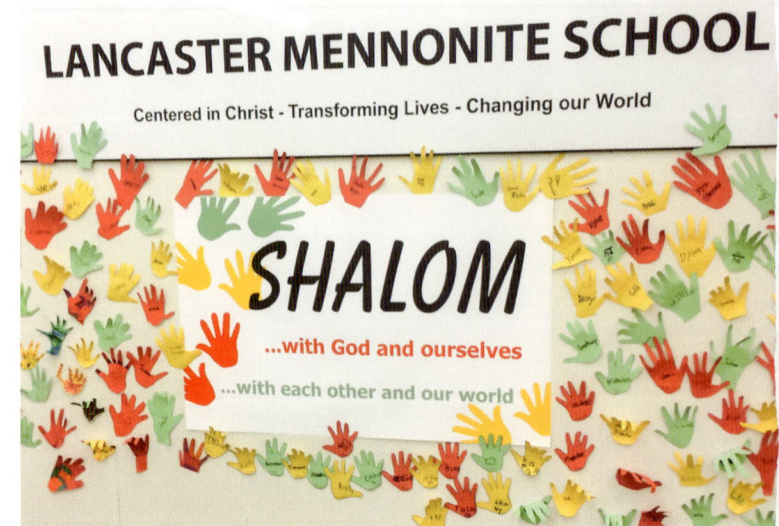